HEART STRINGS
FROM THE BOOK OF HORMAN

Essays on a Mormon Mother's Memories

Hermine Briggs Horman

First Edition

Distinctive Publishing, Salt Lake City, Utah 1991

Published by:

Distinctive Publishing
3600 East 3700 South
Salt Lake City, Utah 84109

All rights reserved. No part of this book may be reproduced without written permission of the author, except for the inclusion of brief quotations in a review.

Copyright 1991, by Hermine Briggs Horman©

Library of Congress Card No. 91-74145

ISBN: 1-880328-24-0 $15.95 soft cover

Cover Design: Denise Fuller
Text Formatting: David M. Muir
Printed by: Roylance Publishing, Inc., Murray, Utah 84123
Printed in the Unted States of America

First Edition: July 1991
10 9 8 7 6 5 4 3 2 1

LITTLE TOWN
by Leone E. McCune

So long this little town was my whole world,
Deep sky, low lying hills, and waters purled.

My home now wears an unfamiliar face;
New owners always want to change a place.

The faces that I loved are there no more;
A modern shop replaced the country store.

The small schoolhouse has long outgrown its need;
New buildings stand where farmers planted seed.

Beloved old church has fallen to decay;
The white spires of a new one greet the day.

All is not changed; the hills remain the same;
The sunset dies with well-remembered flame.

The sun-baked slopes still yield the ripened grain;
The cows trudge to the pasture, down the lane.

And when the valley dons its cloak of white;
The lights glow in the darkness of the night;

But most of all, when lilacs drip with rain,
My memory and my *heartstrings* they enchain.

To my mother's children,

my children, and

their children.

ABOUT THE AUTHOR

Born on a farm in Magrath, Alberta, Canada, Hermine was the seventh of nine children. She admits to fitting the label "little wild flower" affectionately dubbed by her father.

Educated in a one room-eight-grade-22 student-school, she was a child of the Depression and World War II. From these unique environs she experienced pioneering typical of a former generation. Being a teenager during the war brought her employment opportunity for travel. "Sand got in her shoes" at an early age, and resulted in her traversing many lands throughout the world.

While a student at Brigham Young University she traveled and studied in Europe, Mexico and Hawaii. Subsequent travels have included Israel, South Africa, Europe, Korea and China. She especially enjoys a one-on-one experience with her hosts wherever such opportunities permit.

Married to Phares T. Horman, a civil engineer, she quickly found herself proprietor of a day and night nursery, one of their own making! Survival was busy but happy, and the challenge of coping with the needs and wants of seven teenagers (TWO PAIRS OF TWINS HERE!) was largely responsible for involvement in her first book, <u>A Century of Mormon Cookery</u>, which is in its 9th printing, having sold over 40,000 copies. Entrepreneurship, though unexpected, was not accidental. She has been honing her writing skills since winning a penmanship and composition competition in 1938 while attending Lehi School, her one-room educational laboratory on the prairies. From her versatile background emerged a mammoth reservoir from which to draw. We are enriched for her having done so.

TABLE OF CONTENTS

	Page
ABOUT THE AUTHOR	vi
ACKNOWLEDGMENTS	viii
INTRODUCTION	x
OVERVIEW	xi

CHAPTER I
    TENDER VINES 1

CHAPTER II
    SAND IN MY SHOES 69

CHAPTER III
    THE GREEN YEARS 99

CHAPTER IV
    IS MR. HORMAN MR. RIGHT? 133

CHAPTER V
    A PEEK IN THE SHOE 149

CHAPTER VI
    A TIME OF HARVEST 247

CHAPTER VII
    NOSTALGIA 349

APPENDICES:
    A--LEHI SCHOOL 373
    B--THE HUTTERITES 387
    C--PINPOINTS 391
    D--ONE TIME CELEBRITIES 413
    E--TRIBUTE TO MY CHILDREN AND
        MY BROTHERS AND SISTERS 421
    F--FRIENDS FOREVER AND MY "POMES" 431
    G--RESUMES 453

TOPICAL LISTINGS 458

ACKNOWLEDGMENTS

TO MY HUSBAND, Phares, who was subjected to more than his share of TV dinners, soup and sandwiches, while <u>Heart Strings</u> was on the front burner. Thanks for your patience in teaching me the computer, and believing in me.

TO MY CHILDREN, Heather, Susan, Karen, Becky, Briggs, Shelley, and April—thanks for helping to provide the tears and joys of the subject matter, and thanks for just being.

TO MY BROTHERS AND SISTERS, Alice, Beth, Virginia, Ernest, Don, Fred, Emma Lou and Jim—with whom I shared my early Alberta roots. Thanks for adding color and form to a happy childhood.

TO MY MANY FRIENDS, who have, through the years, challenged me to write a book. Thanks for your encouragement in my project and your trust in my ability to accomplish my goal: Cherie Pardoe, Beverly Mercer, Keith and Louise Adamson, Connie and Fraank Fairbanks, Bea Bullen, Ferris Johnson, John and Louise Waters, Shelley Gaetz, William E. Berrett, Tracy Melville and Daphne Sommerfeld. A special thanks to Kirk and Shirley Collins. It was Kirk's suggestion that I add "From the Book of Horman" to my already titled HEART STRINGS. Graditufeld is expressed to Jean Holyoak for her friendship, talent, and the meticulous manner in which she edited this work. She hung in whether the going was smooth or rough. A patient David M. Muir formatted this manuscript.

AND NOW FOR A DISCLAIMER CONTRARY TO THE NORM: Be it known that all names and places used in this narrative are real. No attempt, however small, has been made to protect the innocent. Rather, they are exploited to the max. God bless 'em all!

How to Be A Success
DO YOU THINK I'LL EVER BE A SUCCESS, GRANNY?
WHY NOT!
BUT YOU NEED TO REMEMBER JILL — SUCCESS ISN'T A PLACE, IT'S A JOURNEY! SO YOU'LL FIND IT IN A LOT OF PLACES ALONG YOUR TRIP.
I THOUGHT IT WAS WHAT YOU EARNED WHEN SOMETHING'S DONE!
IF YOU ONLY FOUND SUCCESS AT THE END — IT'S TOO LATE — IT'S ALL OVER.
ENJOY ALL YOUR SUCCESSES — MAKE SURE THAT EACH DAY COUNTS...
ALRIGHT GRANNY!

INTRODUCTION

Are we not all puppets of a sort? Firmly attached to my heart are strings manipulated by a seen and unseen crowd. Some tug tenderly; others with great strength and impatience. Some hurt and others heal. Many lie in the recesses of my memory and surface just often enough to remind me of my age. Others I unconsciously ignore.

If quality of life is measured by that which affects the heart, I must be judged by the succession of incidents I have recorded in this little volume, incidents which brought joy and sorrow to me then and some assurance of a life worth living as I remember them now.

If my reflections stir the reader to make a re-evaluation of his or her own role, the results will have served my purpose. Heart Strings is not necessarily biographical, though some of it fits that description. The author hopes that the timelessness of childhood will captivate the imagination of all who are now, or who have been there. The joy of discovery runs like a golden thread through these enchanted years. Come, join me in a pilgrimage into the past.

OVERVIEW

"ONCE UPON A TIME. . . ."

"She loves children so much. It's a shame she'll probably never have any of her own," lamented one of my sisters.

"She's too darned efficient. She'd scare any man away!" declared my youngest brother.

I overheard these remarks at a family reunion. I had been playing games with the children on the lawn and suddenly sat down on the porch. My family who adored me had unanimously agreed that I was unable to attract a mate or to have children. I was shattered! I could hardly wait to escape the scene. I wanted to examine these painful observations.

I got in my car and hastily left. When I opened the door to get out I realized I could not remember getting in. Nor could I remember driving the few miles from the scene of my poignant family encounter to my apartment.

My tiny, two-room apartment, usually a peaceful refuge, offered no comfort. Intent on changing my clothes, I walked directly to the bedroom and flipped on the radio when I passed the dresser. "Who's Sorry Now?" wailed an accusing voice. I threw myself across the bed, clutched my pillow with both hands, and sobbed bitterly in self-pity.

Even my furnishings, so proudly acquired, mocked my loneliness and fears. Through closed eyes I could still see the picture groupings of others' offspring. My lovely "hope" chest loomed sphinx-like before me. Brim full of treasures, it now represented foolish, optimistic youth to me. A cup and saucer in delicate pink china (part of a service for eight stored elsewhere), decorated the top of the rented piano. Marble bookends supported several classics, but today I saw only <u>How to Pray and Stay Awake</u>. The cuckoo clock sounded a reminder of an old admirer. Every object I saw cast a shadow from the past. Nothing reflected my hope for the future. I was thirty-one and an "old maid," though I preferred the term "bachelor girl." Reared in a family of nine and being the only one unmarried presented some perplexing, though amusing, problems.

I was fond of children. I had thirty-five nieces and nephews with whom I could share my maternal instinct. I was also plagued with their insistent questions. "Don't you have any babies?" or "Where is your Daddy?" they asked. I carefully evaluated any relationship before subjecting male friends to their queries. "Are you going to marry her?" or "Don't you have any babies, either?" To be sure, they kept me aware of my maidenhood.

It was never my intention to bypass marriage and children. I felt that with this one exception I had accomplished everything I had really desired. I had my share of male companionship. How well I remembered my first real love interest, so tender and so intense, which ended with a broken heart. I recalled the casual relationships, the round of parties, dances, shows, and picnics typical of normal youth. Later there were those who worshipped at my feet. But I stepped over their bending forms and ran eagerly to other things.

There was college, a two-year stint as a missionary for the Mormon Church, full satisfaction in my chosen business career where I felt I had "hit the top," and executive positions on an international youth guidance program. I traveled extensively from the Northwest Territories in Canada to the tip of Florida on the North American Continent, in addition to spending several exciting summer traveling in Europe, Hawaii, and Mexico. Life was not only bright and challenging, but it also gave me the feeling I was, indeed, a contributor to this world's need for creative, efficient service. It was at this point that I felt my ability to function as a woman was challenged.

For the first time in my life, I was deeply unhappy. I knew I must get away from the demands of my job and take inventory. I chose an ideal spot, a little junior college where I enrolled in summer school. One could never accuse me of planning a manhunt, for the total enrollment was not more than 200, half of whom were either spinsters or married women taking courses for teacher recertification. The remaining students were young boys and girls.

I decided to come face to face with myself--stripped of pride, vanity or pretense--and hopefully arrive at my moment of truth. I looked about me at the many venerable maiden ladies, and surmised that they, too, had probably lived interesting and varied lives. But I could see that they were plainly marked for "single blessedness." As I studied each face a monotonous crying in my heart said, "Incomplete and unfulfilled!"

When I looked into the mirror, I saw incompleteness and unfulfilled dreams in my own face. Perhaps I was not to know the security of love from a husband and children. This thought broke the dam of tears welling in my eyes. I knew then that these were the tears of a very young girl with her heart broken, mingled with the tears of a bachelor girl in her poignant confrontation with reality. They were tears that washed away complacency forever and left me only with a determination to change my life.

Well, I thought, if there is to be a change, it is up to me. Cruelly, I analyzed myself from a physical point of view. My short-cropped red hair was certainly not feminine; besides, it made me look too self-reliant. I must let it grow. Extra pounds, so innocently gathered around my waist and hips, while not overwhelming, diminished my vulnerable facade. They must come off!

When I returned to my desk in August, there were visible differences. My hair had grown out from the casual short cut worn for several years. A few pounds were gone and I bought some new clothes. The transformation was subtle but sure. I was amazed and delighted at the comments and attention a ten pound weight loss made. They didn't notice my hair until they noticed the ten pound loss! But though I had set my sail, I was not about to be swept off my moorings by glances from the male quarter. A much more traumatic war was raging within. I knew that the smile on my lips and the light in my eyes were discreetly beguiling. I had achieved a dramatic psychological rebirth. I felt the pendulum of my life was swinging a different direction. Changes for me were in the immediate offing.

Within a few weeks of my return, I was introduced to a young engineering student at the University of Utah. He lived in the same neighborhood as one of my European traveling companions. She felt that we "deserved each other." Knowing how I shied away from blind dates, she assured me she had "made it a matter of prayer" before suggesting such a possibility.

I cannot say it was love at first sight, but we definitely were mutually impressed. He was tall enough and old enough, criteria used repeatedly over the years. He was of my religion, which was also important to me. He was well educated and we could converse easily. On the third date, I found myself subconsciously dreaming in terms of "if this works out." His beautiful almond-shaped brown eyes and attentive manner had me feeling like a breathless teenager. Soon the stars in my own eyes were large enough for all the world to see, and I knew that love was sweeter at thirty-one than it had been at any time in my life.

By October I was wearing an engagement ring. To be honeymoon-bound in less than three months suggested the possibility that each date with Phares was something of a summit conference. He assured me in countless ways that he had been waiting for someone "just like me." HE wanted ME to help fill the void in HIS life. Thus happy, giddy, joyous plans saw fruition, and we were married December 20th, despite pleadings from both sides of the house to wait until after Christmas.

I enjoyed abundantly good health and was anxious to devote whatever time was allotted me to the "nesting" and homemaking arts. By the time Christmas holidays were over, there was no doubt in my mind that the "nesting" had begun. From this point on, history had a habit of repeating itself with regularity.

I was still working and intended to do so until our baby arrived. In about the seventh month, the doctor expressed concern as to the baby-placenta position. However, I was confident that everything would, to coin an old phrase, "come out all right." Eventually I was confined to bed to prevent premature labor caused by a condition called "placenta previa" wherein the placenta is positioned so it precedes the baby, thus cutting off the baby's oxygen.

At the next visit to my doctor, I was ordered to the hospital for a caesarian section. I called my husband and announced this change of plans. He was adamant in his reply. "You can't go yet. We haven't even been married nine months! What will people think?" I was not worried in the least what my friends and family thought. Within the hour, we were the proud parents of a beautiful daughter born September 6th.

Heather was the answer to every new parent's prayer. She delighted us no matter what the hour. We awakened her for the approval of every visitor. She was a happy child, and despite interrupting her rest frequently, she fell back to sleep without the customary bottle or cuddling. We felt our cup of happiness was full.

Full it was, but our full capacity was soon to be realized. We moved to a little two bedroom house on Scott Avenue, in Salt Lake City, and thought we would have adequate room for some time. However, the following September, a year after Heather's birth, we boasted twin girls! Twins only because they were born together, for they were as different as night and day. Karen, a redhead like her mother, was right-handed; Susan, a brunette like her father, was left-handed. Their lives paralleled these differences as they grew through babyhood.

Phares was a devoted father and proud of our prolific prowess. His own family of four had been spaced over a thirteen-year period. He wanted our children to grow up together!

The summers are hot in Utah. Having had two pregnancies through the summer, I determined that I would never again carry a child through that season. These words echoed in my mind a year later, when Labor Day was labor day indeed, and daughter number four, Rebecca, arrived.

Was it possible that two short years of marriage had produced four children? I could scarcely believe it when I said it to myself. Four would suffice for some time, I thought. My cup was full indeed, though my diaper pail ran over!

One morning a salesman came to my door and, seeing the many little ones, inquired, "Do you run a day nursery?" I smiled wearily and said, "Yes, a night nursery, too." Sleep at our household was a very scarce item, in fact, hardly heard of at all.

By the time Becky was toilet-trained, we received the news that the twin shrimp boat was about to dock again. Surely we deserved two boys this time! But fortune smiled only a half-hearted smile. We received our first boy along with another girl, both weighing seven pounds each. Phares was overjoyed to have "his" son at last, who received both his father's name, Phares, and my maiden name, Briggs. Shelley was his "wombmate."

It seemed as though these little babies had dangled chubby legs on the periphery of eternity awaiting our invitation. When opportunity finally presented itself, they fairly tumbled out of heaven two-by-two!

I was ecstatic with another pair of twins, but could not find a dresser with two more drawers to sleep them. The reality of wall-to-wall cribs in our two bedroom home was cause for many smiles on our part and much concern from anxious outsiders. Phares was building a bigger home on a four year pay-as-you-go plan, but the need for additional help was urgent with the prospects of six in one bedroom. I threatened to stay in the hospital until the house was livable. He could decide which was least expensive. Fortunately he decided in favor of the home. Now we only had three to a bedroom! But with our usual good fortune, we soon made it four.

The following April, daughter number six, child number seven arrived. We had utilized our favorite girl's names; however, because she arrived in April, that became her name. Since marriage I had often referred to myself as "Fertile Myrtle" and at this point in time, everyone agreed with me!

A ringing doorbell was cause for a miniature stampede. All the little ones stood in full view of the visitor, which caused one to exclaim: "These are not all yours!" in an exclamatory rather than a questioning voice. I confessed, they all belonged to the same mother and father who lived at this address.

Five years and seven children later, I confess that our married life has been intense. The children have been unusually healthy and happy, having avoided family epidemics of measles, chicken pox, and

xv

the usual childhood diseases which might have isolated us for years. Second only to my husband's steady job, I appreciate my automatic washer and dryer almost more than life itself. Supper time bears strong resemblance to mealtime at the zoo. Bedtime is sheer bedlam. But when the crying ceases, and I am able to sanely focus my thoughts, I thank a kind providence for the turning point in my life. I have accomplished the purpose of my creation. Lonesome? No! Unfulfilled? Hardly! Busy? Tremendously! Happy? Indeed!

* * * *

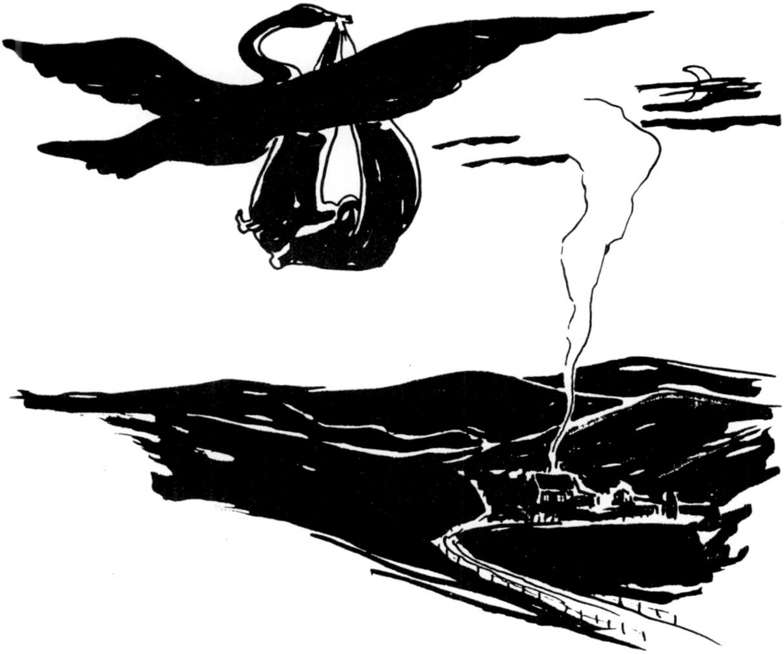

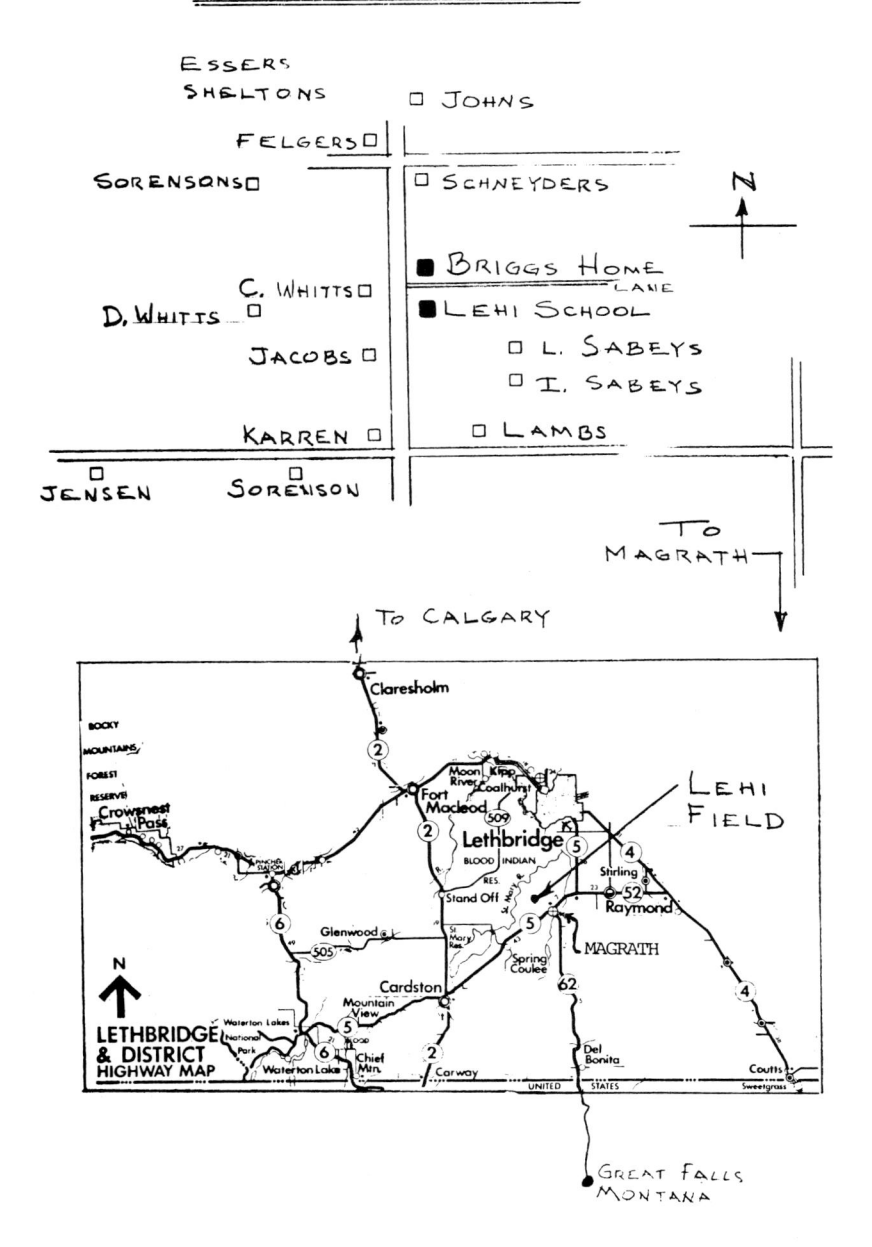

LEHI FIELD

- ESSERS
- SHELTONS
- □ JOHNS
- FELGERS □
- SORENSONS □
- □ SCHNEYDERS
- C. WHITTS □
- D. WHITTS □
- ■ BRIGGS HOME — LANE
- ■ LEHI SCHOOL
- JACOBS □
- □ L. SABEYS
- □ I. SABEYS
- KARREN □
- □ LAMBS
- □ JENSEN
- □ SORENSON

To MAGRATH

To CALGARY

LETHBRIDGE & DISTRICT HIGHWAY MAP

LEHI FIELD

GREAT FALLS MONTANA

CHAPTER I
TENDER VINES

Magrath, Alberta, Canada. I call it "Upper Zion." In my view when the Mormon colonists came westward, those who were too tired to go on, established their "Zion" headquarters in Utah. Those who were more adventuresome and ambitious opted to settle in Idaho. Those who were exceptionally hardy and full of faith pushed the frontier much further by crossing the international line, settling in Magrath, Alberta, Canada!

Alberta is the most westward of the three Prairie Provinces of Canada, just north of the 49th parallel. Magrath is part of the great breadbasket of the world located on fertile plains that slope gently away from the foothills of the Rockies. My father, Azer Briggs, first went to Magrath in 1902. In writing to his mother, he used glowing terms to describe this new land. He affirmed that "the natural prairie grass was as high as a horse's belly."

The buffalo, those giant beasts of the prairie, had fertilized the land for millennia and left a top soil 12-18 inches thick. The original prairie, now visible only on the Indian Reservation, still bears the mark of the buffalo wallows which were low troughs where rain collected. Buffalo rolled in the troughs to rid themselves of flies. The result is a rich humus soil which is unexcelled for the growing of all grains.

Magrath is located in the center of a vast expanse of prairie. Only to the west does one see mountain ranges. On a clear day, Big Chief Mountain dominates the skyline. In summer an alpine haze covers the foothills. Bone-chilling winds of winter and hot breezes of summer have little to impede them; thus their intensity is severe. Warm chinook winds from the west moderate winter's harshness. The openness of the prairie between the Rockies, 60 miles west, and the Milk River Ridge to the south is a colorful patchwork of farms. The Ridge also provides a view towards the international boundary into the United States.

The presence of a clump of trees every few miles signals a farmhouse. Landmark gray and maroon grain elevators point the way to town, five miles distant. St. Mary's River courses its crooked path to the north through the rolling hills beyond which Lethbridge elevators are visible.

Immediately to the west is a hill dubbed by our family "Hill Cumorah." Actually it is no more than an exaggerated pimple on the flat face of the prairie. Every visitor to our farm was taken to its crest. Daddy always allowed time for a few steps among the wild flowers and a sweeping glance of the well-manicured landscape, and then with a broad gesture of his arm, declared: "When Moses was permitted to view the Promised Land, he never saw anything more beautiful than this."

In this pastoral setting on a sunny spring day, a new voice was heard. Though it did not shake the world, it certainly changed an already busy household into a more active one. The date was May 2, 1926. Azer had returned to his sheep camp. Emilie was home alone with six children and expecting her seventh. Even though they were six weeks early, she recognized the familiar pangs of labor. Francis Hacking, her sister-in-law, was called, and she arrived with Sister Poulson, a midwife. Dr. Fowler was summoned from Lethbridge, 20 miles away, and in due time he delivered a yellow, jaundiced, five pound baby girl, Hermine.

I was the smallest of Mother's nine children, but living proof that "the best things often come in small packages." During her entire pregnancy, she and Daddy were in court fighting for their lives and land. Standard Trust was threatening foreclosure on the farm due to the universal problems incident to the coming Great Depression. No doubt this continual stress was responsible for my early, unheralded arrival. Mother said that I was, understandably, born with my fists doubled up.

Thoughts of my parents bring a rush of memories--some sad but more glad. I grew up knowing that I was loved, albeit sandwiched between a darling redheaded baby girl (Emma Lou) and a precocious "apple-of-Daddy's-eye" (handsome Fred). Daddy called me his "little wild flower" which seemed to describe me and my feelings about myself during those early years of growing up in a large family.

In subsequent years I learned that the early pioneers' posterity from Southern Alberta became the literal "leavening of the world's loaf." They served and are currently serving in places of prominence around the world. Having traveled a great deal, I have met people in England, South Africa, Japan, and countless other places, who, upon learning that I am from Magrath, exclaim: "Magrath must be a very big city! I have known so many fine people who have come from there." And when one realizes the numbers who have left their prairie home, one also wonders if any nucleus remains. But the descendants of those stalwart souls who founded this small community are still keeping Magrath on the map. Though I am far removed from the place of my birth, I return at least once a year. I find my heartstrings are pulled like a magnet back to those "who knew me when . . . ."

* * * *

WHAT MADE OUR HOUSE A HOME

Edgar A. Guest said: "It takes a heap o' livin' in a house to make it home." He knew whereof he spoke. The sunlight and shadows of life serve to hallow the spot, be it a log cabin in the woods or a castle on a hill. Our home was humbly appointed on the prairie of Southern Alberta. It was five rooms and a path, but with a family of eleven we provided ample "livin'" in the house to make it home.

My earliest recollections of Mother are when she took me to Utah on a train. The porter was black and very frightening to me. I had never seen a black man before. I was standing on the velvet plush-covered seat when he came by and spoke to me. I was so terrified I wet my pants! Mother was embarrassed but endeavored to mop up the mishap.

Daddy usually took a nap after lunch. We had a couch in the kitchen to accommodate him, and we kids made much fun of his loud snores. One of my earliest recollections is Daddy allowing, even coaxing us, to sit on his "breadbasket" and bouncing us around until we fell off.

At a very early age I was aware that both Mother and Daddy were very committed to our LDS faith and its leaders. We always attended Sunday School and Church (10 a.m. and 7:00 p.m. respectively) while accommodating the milking and feeding chores. I remember knowing that Daddy was very important as he conducted some of the meetings. He was a counselor to Bishop Ellis Heninger, as was Ira Fletcher, and our families were very close throughout life.

Mother always cried when she bore her testimony, so for several years she determined not to express herself until she had more control. I hungered to hear her, but often she would start singing a hymn and the congregation would join in. I never doubted the strength of her testimony, but suspect these were difficult years for her. Life on the farm without much money but with many concerns took its toll on her stamina.

We were taught that there were certain things you do and don't do on the Sabbath. Swimming was a "no-no" as was horseback riding and picnicking. Mother preferred no softball or basketball, but Daddy and the kids prevailed when it was viewed as something that did not take us away from home. Besides, we had already attended our meetings.

Daddy was called upon often to speak. Frequently it was in church; many times it was on the occasion of a funeral. He did very well, using many scriptures, anecdotes, and poetry he committed to memory. It would be less than fair if I did not also relate the early and late hours Mother spent helping him outline his talks. It was a "joint" effort in the best sense of the word.

Mother served several years as a counselor in the Stake Relief Society presidency. Myrtle Passey was president. We attended Stake Conference in Raymond and looked forward to having dinner at one of the "fancy" Raymond homes, where they had indoor plumbing. I specifically remember dining with the Heningers, Brandleys, Snows, Allens and Wings. If a General Authority was attending a neighboring stake conference, often our parents would drive to Cardston or Lethbridge that we might receive of their inspiration. We also took neighbors' kids to church and community affairs which they would not otherwise have been able to attend. Our car was always jam-packed, but we could "double-deck" for anyone who needed a ride.

The farm chores were varied and many. I am amazed at this age to realize the heavy responsibilities I carried at a very tender age. First, I remember gathering eggs, despite the fear of hens and roosters that attacked the head and shoulders of only the redheads. Vividly I can see Ernie running to the house with his coat up over his head, a chicken in hot pursuit, flaying away at him, and feathers flying as he fought off the attacker. I also hated the mites that got on my hands and arms as I executed the egg-gathering detail.

Mother and Daddy were hard workers and wanted us to appreciate the work ethic. As soon as our hands were strong enough, we were taught how to milk cows. Long before that, however, I was taught to ride bareback, and was thus entrusted with taking and returning the cows to pasture a mile and a half away. I must have been small, because I remember climbing the fence to close the gate. The pigs, horses, cats, dogs and cattle had to be fed, and great were the loads we kids carried to accomplish this.

Many a hay-raking or stooking (stacking shocks of grain) project was completed with the promise of a swim in the river or a

*M*y *Beloved Parents*
Azer Richard Briggs – 6 Feb 1882 to 30 Sep 1949
Emilie Sophia Osterloh Briggs – 2 July 1888 to 4 Aug 1976

*D*addy
and
Hermine

*F*ive-year-old
Hermine

6 HEART STRINGS

picnic with Lows or a trip to Lethbridge for an afternoon. At least once every summer we spent a day or weekend at Waterton Park. On one occasion the car proceeded home without Fred who was left on the park swing. I, for one, was overjoyed when we returned to the park and found a tearful little boy who returned to more than one tearful brother and sister.

As a young teenager during the war years, we girls did most of the harvesting. One year Darlene Sabey and I mowed, raked, loaded and stacked hay for all the neighbors. I also shoveled grain to and from the granary to the truck and hauled it to town to the elevator. The truck had no brakes. I pled with Smith Ackroyd, the elevator operator, to drive it up on the ramp for me. He would not touch the wheel when I expressed concern about the brakes! Daddy told me, "Just put it in compound low and you'll be all right." My faith in my father preceded the miracle. I did not kill myself nor anyone else in the process, and the elevator stands to this day!

Of all the farm chores, my least favorite was working in the sugar beets. In the spring they had to be thinned, which meant a man hoeing and a kid on his knees thinning by hand following him. I was always "the kid" and recall getting paid ten cents a row for a mile-long row.

In the summer months the beets had to be irrigated, and that was a pain of another dimension. However, Daddy always performed that chore. Next came cultivating to kill the weeds. Then in the fall they were plowed out in rows. We all donned gloves and grubbies and topped beets with a large machete-like knife throwing them on a flatbed rack, loading on the truck and hauling them to the sugar factory in Raymond. Daddy was there from early morning until the field was vacated at night. There were teaching moments, funny stories, songs in harmony, complaints about slave labor, but it was all worthwhile because everyone felt needed. He praised us often when observing our dexterity in throwing the very heavy beets to their targeted place on the flatbed. We didn't earn much money, but we felt we really earned our new school clothes: a pair of shoes, stockings, skirt and blouse or dress.

When traveling a distance of some proportion, Mother and Daddy usually stopped at the Trading Company for lunch makings. They were always the same: bread, nippy cheese, bananas, and toasted marshmallows. Sometimes Ang Wood in the butcher shop supplied the cheese, cut from a huge 60-80 pound round. Oh, how delicious we found soft store bread, and the rarity of marshmallows

The Briggs Family
Back: Beth, Mother, Daddy, Alice
Front: Fred, Don, Emma Lou,
Virginia, Hermine & Ernie

and bananas, be they ever so brown, almost made us think we'd died and gone to heaven.

When chinook winds thawed the snow and dried up the mud, we knew shortly Mother would solicit our cooperation in spring cleaning. It wasn't a chore we relished, but I remember having fun doing it. Daddy and the boys helped by washing the ceilings and high walls. The girls carried on where they left off. One year Virginia painted the kitchen woodwork while I painted the chairs. We dreamed of being able to calcimine the whole house at once, but it was always done a-room-a-year. The prettiest I ever saw the house was when Mother's room was lavender, the girls' room pink, the boys' room green, and the kitchen and front room beige and yellow respectively.

Daddy liked to see us lighten Mother's load wherever we could. He was quick to suggest our involvement if we didn't grasp the ever-present opportunity. I can still hear him saying, "Now you girls, fly into them dishes!" With no water in the house, other than by pail, that was a chore indeed! First it had to be pumped and brought in, then heated on the coal stove, unless the attached reservoir had hot water in it. It is a wonder anything ever got sanitized, as the water seldom was hot enough to sterilize. However, the tea kettle was usually hotter, and we rinsed the dishes with its water. I especially disliked having to wash the cream separator, which was a daily chore.

Mother is remembered by her peers as a happy person, seldom without a smile. We saw her in all her moods because we caused them. She could be stern when the occasion demanded firmness. She laughed often, with a musical lilt which reflected her lovely singing voice. As a child I thought I had never heard anyone with a voice so beautiful, nor one who could provide a truer, sweeter harmony. She had large brown eyes that literally snapped when she was indignant, an ever-present possibility with nine children at all ages!

Daddy was a reader. He loved history, both secular and Church. His near-annual visits to Utah usually netted a half dozen current or very old Church books. In his later years I remember him in the kitchen, his chair tilted back with his head against the window frame, sound asleep, his glasses on his forehead. Though his formal education was sparse, he could calculate figures in his head with great speed and accuracy, and committed to memory many favorite poems which we all grew to love and have incorporated into our lives. His handwriting was distinctive and legible. I thought I had "arrived" when I practiced his signature sufficient times to duplicate it.

Mother loved learning and did much to imbue us with a desire for higher education. Ever the teacher she was, she encouraged us to use good grammar, write beautifully, sing well, and enunciate our words. Her parting words were: "Always remember who you are."

During the war years, young missionaries were scarce as most were serving in the armed forces. It was during this time that Daddy offered to fill his second mission of six months in Southern California. Those of us in the work force were contacted to see if we could help support him. I really felt it a privilege to send my $20 monthly that he might bring the blessings of the Gospel to others. I am sure he was successful in doing so through the support of Mother and his family. She made a quick trip to California on the occasion of Uncle Karl Osterloh's death. They spent a weekend together, though I have never fully understood how in view of his having a young companion and the mission rules. That will be a topic worthy of conversation when I see him again!

Mother and Daddy were evenly yoked, a blessing in any marriage. This did not mean there was never a difference of opinion, however, as both were strong in their expressions. Though they differed they did not shout at each other nor use abusive language. On one occasion I took Daddy's side on a particular issue. Daddy would not let us berate Mother. He cautioned me and said: "I may not agree with your mother, but she's the best little mother you could ever have, and don't you forget it!"

My parents would not tolerate swearing or profanity of any kind. I know that on rare occasions Daddy let a "hell" or a "damn" slip. The worst thing he ever called me was "You little noodle-head." When he said, "Lord Harry" I thought he was profaning, and I feared for his eternal soul. When we were stubborn he called us "little donkeys."

One winter the family had an inordinate amount of serious illness. First, six-year-old Jim went to the hospital with pneumonia. While there, he contracted chicken pox, which resulted in a "mastoid," an infection in front of the ear. Today we know he had staph infection. It simultaneously spread to Ernie, Fred and Beth, developing into an infection of the mastoid bone behind the ear. Mother and Daddy hot packed, poulticed and prayed around the clock for six weeks. While one of them slept, the other continued the tireless compassionate service for their children.

I remember being the "most-well-one" at home that winter. To ease the tensions and frustrations, on more than one occasion

Daddy asked me to make ice cream. Another night the request was for fudge and popcorn, popped the old-fashioned way with a wire mesh popper over the hot coal stove plate. He wanted those of us who were reasonably well to have some frivolity and attention as well as lighten the burden for himself and Mother. (I fear we all inherited his sweet tooth.) Those were trying, serious times coping with terrible sickness without the benefit of modern antibiotics. But through it all came a reverence and respect for Daddy and his use of his priesthood by administering to us whenever the need arose. He was used as the first resort rather than the last as is so often the case in our world of modern medicine.

Daddy was a strong, athletic man, six feet one inch tall. Despite his 235 pounds, he usually could beat his husky sons at broad jumping and arm wrestling. He was a great wrestler and runner in his youth. One day while driving a six-horse team on the rodweeder, he had the misfortune of having one of the least broken horses cause a runaway. He jump off the seat and reined them in a circle, but in doing so stepped in a hole which resulted in a broken ankle. He had a heart-piercing whistle which was put to good use in calling Don a mile away. He came fast on Jill, a tall bay mare. Daddy flat-footedly jumped on his good leg and swung his broken one over her back! The bone was protruding from his ankle and his shoe was filled with blood. It was a terrifying sight to those of us who watched. Even though in a cast for six weeks, he continued working the beet drill, which necessitated his using that foot to trip the seed. When the cast was removed he had no stiffness in his ankle as is the norm with non-ambulatory patients.

A great deal of Mother's time was dedicated to writing letters. She loved to get mail, especially from her scattered brood. She also corresponded with many relatives and former school and mission "chums." In the winter time she sat on the warm oven door, moving the table over to her, and wrote letters by the score. Her famous "Read and Burn" postscript brings a smile to our lips even now! And how we loved receiving her letters! They were so full of news and advice and clippings from the local newspaper. She also forwarded recent letters from other family members. (How we all could have appreciated a copy machine!) Daddy usually added a note at the bottom, but on occasion initiated the letter on his own. Their letters were treasured and practically worn out with reading.

They both worked to see that each of us had our "needs" filled, and our "wants" once in a while. This must have been a challenge in a depressed economy when crops failed year after year from either drought, pestilence, or early frost. Their lives were expressions of faith. Many times that's all they had.

I remember them best during the years they were 40-65. They were a handsome couple then. But I try to imagine what a truly striking pair they were when they were married. Both had even, straight teeth. Mother's hair was a soft brown with a slight wave. Daddy's too, was brown, and had deep curly waves. He surely cut a wide swath with the ladies, and men today still remember Mother for her beauty. Her nose was absolutely darling! Virginia and Beth most nearly inherited this feature.

Joy, sadness, and strength combine to form the warp and the woof of the fabric of our lives in the home provided by Mother and Daddy. I am grateful for every experience they afforded me, as I am sure they were doing the very best they could to provide me a healthy atmosphere in which to grow. I know that I disappointed them many times, but they came close to the mark of being the kind of parents we all should be. God bless their memories for me and mine.

* * * *

HOMESICK

Homesickness is real. It causes physical pain and pangs. For some the trauma of separation from home and hearth diminish with time. But for me, just a little nostalgia triggers my endorphins, creating an instant replay of the scenes of my childhood.

The name "Magrath, Alberta, Canada" is almost lyrical to my ears. The very sound conjures up happy memories, memories of my farm home which the years only enhance. I see the cows come slowly home from pasture. I hear their gentle lowing in the lane. I see neighbors visiting across a fence in a furrowed field. I thrill at the sight of ripening grain blowing in the prairie breeze. I savor the rich smell of wheat as it spills from the combine to the truck. My mind takes me to pungent fields of new-mown hay, and the sweet scent of pink clover growing high on the ditchbanks. Wind-blown clothes dance on outdoor clothes lines; and Alberta's unacclaimed provincial animal, the gopher, scampers from hole to hole, chattering noisily. The native meadowlark sings praises as he trills, "The Lehi Field is a pretty little place!" I know these words because my mother told me so.

With the changing season, ever-new memories fill my reverie. I become a child again, playing Fox and Geese in a field of virgin snow. I lie on my back and make a butterfly by moving my arms and legs as far away from my body as possible. I skate on the big pond with a chill wind licking my cheeks, hands and feet. The northern horizon is illuminated by the ever-changing formations of the Aurora Borealis. I lie in crisp, frozen snow, and gaze at the immensity of the heavens, awed at their splendor and seeming closeness to me. During recess at Lehi School, I slide down snowdrifts covering fenceposts and build snow forts. I see the mystic shadows painted on evening walls by a kerosene lamp.

I ride horseback to town to take a piano lesson and bring back a school satchel full of groceries. In springtime, while living in town to attend high school, I walk the five-mile distance to be with Daddy and my brothers at the farm. The overwhelming stench of beet pulp and molasses used to feed the cattle permeates indoors and out. My housecleaning efforts are satisfying, but not commensurate with the power of decaying pulp. ONLY that scent makes returning to town more enticing than being at home on the farm.

The poignant smell of the high school gym whets my appetite for more basketball games, either as a spectator or a teenage participant. My voice grows hoarse just thinking of the intense rivalry between high school and senior teams from Magrath, Raymond, Cardston and Lethbridge.

Oh, the wonderful tantalizing aroma of fresh-baked bread, which weekly fills my kitchen. What a sensory experience! Even in maturity when one's tastes become more sophisticated, any other fragrance pales by comparison.

Sunday spells Sunday School in town, where I meet friends not seen on weekdays. Margaret Fletcher has a magic baton which teaches me the songs in the hymnal in such a way that they are recalled by rote all of my life.

The Saturday visit to Magrath's business district, one block long, is always pleasant. At Christmas time, they stretch only one string of lights on the street, but it is enough to bridge the magical chasm of childhood and fill my entire world with "Peace on Earth."

* * * *

"ONE, TWO, BUCKLE MY SHOE!"

It matters not to which generation you belong. If you are female I believe you have at one time or another longed for a pair of patent leather slippers. I was no different. Many of my friends had them, and my life was just not going to be fulfilled until I had my very own. I voiced this plea often, until on my seventh birthday I was taken to the Magrath Trading Company and measured for a pair of those beautiful shoes.

When my parents came to pick me up, I preened before the mirror. Oh, they seemed almost magic! They transformed a normal little farm girl into a lovely ballerina, or a princess, or whatever I wished to be!

I took the precious cargo home in a box and recall going to bed with them close beside me. In the morning I tried them on again, and waltzed through the house as if I had wings on my heels. They had a rounded toe and a little narrow strap that buckled, and they were so shiny I could see my face in them.

While still in this euphoria, I was brought back to reality by the voice of my older sister, Beth, calling me to bring her some soft water. It was summer. The grass was green on the hillside and the river water flowed swiftly down the ditch between the lane and the schoolyard fence. This was our supply of "soft water" which was used for washing hair and taking our Saturday night bath. Cheerfully, with bucket in hand, I skipped off to the ditch where the spiky whisps of brome grass were high. I did not buckle my shoes. There was a little foot bridge across the ditch. I knelt down to scoop up the pail of water, and one of the shoes fell off! I dropped the pail and threw the remaining shoe to the bank. Frantically I jumped into the water, searching desperately for the lost slipper. I ran to the end of the barnyard, feeling the ditch bottom with my hands all the way. Bitter tears of frustration coursed down my chubby cheeks as I checked all the crags along the ditch bank, but none yielded the lost slipper. I never found the shoe.

Can you imagine the feelings of a little girl whose life's fulfillment was so short-lived? My parents were sympathetic, but reminded me that I should not have worn them for everyday, least of all unbuckled. I had to wear my canvas "running shoes" to Sunday School all summer. The remaining shoe was a grim reminder of my folly. Thus at the tender age of seven, I felt that the dark ages of my childhood had set in in earnest.

* * * *

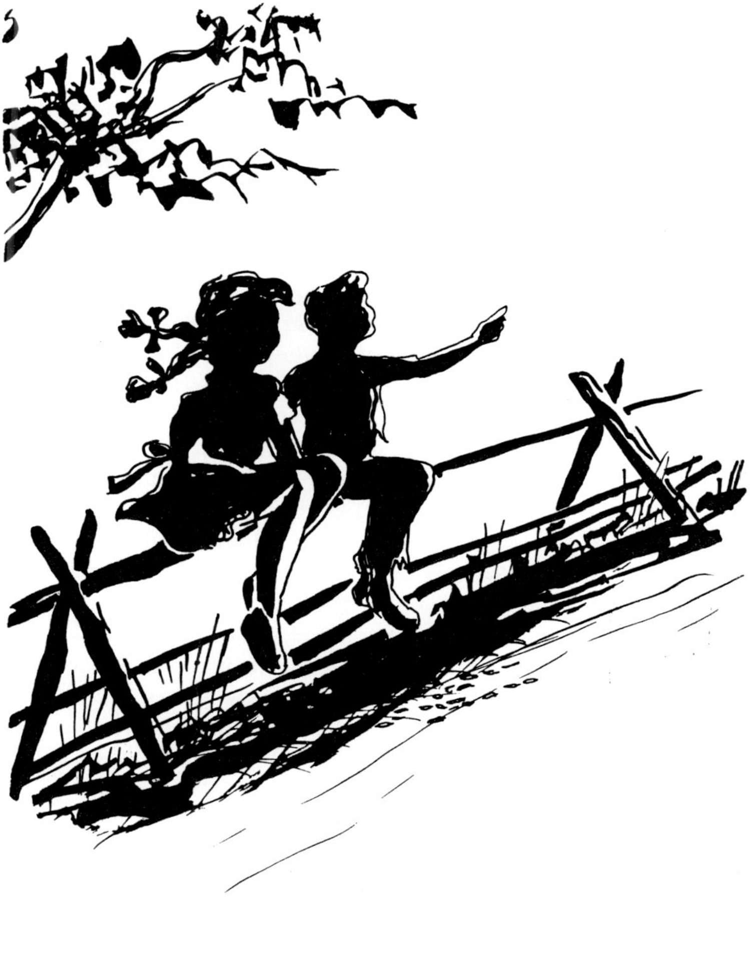

THE FENCE SITTER

The fence around the barnyard was made of pine poles stacked three deep which stood about five feet high. The bark on the poles had long since been rubbed off by the cattle, so the bleached poles were smooth and shiny, except for a few knots. The fence was a haven of refuge enjoyed by kids and cats alike, whether as an escape from a predator (two or four-legged) or just as a way to keep feet dry! It also provided a bird's eye view of barnyard activity, much of which was not for little girls' viewing, but which I surreptitiously enjoyed while straddling the fence.

Springtime was especially exciting, as during that season all the farrowing, foaling, calving and birthing took place. The barnyard became a beehive of activity either waiting for the new arrivals or as a shelter for the young against brisk spring chills or "waiting for a chinook." When the activities went indoors (in the barn), I became a "stall sitter." From the fence or stall, I became educated in the fine arts of breeding, midwifery, castrating sheep and pigs, dipping and shearing sheep, or feeding a calf or lamb from a bottle.

Feeding calves and lambs was accomplished by holding the nippled quart bottle between the poles of the fence. The handfed animals were usually orphans or "bums." Their mother may have died or rejected her offspring. Or had more than she could handle, as in the case of twins or triplets. I became familiar with the latter circumstance a few years later in my own life. They became very tame and followed us everywhere. Of course these were our favorite pets, and it was a sad day when they were sold or sent to market.

I remember trying to ride young calves or colts. This venture was never successful, because without something to grasp, I was dumped in a hurry. However, the anticipation of those few seconds astride a "bronco" were worth the effort. Trying to milk the calves met with the same degree of success.

Each time I find myself near a pole fence a kaleidoscope of activity comes to mind. I yearn to lock my feet between the poles as I lock precious memories into my heart.

* * * *

AN EARLY LESSON IN DISCIPLINE

The disciplining of our family was left to Mother, and she did a good job. We were taught by precept and example the sins of

*H*ermine and Fred in the
Straw Hat Era

*H*ired Man Joseph Melich
& Fred

commission as well as omission. I must have committed my share of infractions, as I remember being banished to the house often, which robbed me of my pleasurable hours spent outdoors. This was punishment enough, but I was also usually spanked, scolded and sent to "my room" which I shared with four sisters at various and sundry times! I was not one to hold a grudge, but bounced back fast and was eager to be on my way to further mischief.

One day I was helping Daddy mend the holes in a granary. The field mice had riddled this particular building, so we quickly used up our limited supply of tin. We returned to the house in search of a tin can; a rather scarce item, as I recall. Daddy found a can, went to the shop for the tinsnips and cut it so it could be hammered into one flat piece. This task was usually accomplished while we sat on the trough.

Unexpectedly Daddy was called to make a trip to town, probably for a machinery part. Of course, I wanted to go. I don't recall the reason he refused to take me, but evidently I didn't understand it. I was furious!

I watched the big truck rattle up the lane without me and my frustration surfaced. I grabbed the hammer and vindictively began pounding the tin into the ground. It was pliable and yielded to my blows. Soon it was bent and riddled with holes.

Anger and strength both spent, I stared in unbelief at what I had done. Now Daddy would be furious! Thinking to destroy the evidence, I took the battered piece of tin and threw it in the pond. As it sunk slowly to the bottom of the cloudy water, my childish spirit also sunk. Knowing I was sure to be punished and sent to my room, I headed in that direction on my own. The interim between the deed and Daddy's return was painful. Self-incrimination nearly destroyed me before hearing the truck rattle down the lane. It took only seconds for him to return to his granary mending.

Discovering the tin missing, he called out, "Hermine! Hermine!" I heard him call, but I did not answer. He came briskly into the house, taking great long strides. Someone betrayed me and told him my whereabouts. He loomed in the doorway of my bedroom and in an irritated tone asked, "Where is the piece of tin?"

"I don't know." My anguished expression told him otherwise. He repeated the inquiry and I repeated the lie. He explained his immediate need to get the job done and asked me again, "Hermine, tell me what you did with the tin."

I had never before lied to my father and could hold back the tearful truth no longer. I blurted out, "I think it is in the pond."

*H*ermine & Fred
Five and Seven Years Old

Daddy didn't hesitate in his parental duty. He turned me over on the bed and put his big, rough hand down firmly (not more than three times) on the place nature seemed to provide for that purpose. My shrieks could be heard as far as Karrens' a mile away! This was the first spanking Daddy administered to me. Though it was not the last, it was one of the three I remember well.

* * * *

APPRENTICE CARPENTER

It was Christmas, 1938. Emma Lou, my sister, and I had received our customary doll, a book, a tiny bottle of Jergens' lotion (free sample sent for by mail), a pair of stockings, an apple, orange, some nuts and candy. We had been over to Sabeys' and down to Jacobs' for "show and tell" and had been told to "come back when we couldn't stay so long." We were tired of Checkers, Rook, and Krochinole, so looked around for new interests.

From a nondescript family project emerged a leftover large piece of plywood, about 1/8" thick. I envisioned doll furniture made from it so volunteered my carpentry expertise for the task. The plywood was too thin to saw with a hand saw, at least the kind available to me, so I begged Daddy for his six-inch pocket knife. He reluctantly gave it to me, cautioning: "Be very careful."

I had drawn the outline of the furniture on the plywood--drafting a complete bedroom and living room set. I visualized each beautiful piece in a specific place in our doll house in the school trees or in the trough. We would surely be the envy of all our friends!

I had successfully cut out a couple of pieces when the knife blade encountered a knot. Working from my lap, I took careful aim, and with the full strength of my right hand, pounded the top of the knife handle. It went through the plywood, the full length of the blade, and into the thigh of my right leg.

I jumped to my feet, screaming. Crimson blood splashed against the kitchen wall. Mother, standing by the stove, knew I had cut an artery. She grabbed a dish towel and efficiently applied a tourniquet, as with each heart beat the blood spurted out like a miniature geyser. (I realize that never does the loss seem quite as profuse as when the blood is your own!)

Had Mother panicked as I did, the results could have been disastrous, but she was well trained as a practical nurse and knew exactly what to do in an emergency. She tightened the tourniquet until the bleeding ceased and then gradually eased the tension until it could be removed. I remember lying on the couch in the kitchen most of two or three days, waiting for the wound to heal. Today it would require three or four stitches!

For some reason, I never finished cutting out the doll furniture. Perhaps a lucrative career in furniture design was wasted because of this incident. I knew better than to ask Daddy for his pocket knife again.

* * * *

SUNDAY SCHOOL SLEIGH RIDE

Sunday was a day devoted to church services after chores were done, of course. To us kids, it was a respite from farm life and an opportunity to see "town friends." The Briggs' car was full to overflowing, but we still managed to pick up several neighbor kids along the way. To say we were "sardined" was a literal statement of fact.

The spring rains made mud of the roads from farm to town, and it was quite a test of faith to subject even a seasoned driver to handling such an experience. It was not unusual to see us walking barefoot, carrying our shoes, as we took little mincing steps in a well formed tire track, leaving the car for someone else to rescue. Occasionally Daddy announced: "The roads are just too bad today," and wails went up from a disappointed population.

In the winter time it was not uncommon for the car to refuse to start despite pulling it with a team of horses. With temperatures dipping in the low 20s and 30s, even a sunny day produced little warmth. If the wind blew, and it usually did, great drifts of snow clogged the roads and almost everything came to a grinding halt. Everything, that is, except my parents' faithful church attendance. We thought our prayers were answered when Mother suggested: "Couldn't we hitch up a team and go in the sleigh?" We kids chorused an enthusiastic approval.

While Daddy harnessed the team of horses, Mother put flat irons in the red coals of the kitchen stove to use for warming hands and feet. Wool blankets were gathered to wrap around us, and heavy hats, coats and mittens were eagerly donned. Wool scarves were placed over our ears and mouths and tied in back of our heads.

Getting settled in the sleigh was exciting. We sat on beds of straw or hay and huddled close together to conserve body heat. Daddy

A Visit from Uncle Floyd and
Aunt Gen Bradshaw from Salt Lake City
Back Row: Aunt Gen, Mother, Beth and Alice.
Second Row: Hermine, Fred, Emma Lou.
Third Row: Ernie, Don and Uncle Floyd — 1935 —

cracked the reins and we glided up the lane. The horses bounded in a slow trot, but the ride was smooth as silk. The harnesses jingled in rhythm to the horses' clomp-clomp, while the horses' breath was like white vapor in the frosty air. Almost immediately hoar frost gathered on our eyebrows and scarves, and our hands began to tingle with the cold. The hot irons packed in towels were passed from one to another. We were reminded to clap our hands to insure good circulation and stave off frost bite. When patches of white appeared on our faces, we knew we were in for a real frost burn, which was painful and often peeled. Accordingly when I discovered my nose was getting frostbitten, I wailed my announcement to Daddy. He only added to my consternation by the affirmation: "Well, if it didn't stick out so far it wouldn't get so cold!" My indignation at this less than subtle reminder more than warmed my chilly person.

The five-mile trip to town was longer in the sleigh, but the exhilaration it afforded was worth the extra time. I loved the feel of feather-light snow on my eyelashes, the sound of the steel sleigh runners on the frozen snowpack, and the intense brightness and clarity of the frigid air. The beauty of these things wrapped me like a warm blanket. Besides, my "town friends" were always envious of our sleigh rides. It was fun to have the shoe on the other foot for a change.

* * * *

THE WINDMILL AND MY MIND . . . .

Characteristically, a windmill pumps water, and in this respect ours was characteristic. We had a large oblong cement trough that originally was the receptacle for watering the cattle. I remember what a smelly, mucky mess it was all winter and well into spring, having the cattle that close to the house. Later a pond was dug on the other side of the barn, so the windmill was no longer employed for cattle use and it fell into disrepair. However, for a time it had its days of glory, and those are the days of which I speak.

The trough was a "special" place, as it was "home safe" whatever the game we played. In the summer when it was not used for water, it housed some beautiful and imaginative play houses. Never was spring cleaning undertaken more seriously as we swept, mopped and dusted to prepare it for our dolls and furniture, rescued from old farm equipment as well as discards from the house. When we outgrew the doll stage, it was planted with flowers which seemed to endear it to us even more, as flowers did not grow easily around the house yet seemed to flourish in this small enclosure. We also used it as a rest-stop between our turns sitting on the ice-cream freezer or turning the handle. And it was dandy to whack the ice into a fine texture in a gunny sack. Suffice to say, it was a landmark on our farm, revered through the years.

The windmill tower was the tallest place on the farm except perhaps the hayloft, but the view was infinitely better. You could see for miles around--the Ridge, the Pot Hole, Hill Cumorah, the Lethbridge elevators. From that vantage point you could trace the route of any vehicle on the road. We climbed the windmill ladder when we thought it about time for Mom and Dad to return from Lethbridge. In the winter we followed the lights and in the summer we tracked the dust clouds churning behind the car. When we felt we had spotted our car, the alert was sounded. We scrambled to get the chores done before they rounded the corner by Schneyders' half a mile away.

I climbed the tower on many occasions. . .maybe when I wanted to be alone, away from the rest of the world, or needed to feel superior in some way. It gave me not only an elevated feeling, but served a rather curious purpose on other occasions.

Since there had been two redheaded boys before Emma Lou and me, Mother was acquainted with the problems of our sun-sensitive skin. Ernie was virtually one big freckle, what with working in the sun-drenched fields. Mother devised a plan disguised as a sunbonnet or straw hat to keep Emma Lou and me from a similar fate. Hats have never been one of my favorite things and for as long as I can remember I have been trying to avoid them. I didn't appreciate the sacrifice it truly was for Mother to buy one initially, much less to replace it through willful neglect on my part. My whole objective during those carefree summer days seemed to be how to permanently separate me from my straw hats. I had been guilty of putting a rock in it and throwing it in the ditch or pond. Rarely did it surface. On other occasions I held it out the car window and as we turned a sharp corner I just accidentally let go! Of course I did not report the loss in time to retrieve it! While herding cows near the corn field, a chore I truly despised, I recall pulling a hat apart out of boredom, one woven strand after another until it lay in a heap before me. I rationalized it as one of the hazards of the occupation!

But my ability to destroy straw hats reached the apex when I hit upon a rather curious scheme to see what the windmill would do to it. I chose a lovely summer day when a brisk breeze was whirling the large fins of the mill, making a whistle as it shook the nearby trees. I scrambled monkey-like up the narrow ladder, eager for a new thrill in destruction! The first revolution caught the crown and began the shredding process which rendered it quite useless in no time! Dismounting the tower, I picked up all the telltale scraps and threw them in a ditch of swift running water. My secret was secure.

I do not remember at what age Mother surrendered in the fight over my freckles, but in time she gave up trying to keep a hat on me. The results were devastating! I freckled daily until I rivaled Ernie for a nose count, but they seemed to match the personality of the little girl dubbed Wild Flower by her father.

When teen years approached, I used lemon juice and assorted drug store creams to bleach out the freckles. When I was about 15, they seemed to merge into one, just leaving me with enough high color in my cheeks that rouge was never necessary. I really didn't mind them all that much and loved it when someone called them "sun kisses." I surely had proof that I was indeed a GREAT lover if they were really kisses!

* * * *

FROM THE HORSE'S MOUTH

In the fall of the year after the crops were off, it was customary to turn the livestock into the fields to forage for themselves. Of course, if the snow got too deep or the winter too hard, they were brought in close enough to receive shelter and feed. They drank water from the big field pond (which was a delightful skating rink in the winter) and one of the boys or Daddy rode out daily to see that an ice-hole was chopped open.

The cattle obviously foraged well because when they were brought in, they were sleek and fat, having gleaned beet tops and grain from the harvested fields. Months of freedom had the effect of making the horses extremely wild and almost impossible to catch, unless driven into the barnyard or a small fenced area.

This particular spring I was probably 10 or 12 years old. I loved horses and spent many happy hours on horseback. An urgent message came over the rural telephone line for Sabeys. They lived about a mile through the field to the west. They had no phone, so it became our job to deliver the "message to Garcia."

Daddy and Ernest were in the barnyard, preparing to go into the field. I was elected to deliver the message, but all the horses were out. I volunteered to go out and catch Joe, and then take the message. Both Daddy and Ernie laughed at the remote possibility of my catching a horse under the circumstances. They knew as well as I that an approaching footman was all horses needed to make them break into a dead run and frisk around the field as if playing a game of tag--with the horses always in the lead!

Undaunted, I took bridle in hand and set off across the stubble to the north end of the land, where I saw the group of horses. As I approached them I called out to Joe. He pricked up his ears and took a long look at me. Perhaps his rapt attention was responsible for the horses not breaking into an instantaneous gallop. When I was close enough to him I cracked the reins and gently called him to me. The rest of the horses dashed away; but Joe, obedient as if confined in the barnyard, came to me, trembling.

I bridled him, led him to the nearby fence, and jumped on his back. I wasted no time getting home to boast of my conquest. To say that I was proud, excited and thrilled to death, would have put it modestly. But when I learned that Daddy and Ernie had watched the procedure through disbelieving eyes, I was on Cloud Nine! I promise you that "Hermine" stock went up that week.

Suffice it to say, "Garcia's" message was promptly delivered, along with the glowing report of how I caught Little Joe.

I should add that Ernie was responsible for teaching several of our saddle horses to come at the crack of the reins, so I will share a minute part of the honor with him for this exciting event in my young life.

* * * *

RIGHT BETWEEN THE EYES

The Royal Canadian Mounted Police was a respected presence in our town. Bill Ellis was large of stature and an imposing figure in any crowd. In full uniform he was intimidating enough to stem even the thought of a misdemeanor. He was our one-man law and order official.

As we saw the dark blue car with the large R.C.M.P. crest come down our lane, we experienced instantaneous fear and trembling. Don and Daddy were in the grain tank putting formaldehyde on wheat as a rust retardant for planting when the car pulled into the yard. Bill Ellis and another man got out and engaged Daddy in conversation. I knew Daddy shot a dog the day before which had killed our sheep. When I saw Bill and the stranger walk toward Daddy, I ran to his side as if to protect him from arrest. The stranger raged on in a very authoritative manner and recounted the value of his dog. He demanded reprisal. The fact that two dogs, both his, killed OUR sheep on OUR property was waved away with dispatch. Daddy remained calm throughout the tirade. Finally Bill Ellis interrupted, and trying to establish where the shooting occurred, asked:

"Where did you shoot the dog?"

"Right between the eyes," Daddy replied matter-of-factly.

* * * *

IN PRAISE OF LEHI SCHOOL[1]

Today we hear a great deal about the needs of the individual child: the impact of the learning experience, the pros and cons of the open classroom, individual differences, the deprived child, the gifted child, the special child, and sex education in the classroom. Such rhetoric was foreign to my education at Lehi School. Still, I am convinced that this little one room, eight-grade establishment provided adequately and happily my personal needs from 1932 to 1940.

Lehi School was a small white frame building of about 2,000 square feet. It had a rather boxy appearance as did most one-room schools. It had ample windows on two sides of the building to shed sufficient light on our studies. Never were they covered with blinds or curtains. I guess the Board of Trustees figured we needed all the light and sunshine we could get!

The desks were wooden, the type with armrests on the right side with no provision for left-handers. The desks were equipped with inkwells and also a bookrack underneath the seat. They were arranged in rows by grade. Never were the rows longer than four or five desks. My grade never had a row longer than four desks and that was probably for only part of a year.

The first three years I attended school my grade level consisted of Darlene Sabey, Betty Cheeseworth, and myself. Ron Passey, Maxine Aldrich and Keith Bennett were in my grade at short intervals. Johnnie Brunner was in grades 6, 7, and 8 with Darlene and me. Emily Schneider was in our class the last two years. I always stood first or second, but never third! Darlene and I were very competitive, not only in academics but in sports as well.

The schoolhouse was heated by a coal furnace in the quarter basement built to accommodate it. In the winter months we crowded round it to thaw out our hands and feet, and left our outer clothing on or near it to dry. Most of the students who lived two or three miles away rode horses. The remainder of us walked, as the distance was never more than a half-mile. The Briggs family lived just across the fence, while the Sabeys and Brunners lived about a half mile through the field. Everyone carried a lunch bucket (lard pail) and noon time was festive as everyone traded sandwiches. We Briggs kids didn't always stay for lunch but felt we were missing out on the fun, so

---

[1] Lehi School was so-named because most of the residents of the farming community which it served were originally from Lehi, Utah. It was the hub of our school and social activities for two decades. See Appendix A.

Mother frequently made us a sandwich. I remember trading Darlene a peanut butter and honey sandwich for an egg sandwich on a regular basis. An apple was generally the fruit of choice as other fruits were very expensive. Mother frequently bought dried fruit (raisins and prunes) which were often included in a lunch. The teachers were very emphatic against chewing gum while in school. I recall once being accused and I responded, "No, I don't have any chewing gum. I am just soaking a prune for recess."

The three R's were paramount. We recited our multiplication tables silently and aloud until we knew them by rote and could almost break the sound barrier for speed when reciting them. Daily trips were made to the blackboard to demonstrate our memory and skill. If our performance was less than impressive we were frequently detained during recess or stayed after school until it improved.

We spent as much time improving writing skills as learning the multiplication tables. We were taught to use free arm movement and countless were the pages filled with exercises making ovals and up and down movements with a "nib pen" dipped in the inkwell. All of the pupils learned to write legibly if not well, which is a crying need in succeeding generations. Judging by his penmanship, I tell my son that he qualified as a doctor very early in life.

Reading was a pastime we enjoyed whether we wanted to or not. It was a requirement not taken lightly. We had to memorize many poems, long and short, and I can recite them to this day. We read the classics, looked up the new words, used them in sentences, and wrote the entire poem in our notebooks, including punctuation, by memory. We were also graded on our handwriting and spelling for anything we handed in. Although the school library was small, most of us became voracious readers and read everything we could get our hands on. Mother and Daddy never let us say we were bored. We were given books of all kinds to occupy our minds, as if there were not enough chores to keep us busy! I remember reading many of the classics several times. Books were my cherished possessions and many of them are still in my home library. Jack London, Louisa May Alcott, Robert Louis Stevenson, Harriet Beecher Stowe, Mark Twain, and Tennyson are still some of my favorite authors.

If we needed help while the teacher was busy, a student in one of the higher grades tutored us, an honor bestowed on the first one to finish his own work. This solved the problem of a student having to wait his turn with the teacher.

Recalling our studies in geography, social studies and science, I am aware that these subjects were very much book-oriented because visual aids were almost non-existent. I recall two "visual aids." One was an apparatus depicting the earth and all other planets revolving around the sun, the other a Bunsen burner. These two items were the nucleus of any experiments the teacher wished to demonstrate. Our world was also expanded by many large relief maps which hung above the large blackboards.

Current events were discussed daily, though none of our parents were subscribers to daily newspapers. During World War II, I remember listening to the BBC news from London each morning. My teacher, Sarah Gibb Low, had a little radio that was our lifeline with the world we did not know. Her interest in events in Europe was more than passing, as her husband, Lorin, was serving with the troops on active duty. I have several scrapbooks chronicling events of WW II, including the newspaper the day the Canadians declared war on Nazi Germany. The maps printed by the newspapers put each theater of war in perspective, and showed what territorial lines were being changed by aggression. We vicariously lived the war. Few families were untouched by it, having members who served in one capacity or another. Many did not return.

Discipline might have been a problem at times, but was usually short-lived. Having older brothers and sisters in the same room was a natural deterrent to misbehavior. Also, the teacher was not hindered from the use of a leather strap applied to the hands or bottom. The strap hung on a nail in front of the room. It represented "The Board of Education" for those who were not sure who was in charge. The younger students were very much intimidated by seeing it administered to the older ones. However, on several occasions I can remember Darlene and Betty and I standing in front of the classroom to receive five hits with the strap on our hands for completely failing a test on addition and subtraction. I think we each had twenty or more problems wrong. Betty cried before even getting one hit, and Darlene and I got the giggles, which meant we got more hits because we laughed. We sobered up eventually. Mr. Blumell said it hurt him more than it did us, but we didn't believe him. We usually performed scholastically better than that.

Personality conflicts with the teacher had little opportunity to foment as siblings kept surveillance of a testy situation and reported same to parents. Case in point (which I do not remember but had relayed to me): Alice felt the teacher had dealt unfairly with Virginia so she took him to task after school. "What did Mr.___ say?" inquired Mother. Alice replied: "What could he say? I had him in a corner!"

Our teachers were extremely versatile. Though only "normal school" trained, they made an earnest effort at far more than the basics. Emerson Blumell taught me to read and write, since he was my teacher from first grade through third. He was handsome and his handwriting was beautiful. I tried to form my letters as he did his. He praised honest effort and my handwriting improved accordingly. My sister Beth taught me in fourth grade. She brought a feminine dimension to the classroom that I had not known. All the girls wore overalls to school, but she wore a dress and looked and acted very much the "school marm" part. She had a lovely singing voice and music appreciation was added to the curriculum through the use of an old phonograph, the kind you cranked. When the crank wound down, it emitted some terrible noises which created much frivolity! Jim Blumell (Emerson's younger brother) taught me in fifth grade. He, too, was a very good teacher, and a fine athlete. I recall that both he and Emerson could hit the softball or baseball clear across the fence of the school yard. We loved having them play with us.

Sarah Gibb Low taught me in grades six and seven. She could sing like a meadowlark. In addition to being well-versed on the basics, she continued our musical training by teaching us countless folk songs which I, in turn, taught my children.

My eighth grade teacher was Irene Dow Minion. Though tone-deaf, she knew the rudiments of music, and thumped many a new tune out with one finger on the "prehistoric" piano in the classroom. I stood a head taller than she, so from a picture point of view, I looked like the teacher and she the pupil.

Vinessa Tanner Hamilton was one of our infrequent substitute teachers. She was a rare commodity in that she was the only teacher who played the piano. She taught us "The Santa Claus Express," still one of my favorite Christmas songs.

Our social needs were also nourished in our cocoon environment. Each Friday afternoon for the last hour of the day, the students presented a program wherein individuals sang, recited, told a story, or expressed themselves in their own ways. The teacher also participated with a presentation of his choosing. We frequently heard the same numbers over and over again, but no matter. It gave each person expression and we clapped as if the rendition were new. I recall Merlin Sorenson giving a reading in Danish dialect of "Daddy's Tracks." We never tired of hearing it. Other Sorensons, Delyle and Haroldine, had lovely voices. Darlene and I often teamed up for a duet taught by our older sisters. We were notorious for getting the giggles during our renditions, but we still were asked to perform, both at school and in the community. In retrospect, I am confident that Magrath never suffered from a dearth of talent for such events. Why they kept asking us is beyond me, other than our price was right!

At Christmas time and at school's closing in June, the students prepared a program for parents and townspeople. It usually involved a play and many choral numbers. My, how we practiced and practiced so we would not embarrass ourselves or our parents:

The stage was made by borrowing the neighborhood supply of sheets and stringing them on a wire suspended from the ceiling. It was a great honor to be the opener and closer of the curtains. Refreshments were usually punch and cookies in the summer and hot chocolate and cake in the winter. Those who drank coffee brought their own. Then a live combo of a pianist, a violinist and a drummer provided dance music for the evening. How we looked forward to these two events because we had opportunity to dance with our favorite beau, our handsome teachers and our fathers. It was an accepted fact that some of the parents were imbibers, and they were given that privilege outside the school building. They usually returned much happier and ready to participate in the dancing. At times the party became somewhat raucous, but we felt the excitement was part of our education! And besides, it was quite thrilling to have an ever-so-slight brush with sin.

In the spring we participated in the regional festival, which was a competition in both music and elocution. After hours of practice before the studentbody and my mother, we were transported by parents to the big city of Lethbridge. Mother was a good musician as well as knowing drama, so she enhanced our winning opportunities tremendously. Our school came away with more than our share of firsts, seconds and thirds, with many of them being awarded to the Briggs kids, probably because we always had three or more attending Lehi at one time. It was while Beth was teaching that our chorus won the silver cup for participating, an honor which we retained for three years under Sarah Low. We were supposed to get to keep the cup, but no one seems to know what happened to it. Since it was silver, it should have substantial worth at this writing.

Another annual event of much anticipation was the track meet staged in the spring. Competition was keen within grades, but became epidemic when students from Farmhill and St. Mary's one-room schools were invited to participate. On other occasions we had softball competition with these schools and Lehi was always the victor because "we had such big boys." A wiener roast usually ended the day's activities. Of credit to our teachers is the fact that they were the innovators of such events. The teachers at the other schools rarely instigated anything to which Lehi students were invited.

When the school grounds were dry enough, we played softball, baseball, or Danish ball. Every student was needed because without every one, we could not make up two teams to play. There was no provision for the kid who just "didn't want to play" or the one who "didn't feel good." We were each too important to the team no matter how poor at the bat! If the weather was inclement, our recesses and noons were spent playing with rubber guns in the barn. Fathers or brothers carved guns out of plywood or pine, and bullets were rubber rings cut from tire tubes. They stung like sixty when hit at close range, but our rule was it had to be a hit below the head. Of course some of us were poor shots, and sometimes a stray bullet hit the head, but we lived to tell it!

Basketball hoops were installed during my seventh year at Lehi. How we loved to practice foul shots and play basketball and "freeze-out." It was a novel change from the usual ball games or Kick-the-Can played in the school trees. We had a lot of fun and a good physical workout. I recall that these same basketball standards were completely covered with snowdrifts in the winter, as were the trees and fenceposts around the schoolhouse. We had great fun sliding down the drifts and were loathe to see them disappear with warming weather. However, it made basketball once more accessible to us--as soon as the mud dried up, that is! Being as close to the school grounds as we were, the Briggs kids enjoyed playing basketball all summer. Also there were many evening games of softball that we enjoyed with neighbors and hired men.

My first "lucrative" employment also took place at Lehi School. For three years I was the "janitor." This entailed daily sweeping of the floor (using oiled sawdust called "dustbane") to cleanse the floor, dusting the desks, cleaning the blackboards with a wet cloth, cleaning the erasers by pounding them on the outside of the building, emptying the wastebaskets in the furnace, and filling the water pail from the cistern by drawing the water up with a rope. I also cleaned the washbasin and washstand. We all drank from a common dipper and wondered why we all caught the same colds! The above details could be accomplished with dispatch in little over an hour, but the real test of character came during the winter months. At that time I got up at 5:30 a.m., made my way in the dark to the basement of the school building, built a fire in the furnace, and had it sufficiently warm by the time school started. Of course I had to return several times during the day to put on more coal and try to "bank" it at night so that the building remained warm. It was also important to keep temperatures up for the comfort of the teacher living in the built-on "teacherage." On weekends I did not maintain the furnace because the teacher was usually gone to town. However, that necessitated having to build a new fire on Monday morning. It was not infrequent to see temperatures dip down to 20 and 30 degrees below zero for several weeks. I felt a grave responsibility for the comfort of many besides myself. And for this grand and glorious privilege, I was paid $5.50 a month for the first year, and $7.50 a month the last two years. Talk about child abuse, child labor laws and non-union labor!

However in spite of these drawbacks, I was thrilled to have the means of earning some money of my own. From this early beginning, I found I could pay tithing and buy "all" of my own school clothes! I am confident "all" is a misnomer, but the wardrobe of a little tomboy like me was limited to a pair of overalls, a too-short dress used as a blouse, and a sweater. I know my wages did not cover my sturdy one pair of shoes. But I bought my first wristwatch at a second hand store in Lethbridge for $7.50, a whole month's wages! It gave me a great rush of independence. Today my title would be "Maintenance Superintendent" or "Custodial Engineer," but at Lehi School I was just the janitor.

* * * *

SEX EDUCATION (?) AT LEHI SCHOOL!

The school grounds were yellow with dandelions. Gophers scampered from hole to hole, stopping occasionally on hind legs to better chatter to one another as they surveyed their domain in the school yard. The trees bordering the school property were dressed in delicate shades of leafy green. Spring fever had reached epidemic proportions at Lehi, and recess held great excitement with our softball games. We were reluctant to answer the calling bell that summoned us to lessons. Sarah Gibb was my teacher and I was in sixth grade. She was fun-loving, young, petite, and very pretty.

In answer to her bell, we ran toward the classroom. We were distracted by the sight of a cow on her front knees, on the Sabey side of the fence. Some of us were aware she was giving birth, and to-the-man we all lined the fence to watch the phenomenon. The forelegs were well into view as we came on the scene. No one spoke. We all stood as if transfixed before the miracle of birth. Her mammoth belly heaved with each contraction. She moaned and salivated, and we

The Briggs Lineup: Jim, Emma Lou, Hermine, Fred, Mother, Virginia, Beth, Alice, Don, Ernie and Daddy (1937)

Hermine at farm swing, Reading *Little Women*

36 HEART STRINGS

Lehi School Entry in 24th July Float, 1937: Sarah Gibb—teacher, Hermine Briggs—nurse, John Brunner—scientist, Arden Olmstead—artist, Haroldene Sorenson—basketball, Tom Karren—hockey

Chorus Winners of Silver Cup – 1936
*Teacher – Beth Briggs, Leonard Whitt,
Merlin Sorenson, Fred Briggs, Gordon Sabey,
Roy Rollingson, Hermine Briggs, Darlene Sabey,
Arden Olmstead, Emma Lou Briggs, Ron Passey,
Haroldene Sorenson and Tom Karren*

Friends Forever!

Hermine Briggs and Darlene Sabey

– 1937 –

Lehi School – 1941 Teacher, Irene Dow Minion. The tallest one there is Hermine.

The
Rope
Twirler
Hermine

*M*agrath
Girls' Basketball Team
  Victor Bohnet, coach;
Norma Ririe, Haroldene Sorenson,
Dorothy Tanner, Darlene Sabey, Nora Carter,
Ruth Anderson, Hermine Briggs and Herta Mole

Lehi School Silver Cup Chorus Winners – 1938

Back Row: Jim Briggs, Arden Olmstead, Gordon Sabey, Grace Peterson *(accompanist)* Hermine Briggs, Darlene Sabey and Tom Karren.
Front Row: Mike Schneyder, Annie Brunner, Haroldene Sorenson, Sarah Gibb *(teacher)*, Emma Lou Briggs, Emily Schneyder, and Johnnie Schneyder

Special Friends at Waterton Park Hermine, Dorothy Tanner, Darlene Sabey and Norma Ririe.

A Waterton Holiday — Front: Beth and Norma Ririe
Back: Hermine, Dorothy Tanner and Darlene Sabey

*R*iding my Favorite Horse, Stroller – 1940

Good Friends — Daddy & Jim (1942)

Appleblossom Time on the Farm – 1941 Jim, Hermine and Emma Lou

*At the Farm
Hermine
– 1941 –*

46 HEART STRINGS

Briggs Sisters – 1943
Emma Lou, Beth, Hermine and Alice

*Fred
and
Hermine
– 1941 –*

*Hermine,
Daddy
and
Emma Lou
– 1942 –*

pressed as close as possible to catch a glimpse of the emerging curly head. It seemed but a few minutes before the whole body slid out. It was a beautiful bald-faced heifer, wobbly legged, with huge brown eyes. An air of excitement bathed each of our group of youthful spectators. The cow bellowed relief and licked her baby dry. The whole procedure must have taken about 45 minutes.

Mission accomplished, we simultaneously became aware that school was supposed to be the subject of the day. With this realization we turned to run to the classroom, fully expecting a scolding for our tardiness.

Imagine our surprise as we unexpectedly bumped into our teacher, Miss Gibb, who had surreptitiously joined the onlookers at the fenceline. She said nothing, but smiled. Her countenance seemed to convey the thought that a very important lesson had been taught during those golden moments. Perhaps our sweet unmarried teacher from the city had learned more than her students.

* * * *

LITTLE BROWN JUG

When I was a little girl I recall an oft-sung song: "Ha ha ha, you and me, little brown jug how I love thee."

Depending on one's point of reference, the song had many meanings. In my mind's eye there was only one little brown jug, and that was the kind that was called a crock. It was heavy with thick sides. When initially purchased it might have been filled with kerosene for a wick lamp or with vinegar for making dill pickles in the fall. These were the days of prohibition, and to those who imbibed, perhaps their homemade brew gave greater meaning to "little brown jug how I love thee."

My sister, Emma Lou, and I shared the girl's room, which was an add-on without foundation. In the winter the windows were so thick with frost you could scarcely see daylight through them; the atmosphere so cold we used to say we could read each other's conversation! Our bed was piled high with homemade quilts and overcoats. I marvel that we could breathe at all with such heavy coverings.

About an hour before retiring, we boiled water in the teakettle on our coal stove and filled the little brown jug to the top, corked it, and put it at the foot of the bed, covering it with mounds of bedding.

If we perceived the night as extremely cold, we added hot flat irons to other portions of the bed to warm the frigid mattress. Then "getting ready for bed" began in earnest. We stripped down to our woolen long johns, donned at least two pair of flannel pajamas and put on a sweater and wool socks. A wet cloth was wound around our necks with a dry one on top to ward off sore throat. A wool scarf was tied around our heads to protect overly-sensitive ears. As we clutched a hot bottle to our bosom, we even cheerfully entered our deep freeze bedroom, looking for all the world like a couple of Russian babushkas!

If prayers were said, I am sure they were either relayed in the kitchen with other family members, or mumbled under covers. No one in his right mind would kneel on the freezing floor as we were taught to do. "If I should die before I wake" was not part of our normal litany, but in retrospect, it might well have been!

Stealthily we slithered underneath the covers so that none of the precious heat from the jug could escape. The area around the jug was somewhat warm and our feet eagerly found the source of heat to ensure comfortable toes for the duration of the night. Whoever faced "out" owned the hot water bottle, since the other party, lying spoon-fashion, kept the backside warm. The individual on the "inside" tucked blankets around neck and torso and well under the body. With an arm around the waist of the outside sleeper, sweet dreams were not long in coming. So tight was our adolescent cocoon that without waking or having verbal communication, this twosome executed turning over perhaps a dozen times, scarcely moving the blankets while retaining the spoon position. Morning always came too early, but the refreshment of a good night's sleep found us eager to face the dawn.

Fifty years later I marvel at our youthful stamina. I am confident that we could have slept in warmer quarters in the front room had we chosen to do so. But it seemed to be an exercise that went with the territory. We had long waited our turn to exclusive rights to the "girl's room," and it was apparent that rain, sleet, hail, snow, or temperatures of 20-30 below zero would not remove us from that proffered, yes, even hallowed place.

Memories of the little brown jug still warm my heart.

* * * *

A HAREY STORY

The call of "Daddy's coming home" sent us scampering to the door. Daddy wore bib overalls and a sweater or denim jacket. His pockets fascinated me as they usually contained something of a surprise. If he had been to town, we were assured a stick of licorice which he would cut up with his long-blade pocket knife. One day as he returned from the fields, his pocket produced a fluffy little wild duck. Frequent were the stories of uncovering a skunk's nest with little ones, or a meadowlark's nest, or a colony of field mice. He had a reverence for all living creatures. Perhaps that is why he was happy on the land, and he instilled this same love in his children.

I followed him like his shadow wherever he was going by whatever means. I can remember being with him in a horse-drawn sleigh, a grain tank for a load of coal, on a flatbed hay or beet rack, on the tractor, combine, cultivator, in a truck and car. Any mission was not nearly as important as "just being with Daddy." I was usually his errand girl as he mended fences. I would spend the entire day outside with him. Some of the most memorable lessons of life were literally learned at his knee because the work he was doing was mostly on my level. In the fall and winter, he'd usually spend two or three days mending harnesses. I enjoyed sitting on a saddle thrown over a saw horse and pretending I was on a wild bronc, racing horses-- enjoying all my childhood fantasies while he did his stitching.

When I was about eight or nine, Daddy and I were in the truck picking up stray bundles of grain that had been missed by the binder. A little rabbit flitted across our path and retreated to the safety of the nearby strawstack. "Would you like to take that home to show the kids?" he asked. "Would I!" I shouted, my eyes dancing with anticipation.

He stopped the truck near the stack and told me to watch the hole into which the rabbit had gone. Daddy went around the opposite side of the stack and shouted his confirmation that the hole went all the way through the stack. "I'll put the pitchfork handle through the hole. You put your hands over the hole on your side and be sure to catch the rabbit," he instructed.

The seconds of anticipation were painful--then reality hit me. The rabbit bounded out of his hole. I snatched at him with the speed of light. I screamed and squealed and danced with joy at my wriggling unhappy prize. Daddy came on a dead run and took our bunny booty from me, depositing it under the seat of the truck so it would be safe until we got home.

Never was a little girl more excited! I recall trying to relate the story through great gasps of breath and laughter to Mother, Jim and Emma Lou. I was the envy of my peers for a day or two. Then we turned the rabbit loose in the field. But I was just as proud of my catch as if I had captured it single-handedly!

* * * *

IF WISHES WERE HORSES, I'D RIDE AGAIN

Countless are the horses that my short or lengthening legs have straddled. Some I hold in beloved memory; others with mixed emotions. A favorite with all our family was Mother's "Pet." She was probably the first horse I rode and was so gentle that even if a child fell off she would stand stark still while the child scampered to safety. She stood tall and stately and had a dark brown coat. Her mane stood in short tufts at the base of her neck because we yanked it off as we "swung on."

Long before I was of school age and could swing on, I rode Pet up and down the lane, hours on end, until someone took me off for lunch or dinner. The horse must have been at least 16 years old prior to my arrival, because I remember she was always old. She had very expressive big eyes and seemed to understand that her role in life was to make enjoyment for children. Never did she forget it or betray the trust put in her gentleness.

Dixie was another story! She was a pinto mare and a typical Indian pony. She had her ears pulled back constantly and was ready to bite should anybody allow opportunity. She tried daily to buffalo her youthful mounts. If I were trying to climb on via the fence or swing, she would take off before I could get a leg over her back. If I were swinging on, she would turn in a circle so that I couldn't get on. If I tried to make her run and she didn't want to, she would try to rub me off on a barbed wire fence. She only ran willingly when accompanied by another horse. If I were heading home and was almost to the lane, she would break into a dead run towards the barn. Whether the barn door was open three inches or three feet, she would scrape through. It must have presented quite a sight: the horse running full tilt, her neck straight out, ears back, tail extended, while I was doing a balancing act with my legs in the air!

If I tried to get her to lope, she would literally get her back up and trot a most miserable hard trot guaranteed to jar my innards loose until I gave up and let her walk. No amount of rib kicking had any effect on her. Without a doubt, she was one of the most ornery critters in my experience!

On one occasion, my brother, Fred, forgot to feed the horses in the barn. It was dark and Daddy reminded him of his waiting chores, specifically feeding the horses. I willingly accompanied him on most errands, so it was natural that I got summoned on this one. He was in the manger feeding Dixie. I came up behind her and slapped her on the rear. Most horses would have kicked in the direction of the offense, but not Dixie. She reached for the body ahead of her and grabbed a big bite out of Fred's back. His shrieks could be heard at the house--and of course, I was in big trouble for having caused the incident! He wore those teethmarks down his back for many weeks and a bruise remained long after the initial teethmarks were gone.

I remember her trying to scrape me off on the fence as I was returning from taking the cows to pasture. In vain I tried to gallop her, but could not get her off that miserable trot. I saw a hefty piece of wood from a broken post. I got off, picked it up, and was determined to let her know who was boss. I got back on and laid it to her. The shock was so great that she made a lunge that threw me off. I lit in the barrow pit, hitting my side on a rock which knocked the wind out of me. I rolled around for several minutes before I was sure I was not being "called home." She kept about two horse-lengths ahead of me all the way home and wouldn't let me catch her. I ended up walking the entire three miles.

She had one colt, Pinto, who was one of the prettiest little fillies we had. She carried herself with pride and was a much better saddle horse than her mother. She was very spirited and in the process of being broken, she ran away with several of us. We sold her while she was young, fearful her disposition might reflect some inherited genes.

Probably the most handsome horse I rode was Stroller. He was a beautiful dapple-gray gelding. He was sleek and fat, a big horse, but I always felt he was the envy of his peers. He developed a single foot gait that was most pleasant and made the rider feel she was almost floating on air. Smooth is the only word that describes it. The single-foot gait had two speeds before breaking into a run. He could easily out-pace any horse on a trot, and for being as big as he was, didn't take second place to any on a gallop--at least to any of my friends' horses, which surely were in a class of their own: this was true of horses in the neighborhood with the exception of Darlene's "Old May," who was mostly thoroughbred and had won some races at the local track. We thought she was magnificent, but I preferred riding Stroller.

His one bad feature was that he shied at anything that startled him. I recall coming from Felgers' on a gallop. As we came to the summit of a small knoll, a canvas dam was swung over the barbed wire fence. He shied. I fell off in the soft dirt along the country road. He was frightened and made his way home without me, try as I did to catch up with him. I did, however, catch him about a block from home so that I arrived with my dignity intact. I didn't have to admit being thrown unless I wanted to! My brothers gave me a bad time about the horses, so I had to protect my reputation as a horsewoman.

Lest my readers think I was easily thrown, let me explain that these experiences were all had while riding bareback. It takes a much better rider to ride bareback than with a saddle. We were raised to ride bareback with a blanket to protect our legs from sweat, but that was only if we were going some distance. It is a much more comfortable ride. However, if a horse is going to throw you when you are bareback, there is little to do but give him his wish. After all, you have nothing to keep you on except leg muscle and determination, neither of which is too effective if the action cannot be predetermined.

Another experience involving Stroller came when I was riding near the river on the Felger property. I had just descended one of the rolling hills when all of a sudden I found my feet touching the ground. I instinctively jumped off, realizing that Stroller was up to his belly in quicksand! I lashed his rear with the reins and only because he was such a big, strong horse was he able to extricate himself. I was scared, but I know I was very cautious thereafter when riding in that terrain.

Jill was a big bay. She stood taller than any horse I had ever ridden. She was part thoroughbred and we bought her from Cliff Merkley. Since I was not yet full-grown, I had difficulty bridling her, especially if she didn't want me to do it. She stretched her already long neck just enough to make it practically impossible to get the bridle over her ears. I took the problem to Daddy. He was confident of a solution. "All you need to do is stand on the manger and whisper in her ear." I laughed and asked, "What good will that do?"

"You just try it," he replied.

I decided it couldn't do anything but improve an impossible situation, so the next time I wanted to bridle Jill I did just as Daddy advised. I stood on the manger, took both ears in my hands and whispered in them. It worked like magic! She put her head down and I was able to bridle her. I don't know how long it was before I realized it was not my plea shared with her, but rather the tickling in her ears that made the difference. But I was confident that my Daddy was as wise as Solomon.

Jill was a spirited horse and a lovely one to ride. However if something frightened her, she reared. That was scary for me to watch as I was afraid her powerful legs would come down on someone. Of course, if I were on bareback, I automatically slid off.

Work horses I hold fondly in my memory are Kate and Duke (roan mates); Prince, the white sway-back; King and Star (big dappled Percherons); Nora, a big fat black mare who jogged someone overhead into the pond; Blackie, an ornery work horse-saddle pony who often balked; Old Fly, who died pregnant from sleeping sickness despite our long-suffering efforts to heal her and save the colt. Daddy did a caesarian section on her, but she was so far gone that the colt could not survive. We kids relived the trauma of the event for many weeks. Most of our work horses were saddle-broken, too. Fred and I plowed the garden each spring with me riding Prince while he guided the plow. His sway back was more comfortable than any saddle and made him just right for the job.

Another vignette has been devoted exclusively to another saddle horse, Little Joe. His counterpart was Pearl, who was aptly named. She was a well-trained white mare and a beautiful, fast little pony. Since she belonged to Ernie, we usually admired her from a distance. It was Pearl that he first taught to come to his call, and we all thought that was fantastic! He also taught her to "nicker," which is horse talk for talking back to him. Ernie had a special gift for working with horses and is still enjoying raising and training them.

Horseback riding is still one of the most pleasurable events of my life. It gives me an exultant feeling to be master of something so strong, majestic, and powerful as a horse. The wind-blown hair across my face, the smell of horse sweat, the green sea-like foam from the bit tossed in the air heighten my sense of freedom. In retrospect, it stirs the desire to once again combine the motion of one's body to the rhythm of the horse's gait. Yes, if wishes were horses, I'd ride again!

* * * *

FARMING AND "LIKING" IT

I thought of naming this essay "Hired Men I Have Known and Loved," but with the stories extant about the farmer's daughter, thought better of it. But the hired men surely added color to the scenes of my childhood.

First, I remember Joseph Melich, an emigrant bachelor from the Ukraine, who spoke no English until my school teacher mother spent many evenings, over a period of years, teaching him. He was not old, perhaps thirty, and was as gentle as a lamb with Emma Lou and me. He had soft brown eyes and was very kind, as well as a good worker. He stayed with us for several years. Like the hired men who followed, he lived in the bunkhouse. He eventually bought a homestead in Northern Alberta, had some difficult years, and died a bachelor in 1972.

Two Swedish brothers, Eric and Hilmer Chronholm, came later. I remember their crude manners at the table and the demand: "Pass every ting dis vay!" They had healthy appetites, and we children were cautioned that the "meat was only for the men." How Mother kept a full table for the multitude she usually had to feed was a miracle! I think she did very well with modest means and no corner supermarket or 7-11.

A married couple came to us from Hungary, Louisa and Joe Sebjen. There was a mean streak in both of them. Louisa taunted cute little brother Jim with: "Come see. Lotso canny, pocket." After being disappointed a time or two, Jim came back with the retort: "Lotso canny pocket all gone!" She wanted him to kiss her but he never took kindly to the idea. However, she never despaired of getting him to come to her for that purpose. He became wise to the ways of women at a very early age! We kids tried to steer clear of both of them, as we didn't relate well to them. In the post-war era, Mother received a pathetic letter from Louisa from Hungary, telling of their destitute conditions. Joe had died, she had a 14 year-old son, and they feared starvation. The Russians had confiscated all they had and she was penniless. I don't know what Mother and Daddy sent her, but I am sure Louisa was a recipient of their generosity.

Most of the hired men worked through the spring or the harvest, but one hired man stayed year-round, going to his home in town only on weekends. His name was Nick Leock (pronounced "Like"), and like him we did!

The first time I saw him was scary. Fred and I had stayed home from church to do the chores. We had milked the cows, fed the pigs and horses, and returned to the house. It was dark outside as we washed supper dishes. I washed and Fred dried. We put them away by the light of a kerosene lamp, singing at the top of our lungs. Fred picked a good harmony and carried the melody. We knew all the hymns by heart, as well as many school and folk songs, and we were going through our entire repertoire. Suddenly without warning (which we no doubt had, but could not hear for our singing), the kitchen door opened. From the evening shadows emerged a rather grotesque figure. His dark face had a huge ugly scar the full length of his cheek and across the forehead. I don't know how I stifled a scream, as I vividly recall the chill down my spine. The tenseness of the moment was broken when he said: "I knocked, but I guess you didn't hear me. I'm Nick, your new hired man." His gentle voice put us at east at once, and from then on he became an integral part of our lives.

He was an unusual hired man. He was clean and didn't smell of tobacco. He knew how to cook and was willing to do so as the need arose. This endeared him to Mother. He was a good mechanic, a general fix-it man, and was also capable in field work. This endeared him to Daddy. But most important of all, he loved to play with kids, be it Kick-the-Can, Hide-and-Seek, Run-Sheepy-Run, Pomp, or softball. He endeared himself to us kids. As long as his days were, he never seemed too tired to play with us. The long hours of sunlight in the spring and summer were sweeter because of our association with Nick. We shared our secrets with him, our joys and disappointments, and we knew he understood. And I am still sure he did, though he had no children of his own.

Emma Lou was a cute, cuddly little girl, and Nick enjoyed providing her safety as she ran to his waiting arms. We all knew no harm or reprisal could be administered as long as Nick was around.

When I was thirteen, Mother and Daddy went to Utah and left me and Nick in charge. This fact justified my parent's complete trust of Nick in his relationship with us children. It was October, and I was preparing my entries for the school fair. I had countless exhibits of garden vegetables, cookies, fudge, and baking powder biscuits. If I needed help, Nick was right on the job. I had put my entries on the porch awaiting the car to take us to the fair in Spring Coulee. In an unguarded moment the dog ate one of the biscuits. I had no more to complete the three needed for my exhibit. There was no time to bake another batch so I went to the kitchen and took one of Nick's that he had made for breakfast. When the judging was complete, I was awarded first prize for my biscuits! Only one of them had been sampled, and I feel sure they tasted Nick's and awarded the prize accordingly. But I was too proud to confess, so took the prize money with eager hands.

I also won with my fudge, penmanship, composition and many prize vegetables. I received $25 in prize money. This enormous amount nearly qualified me for a summer school scholarship to Olds Agricultural College. The girl who won admitted to entering much of her aunt's trousseau. At least my entries were my own...well...nearly my own. All but one biscuit!

On more than one occasion Nick was called upon to sew on a button or mend a tear that needed immediate attention. He was the first man I had ever seen use a sewing machine. We didn't have to ask him to do things; he volunteered wherever he saw a need.

Knowing Nick we learned to love people for themselves, not for any particular physical feature they may or may not have. As soon as we got to know him, we never noticed his terrible scar. Today, thoughts of him bring memories of his kindness and gentle ways.

Nick left us reluctantly, and we truly hated to see him go. The years were hard and the $40-50 per month paid him was sorely needed to keep kids in college and on missions. I am still amazed that a man of his caliber worked for such low wages, but I am glad that he did. My life was enriched for having known him.

* * * *

DADDY

Daddy had a way of making each of us feel that we were his favorite. During my childhood I loved tagging along with him, because he was full of stories and exciting events of his own making. I recall how important it was for all of us to get our chores done so that we could attend the air show at the newly established Lethbridge Airport. There were thousands of people in attendance as we all stood to watch the small private planes go through their maneuvers. It was not much of a show by today's standards, but the sight of a plane in the wide open prairie sky was most unusual. Many people sunburned the roofs of their mouths that day! We did not realize that in less than three years the skies would be filled with all sorts of planes, large and small, as the Lethbridge Airport became a giant bombing and gunnery school for airmen from the British Commonwealth of Nations. What seemed a miracle and a rare event one day became common place the next. World War II forced us all to mature too quickly.

Daddy was fiercely loyal and patriotic to both Canada and the United States. He served in the Spanish American War in his youth, and would have served again had he been called upon to do so. He was proud of his family, whatever their particular contributions to the war effort. Ernest served six years in the Royal Canadian Mounted Police. Fred was a flight engineer in the Royal Canadian Air Force, but did not see active duty because the war was drawing to a close. All of us old enough to work, either on the farm or in the work force, were in war-related jobs.

* * * *

THE GREAT HORSE RACE

It was July 24th--the premier event in Magrath's holiday celebrations. First of all, it is a holiday of historical significance to Mormons worldwide, but locally it heralded the early beginnings of this small Mormon-found community.

Traditionally the first event of the day was a pancake breakfast catered by the Lion's Club. Next came the colorful parade comprised of a band, hundreds of costumed children, a couple of floats, many decorated bicycles, cars and horses, and spanking new tractors and combines, and the latest from the local farm implement stores. The parade went up and down Main Street to make the event last longer. At 11 a.m. a patriotic program was staged at the Assembly Hall followed by a picnic lunch. Sports events followed at the fairgrounds, which included a rich offering of all kinds of races for adults, children and horses. The last event in the grandstand was a baseball game, and we capped the day off with a movie and dance in either the Assembly Hall or at the open air pavilion.

Few events in our rural life were more eagerly anticipated. It was an amalgam of titillating experiences for us farm kids. Daddy usually gave us 25 or 50 cents (depending on how good the harvest had been the year before). On occasion I won a foot race, which added 10 or 25 cents to the enjoyment. With reckless abandon, we indulged ourselves in a bottle of pop, cracker jacks, and ice cream cones, with a candy bar--all novel to our normal diet. Making this vast investment last all day was the real challenge.

One memorable 24th makes all others pale by comparison. I refer to the time Jim entered Buck in a horse race. In retrospect, I presume this was the beginning of Jim's growing independence, his flamboyant personality, his lack of fear in gambling against great odds, his devil-may-care philosophy, and certainly his great show of optimism.

Now horse racing on the 24th was very serious business. Horses from the Indian Reserve were great contenders, with local entries of thoroughbreds by Charles Harker, Cliff Merkley, Sabeys' Old May and Trixie, plus a few other spirited mounts. The purse was adequate incentive--$50 for the winner, $35 for second place, and $25 for third. That sounded like a sizable bank account in those days. On a long shot, perhaps 10 year-old Jim saw a fortune to be made.

Now Buck was another story. To describe him is a challenge. He was two-thirds work horse and one-third saddle horse, though he excelled at neither. He was a big horse with a thick neck and short mane. His disposition was cantankerous and his gait miserable. However, he could run fairly fast, but even a novice judge of horseflesh could discern he was outclassed this particular day. The "real" horses had either light jockey saddles or just blankets and pranced at the starting line. Jim was mounted in a heavy conventional saddle, on which he had ridden from the farm that morning. Buck stood at the starting line with his ears pulled back, posed as if awaiting a horsefly attack. The cap gun sounded and they were off in a cloud of dust.

It was no surprise when, as soon as the air cleared enough for us to see, we noticed Buck was bringing up the rear. However, it seemed he had eaten just enough dust to inspire a new course of action. He lit across the field diagonally, despite Jim's best efforts at keeping him on track, running as if his life depended on it. Jim protested using the quirt and reins with all the strength he could muster. Buck only extended his stocky neck and legs and continued on, "hell bent for election."

He crossed the finish line with Jim straining in the saddle, still lashing with his quirt first on one side and then the other. However, he did have the distinction of crossing the line first. The grandstand assembly clapped and cheered long before the "real" contenders arrived to claim their purse.

Youth must try their wings and at this particular time, Jim no doubt wished he was mounted on them instead of Buck. Memories of July 24th will always bring a smile to my lips as I replay "the greatest horse race of all."

* * * *

HE WHO LAUGHS LAST. . . .

Regardless of how many saddle horses we had, we were usually one short to fill the demands of a big family. It was something like the car situation in most homes today! In the summer months the horses were kept in the horse pasture. This particular enclosure was little more than modern-day environmental protection to utilize the brome grass and preserve the ditch which ran the length of the half-mile pasture.

My best friend, Darlene Sabey, came over and together we devised a plan to get a horse and ride to Herman Johns' for a candy bar. Only one horse, Pearl, was in the pasture. I went to the barn for a bridle. I met Fred enroute, who informed me he needed the pony. We had a little verbal altercation at the end of which I was confident my need was far more pressing than his. Being one of the youngest in the pecking order, I often felt the boys concocted reasons to interfere with my freedom in choosing which horse, as well as when, to ride.

Securing the bridle, I felt my cause half won and proceeded to the pasture where I caught Pearl, a lovely white mare. Darlene was with me, and we knew that a quick get-away was imperative.

Across the barnyard I could see Fred approaching. I led Pearl to the edge of the ditch bank to jump on her bare back. In my anguish and haste, I put twice the spring necessary into my jump. I completely flew over her and landed in the ditch on my back! It was not a full ditch but a muddy one. Fred arrived at the scene just in time to see my fantastic leap. We were all hysterical with laughter as I got to my feet quickly to survey my mud-clad apparel. Fred took the loose reins and led Pearl away for his purposes. I ran to the house for a change of clothes, laughing but piqued.

Darlene and I rode double on Old Ginger to our destination. I could hear Fred guffaw until we were out of the lane. Reprisal would be sweet, I vowed. To this date I confess that I never did quite get even with him!

* * * *

"HACKING" IT

As our family grew up, I am sure that we were aware that Mother and Daddy had several brothers and sisters. However, it took years for me to learn the concept that we had cousins other than the Hackings. You see, they were the only ones who lived in Canada, and for many years they were the only ones I actually saw. There was Reed, Edith, Earl, Lexie, Wayne, Beth and Dorothy. We envied their curly hair which all but Lexie had. So the Briggs' had been "Hacking" it long before the term came into common usage.

I alone had the pleasure of spending summers with Aunt Francis, Daddy's sister, and Uncle George "A" on the ranch. My earliest recollections are at the ranches near Caldwell and Mt. View. Later they moved to Glenwood, where Uncle George A continued with his small herds of sheep.

I was aware that in the early days of his ranching he had owned huge herds and had lost several fortunes due to drought and depression. There had also been a prairie fire which destroyed an entire herd of sheep near Medicine Hat. Although they lived in Magrath for many years and owned a grocery store (destroyed by fire the same year as the flock), I was too young to remember them in that environment. I recognized the lovely homes that they once owned in town. However, I remember them best away from Magrath as that is when they became special to me.

Aunt Francis was a hard worker, very adept with a needle or working in the kitchen. She usually kept a boarder and sold cream to supplement her income. When my cousin Dorothy was not there, I got the job of milking her cow. Many were the clothes we wore that Aunt Francis had made from something else. She moved briskly about her tasks, and I felt it a compliment when people said I did something "just like Aunt Francis."

She was determined that each of her children would play the piano. She had the teacher come to her home and give lessons to other students, which in turn paid for her childrens' lessons. During my summer stays with her, I was awakened each day at the crack of dawn with one of the Hackings on the piano. I believe they had to get up at 5 a.m. during the school months, but were given an hour's reprieve in the summer, making it 6 a.m. when they hit the ivories! They all learned to play well enough to give great service in their respective communities due to Aunt Francis' frugality and perseverance.

I mourned her not having a child my age. Dorothy, her youngest, was five years my senior. Still, we had many good times together. She frequently took me swimming in the canal, and we had thousands of games of Rummy, I Doubt It, Fish and Rook.

Uncle George A was a kind, soft-spoken man, and Aunt Francis' "jawing" affected him like water on a duck's back. Weekdays were spent in the sheep camp and he returned home on the weekend. Sometimes I felt that he was glad to return to the quiet of his camp! On one occasion he took me with him to track a coyote who had preyed upon his herd, and who, he was confident, had a den of pups. He knew the way of coyotes, having lived with them during his sheep-herding years. He watched the bitch circle the herd and then zeroed in on the location of her den. Sure enough, we found two cute little balls of fur. I was enchanted with them and cuddled them close to me. He saw them as potential threats to his livelihood. He killed the mother with one shot from his .22, but compassionately waited until I was not around to kill the pups.

I stood in awe of Uncle George A. First, because he never brushed his teeth, but cleaned them with a toothpick. They were pearly white and he had all of them when he died in his seventies. Further, he rarely felt that his hair needed combing. I recall Aunt Francis trying to get him to "clean up" but he felt his appearance quite acceptable for sheep company! He met her specifications only on Sunday when they both went to church. Uncle George A loved mutton in any way, shape or form. While he relished it, I shuttered when the tallow stuck to the roof of my mouth, making it quite unpalatable. Mutton stew was his favorite, and I confess that Aunt Francis made a very savory pot.

It was a great occasion when our two families got together. We enjoyed outings at Waterton in the summer, and two or three day sleep-overs during the Christmas holidays. A daily marathon of Rook took place with the children, with the parents joining in the evening. The spirited chatter was more pleasant with the passing of hand-dipped chocolates, fudge and popcorn.

We were aware that Uncle George A and Aunt Francis took the game more seriously than did Mother and Daddy. I recall Daddy's oft-heard comment, "Melia, what do you want to do that for?" And as the cards were cut, Daddy commenting: "Shallow cut, sore shins; deep cut, the dealer wins." And when it came to bidding, hearing him say: "Bid 'em high and sleep in the streets." Games went on until the gasoline lamps merely made a soft glow in the room.

Then it was time for us all to "hit the hay." This was before the days of sleeping bags, so many beds were made on the floor (as cold as uncarpeted floors were). We always had three to a bed wherever beds were utilized. And oh, the mounds of food we'd consume! A second table was always necessary to feed the multitude. Often we had a turkey dinner, complete with all the trimmings, finished off with homemade ice cream, pie and cake. Mother praised Aunt Francis' cooking, but Aunt Francis returned the accolades when the spread was put on at our house.

Another special occasion was when the Briggs family attended the Hacking weddings. Their children married before ours of the same age; therefore it was a new experience for us younger ones to attend a wedding reception. If something interferred with our going, there was great disappointment for both families. They made us feel that the show simply could not go on without our support.

Aunt Francis loved to sing. When we were alone she asked me to teach her a song. I remember her learning "There's An Old Spinning Wheel in the Parlor," "Santa Lucia," "Church in the Wildwood," and "Home on the Range." She carried the melody, and I sang harmony. We spent many enjoyable hours with me being the teacher and she the student. It was good for my fragile adolescent ego. I also remember her asking me if I thought I would have red hair in the next world!

Uncle George A and Aunt Francis eventually left Glenwood, sold their sheep and moved to Cardston where they lived a few years prior to their deaths. With their passing a golden era ended in family relationships. By this time we were acquainted with other relatives in Utah. However, we experienced so much growing up with the Hackings through good and bad times. We shared such a tender, unique bond with them. The Hackings will always be special to all of the Briggs clan.

* * * *

TROUBLE! TROUBLE! TROUBLE!
(Right here in "The Garden City")

Camping at Waterton Park was the highlight of the summer. My girlfriends[2] and I, all 14 and 15 year-olds, were planning the outing. My older sister, Beth, had parental approval as chaperon. To finalize plans we needed to go to town where we would decide each person's contribution whether it be tents, cookies, root beer, canned stuff or whatever. We had permission to take the big green Plymouth, a treat not often afforded us.

We met at Norma Ririe's, and happy, giddy, giggly plans tumbled out. As I recall, we figured we'd each have to contribute $5.00 to the kitty for our needs for the week.

While taking two of the girls home, we encountered two likable ladies (much our seniors) who were sisters, Winnie and Effie Sabey. They were headed in the direction of our drive, so we offered

---

[2] Dorothy Tanner, Norma Ririe, June Gibb, Hope Alston, Leola Bennett, Darlene Sabey, Ruth Anderson, Lillian Karren, Ruth Bingham and Dorothy Dean Anderson.

them a ride. They enthusiastically told us about the face lift recently given the local pool hall and were excited to meet their girlfriends there for a game that evening because it had been declared "Ladies' Night."

Now the very word "pool hall" conjured up all sorts off racy images in my young mind. We teenagers giggled as we passed it on many occasions. We were conscious of the "undressing" we took from downcast eyes of the ne'er-do-wells (anyone not of our faith) who flipped cigarette butts to the sidewalk from their perch upon the red benches out front. Part of the pool hall's drawing power was due to the fact that a bootlegger occupied the top floor of the pool hall, and he shared a common outside door. Daddy was adamant that the boys never go in, not even to wait for a ride home. "There are better places to wait," he cautioned. "Were the pool hall to burn down tonight, thousands would be rendered homeless" embodied his appraisal of this establishment. He was intent that his progeny know they had a better home. A visit to a house of ill repute could not have met with more disdain.

However, tonight was Ladies' Night. Surely the indictments against it had disappeared with last year's smoke-stained paint. Tossing discretion to the winds, we followed the "big girls" inside.

As is so often the case, the anticipation was far better than the real thing. There was nothing unusual about the oblong big room. Instead of the acrid smell of smoke, it reeked of new paint on the walls and oiled sawdust on the floor. Two pool tables stood beneath drawstring lights. The gaudy-colored balls were enclosed in a wooden triangle. Behind the tables the walls were lined with cues. At the end of the room nearest the door was a counter filled with candy bars and cigarettes. An old-fashioned cash register was atop the counter. A large brass spittoon, newly polished, sat adjacent to the door. While the older girls played, we watched in amazement.

One of the mothers of our group, Norma Alston, was blessed with a sixth sense in knowing where and when any of her offspring were in moral jeopardy. The KGB would pale at her innovative means. Once the truth was discovered, she was willing to share all such "privileged information" with other parents similarly concerned. Hence, it was no surprise that upon our arrival at the farm, our parents had full knowledge of our "sins." We were lectured on the power of example. While I was just a hair less guilty than Beth, "she should have known better" because of her age. They wondered if she was a fit chaperon for the campout, or if the campout should be executed at all. We both expressed our willingness to wear the scarlet letter if only plans could go forward as scheduled. Happily, they did. The plans, that is.

But forty years later, I am confident that neither of us has ever gone inside another pool hall. We have, however, hidden the scarlet letter.

* * * *

"Adolescent Hesitation" seems a fitting caption for the independence emerging as youth strains to cut the apron strings. The world of Magrath seemed too confining for a fledgling eager to try her wings in higher and bluer skies.

HEART STRINGS 67

Hermine in Edmonton, Alberta, – 1942

CHAPTER II
SAND IN MY SHOES

Edmonton, Alberta

Sisters Alice and Beth had secured positions in Edmonton, capital city of Alberta. A complete hail-out on the farm, July 24, 1942, posed a disastrous scene for the year ahead. At their suggestion and with mother's apprehensive approval, I joined them in Edmonton to continue high school. A bright, new world opened to me, one so challenging and awesome, I knew my security under the wings of home was gone forever.

Living in a small LDS branch shepherded by President Nathan Eldon Tanner, I became acquainted with many great and wonderful friends. Both President Tanner and Solon E. Low were well-known and respected members of Parliament. The warmth and closeness of the branch was quickly evident as its membership was a homogenous group comprised of fulltime missionaries, college students, Canadian and American service men and women, government employees and many fine and great stalwart families. My special friends were Beth Tanner, Bernard Critchfield, and Ralph Walker. I found the association with the missionaries especially stimulating and determined that one day I, too, would serve a mission.

To ensure a little spending money, I secured a Saturday job clerking at the famous Hudson Bay Department Store in the stationery department. I loved meeting the public and for an eight-hour shift, my take-home pay was six dollars! However, it was little more than streetcar fare to school. Riding the streetcar and attending as well as succeeding in the 600-student Victoria High School added new dimensions to this adventuresome youth. Further, I worked at the Mission Home one night a week ironing shirts. Frequently I ironed as many as 40 shirts for the missionaries living there. I had ample opportunity to improve my skills and speed for which I earned $2.00 per hour.

As an example of a big sister striving to do her duty toward her younger one, I include the "Do's and Don't" list prepared by sister, Beth.

DOS AND DONTS

We *Beth Briggs*
and *Hermine Briggs*
do solemnly declare, in soberness of mind, knowing the consequences of breaking this declaration, that we will keep the following resolutions, to the best of our ability, to say nothing of our will-power. With the noblest of intentions we resolve to save our pocketbooks, or at least one of ours, and salvage what is left of our figures and promote the cause of Christmas presents etc. Therefore we say we will keep these in as much as we are able, but if it comes to a question of saving someone's pocketbook, other than our own, we are not obliged to stick with this covenant. If the above persons find it necessary to use their books for the sake of friends and influence, then they are not obliged to stick with it either.

1. No more candy, popcorn, icecream, hamburgers until after Christmas.
2. No more light lunches after supper.
3. No more than 2 apples a day.
4. Go slow on the peanut butter, honey and jam.
5. No more than 3 slices of bread a day, unless in sandwiches.
6. Be in bed by 10:30 the nights we stay home, and by 12 other nights than Saturday.
7. Study at least ½ hour each night.
8. Get up not later than 7:15 on week days.
9. Leave for work and school not later than 8:10.
10. Write home at least once a week.
11. Write Dorothea at least once a week.
12. Attend mutual, Sunday School and Church once a week.

BETH   HERMINE

German and Italian Prisoners of War from the Lethbridge Encampment. Daddy is at extreme right on back row: Jimmy is in the front row — next from the end.

POWs stand at fenceline which separated them from our yard on the other side. Note the tent encampment.

Introducing the First Sister-in-law
Back Row: Hermine, Betty Spence, Emma Lou and Mother
Front Row: Alice and Beth

*E*rnest Briggs in his Redcoat (RCMP)
Royal Canadian Mounted Police

Fred Briggs, Flight Engineer, Royal Canadian Air Force

Daddy and Ernie in the R.C.M.P.

*D*on Briggs while on
Western Canadian Mission

Calgary, Alberta

World War II was raging and the urgency "to do one's part" in the war effort prevailed over my continuing in school. A good friend, Dorothy Tanner of Magrath, wrote and expressed a similar view. Together we devised the parent-shocking plan of attending business school the following year. As secretaries we would be prepared to "do our part." Henderson Business College was in another burgeoning city, Calgary, Alberta. In the fall of 1943, Dorothy and I enrolled.

Living in a dark and dingy one-room apartment was not "up to our standard," but it was all we could get for the amount we could afford to pay. Wartime housing was at a premium everywhere. It was close to school; and since we spent very little time in our apartment, we made the best of it.

We loved our studies and fellow students who hailed from all over the Province. We also had excellent instructors, two of whom were LDS, Dorothy Nurse of Raymond, and Margaret Leishman of Magrath.

Our social life revolved around weekend dances in numerous locations where we met servicemen from every county in the British Commonwealth. It was common for every girl to write to several servicemen, some new-found suitors and many childhood friends. It was our patriotic duty!

I wrote the following two poems while attending business college in 1946-47:

A LETTER TO SANTA CLAUS

Dear Santa:
Have you ever gone to business school?
And tried to learn the golden rule?
Well, that's what we're trying to do
And we're asking a little help from you. (We need it!)

We're sorta big to ask for toys,
We'd really sooner have real boys,
There's a manpower shortage, don't we know!
So for this Christmas forget the beaux.   (See if you can,
we can't!)

We're sorta awful low on cash,
So when on Christmas Eve you dash
Into our place of ice and snow,
Just sorta tuck it in the toe. (If there is one!)

On you we have to so depend
Cause no one else wants to lend.
I guess our credit's not up to much,
At least it seems regarded such. (Wonder why?)

Dorothy can't afford to buy for me
We're alike, she's broke you see.
So whatever she was going to get
You can have a chance on it yet! (Probably was a hanky!)

Perhaps to you, this is out of place
But honest, look at Dorothy's face!
We're half starved, don't look at mine!
We eat soup and water all the time! (And that's no lie!)

There's a shortage of materials we know
But we're really not fussy, so
Don't worry about what to bring,
We'd be grateful for anything! (Well, we would!)

THE SNOW STORM

The wind was all a-flurry
    The clouds were dashing 'round,
The windows were a-shaking,
    The sun peeped through and frowned.

And then the scene was changing,
    The atmosphere was still,
The wind withdrew reluctantly,
    Stopping the windmill.

The snow flakes were a-coming!
    Each racing to the earth,
Each filling well their purpose
    A new earth given birth.

Each little snowflake took its place
    On every shivering tree,
Bending down the wilted flowers
    A "Keep Out" sign for the bee.

The lawn grass, like the rabbit,
    Changed its color with the season,
Turning a lovely, fluffy white,
    The snow storm is the reason.

The garden plot, which was so bare,
    Now looks so nice and warm,
The old white hen stands on one leg,
    Adding to her charm.

The cattle stay in the corral,
    The rabbits play hide-and-seek
The rooster's crow is unmolested,
    The cold car brakes now squeak.

From the chimney, smoke is curling
    In a path of winding charm,
'Tis the long awaited rest time--
    Winter on the farm.

*B*obby Soxers, and all sixteen
years old
Hermine, Norma Ririe
and Dorothy Tanner

Hermine in Edmonton
– 1943 –

*S*ecretaries in Embryo
– 1944 –
Hermine and
Dorothy Tanner
Calgary, Alberta

HEART STRINGS 79

80 HEART STRINGS

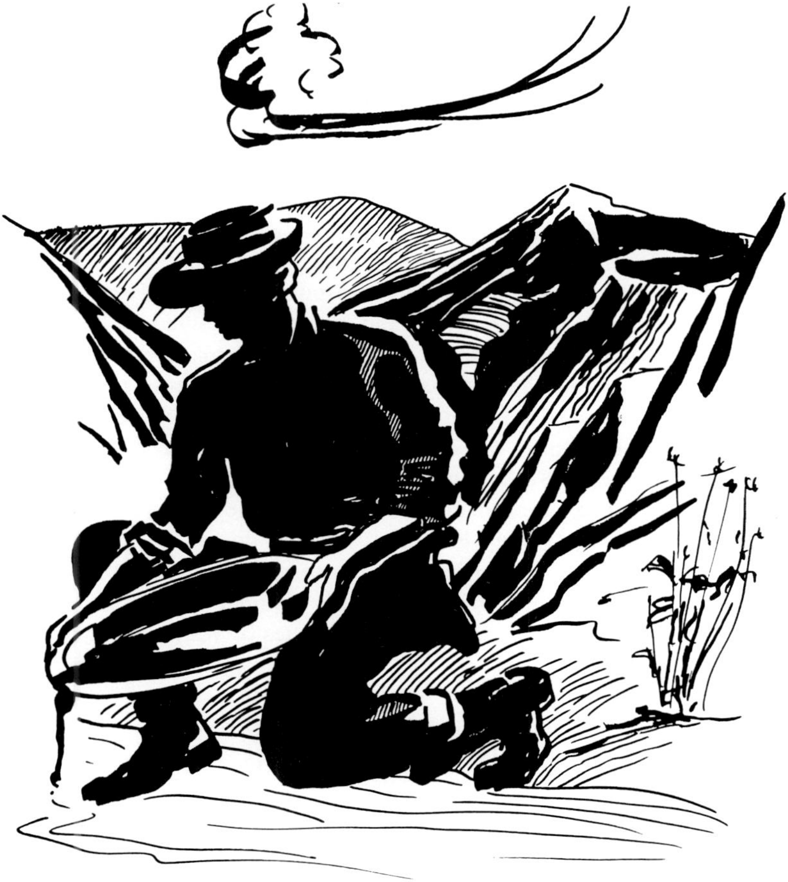

Whitehorse, Yukon Territory

As soon as a business student felt confident in his skills, he usually joined the work force. Though my skills were less than wonderful, after nine months I qualified for employment as a secretary with the U. S. Air Transport Command (Army Air Force) with headquarters in Whitehorse, Yukon Territory. I was flown to Whitehorse in a D-47 accompanied by 36 servicemen. The plane had no frills, just bucket seats!

The culture shock was what most girls pray for: a 100 to 1 male ratio! My near-Victorian upbringing was put to the test in many unique situations. It was gratifying to have a big sister, Alice, as a roommate. We often double-dated despite the twelve-year age difference. She was my best friend and mentor. We lived on the air base and our "barracks" was one in a line of barracks for enlisted men. There were four girls to each apartment. This was my first experience at sharing living quarters with girls whose values were different from my own. I was eager to learn from them, and was not intimidated by them. We had wonderful times together.

With the cessation of hostilities abroad, the military base on which I worked was slowly but surely closing down. All civilian travel was "frozen" to give priority to returning servicemen. It was much like watching a dear friend die with terminal illness. It was painful, but here I played out some uncertainties of youth.

* * * *

MY "FIGHT WITH JOE LOUIS"

Due to the nature of my job in Aircraft Maintenance and my sister Alice's in Priorities and Traffic, we kept a visual log on the VIPS coming or going on our base. Alice was working late but called me to the hangar for a good "look-see" of a real celebrity. "You'll recognize him when you see him," she promised. Eagerly I took the bait and upon entering the service area of incoming traffic, saw only one person sitting alone at a table. He was a M/Sgt and black. I knew instantly that I was about to meet the "Brown Bomber" as he was called in the Big Little books of my youth. It was JOE LOUIS, HEAVY WEIGHT CHAMPION BOXER OF THE WORLD! Yes, I must have his autograph!

Since no one was around, I was not timid in my approach nor my request. He was very cordial and asked me to sit with him and have a Coke. Though I felt awkward, I was delighted to oblige. We engaged in small talk during which time he mentioned he was waiting for billeting. Evidently Special Service personnel had not met his prearranged flight, nor were they in any hurry to make amends for their faux pas.

After barely an hour of excuse-making on my part, I went to a phone and attempted to right the situation. I made several phone calls to those I thought could help. I was rebuffed. Apparently there were no barracks for blacks among the enlisted men. Special Services next appealed to the officer in charge of officers' quarters. He was not cooperative; however since officer's quarters were private, they agreed to accommodate Sgt. Louis with the proviso that he eat at the enlisted mens' mess. This scenario took three hours to play itself out. By then I was steaming with indignation. I was embarrased for him as well as the poor performance demonstrated by the military.

The irony of the situation was obvious. The same men who in civilian life would pay a week's wages to see Joe Louis box, would not, in a military setting, provide him with even the bare essentials for soldiers or the usual amenities afforded the most unknown USO performer! His exhibition bout the following day had mediocre attendance.

The status for men of color in the Armed Forces has improved since 1946, proved by the fact that General Colin Powell is currently Army Chief of Staff. I hope that the citizens of this great nation have likewise become a bit less color-blind. My "fight with Joe Louis" was against discrimination, my very first, but certainly not my last.

* * * *

A BEAR-FACED STORY

Consistent with the habits of youth, Chuck, a GI, and I decided upon an evening stroll in the wooded hills of northern Alaska. The sun was smiling a reluctant farewell on a crimson world and the lengthening shadows of stately pines beckoned us.

Enthralled with the radiant sunset, we walked slowly skirting the airfield. Conversation seemed unimportant and was made difficult by the frequent interruption of the slow drone of a C-47, the lightning zoom of a jet, or noisy P-38s landing and taking off in precision formation.

Shortly we came upon a narrow footpath that wended its way through the dense forest growth to the distinctly marked timberline. A spring breeze, fragrant with alpine scent, played among the treetops and a bald eagle hung motionless, silhouetted against the sky. The silence was broken by a honking sound completely foreign to my ears. "Sounds like a bird of some sort," I said wistfully. "No," replied Chuck, "sounds more like a bear."

The very thought of being on the same five acres with a bear in this country was enough to make my blood run cold. However, I tried to dismiss the fearful thought. After all, I mused, I had been out with wolves before, why should a bear scare me!

My peace of mind was short-lived as the crackling of twigs and a repeated honking sound came closer. About five yards ahead the path widened, and instinctively we ran toward the spot. The appearance of a mammoth brown bear in the clearing suddenly halted our footsteps. Walking on his hind legs, he took on gigantic proportions, and lumbered across the path and into the woods. My head felt dizzy and the pounding of my heart seemed to wrack my whole body. I turned to run, but a firm hand in mine jerked me to my senses and Chuck's unsteady voice cautioned, "Don't run, he'll chase us!"

We didn't run, but two frightened people left some hasty tracks for Bruin's perusal. We neither stopped nor looked back until the friendly lights of the airfield assured us we were out of bear country.

* * * *

TO THOSE WHO ENTER[3]

The Yukon, where men are still pioneers, where the temperature often drops 25 degrees in half an hour, and where huskies are still used to discover and explore new and dangerous trails.

The first impression is one of disappointment, for one sees no dog sleds. Wasn't this the promised land of ice and snow and dog sleds? One is surrounded by tall majestic pines. In the background are the rugged Rockies. The snow is piled high on both sides of the well-built roads.

---

[3] This article was written at the request of the local newspaper in Magrath, Alberta, Canada.

HEART STRINGS 85

Transport Plane of the North   C-47

3rd and 4th Echelon Maintenance Personnel, August 1946

Base Chapel, Whitehorse, Y.T.

Womens' Barracks on the Air Base

*W*hitehorse Paddle Steamer

*S*cenic Beauty —
"To those who enter..."

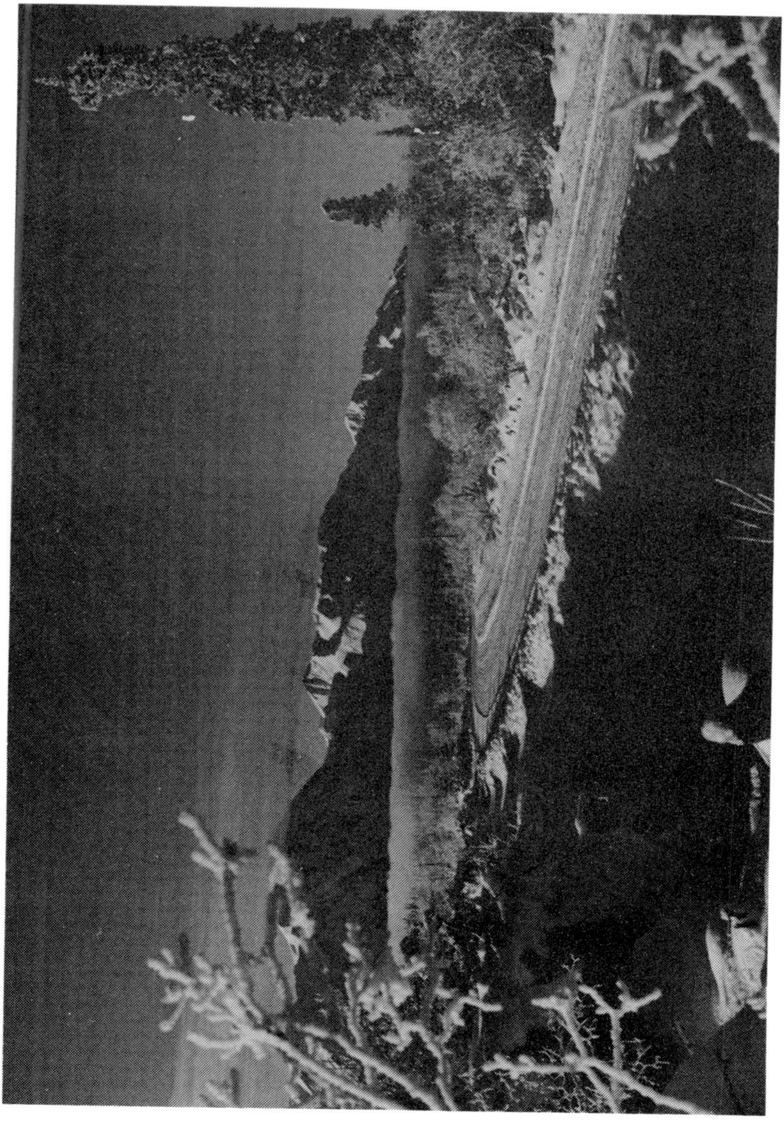

Whitehorse Townsite – 1945

The Yukon might be called the "land of the rising sun." At approximately 10 a.m. during the winter season, the eastern sky becomes aglow with a blend of colors. Slim warm fingers reach far into the sky. The mountains take on a deep blue shadow. The light slowly fades as the sun ascends further up to warm the giant bombers whose engines make a cold drone as they travel, seemingly motionless in the still, frosty air.

During twilight, snow gently wafts to the ground, covering the earth with a fluffy soft coat. The spruce trees look very sedate under their snow mantle, as they hold their slender shapes. Although there appears to be no wind, the snow is drifting as it falls.

This is a skier's paradise. At the stroke of dawn, many GI Jills and Joes are seen with heavy parkas, mukluks, and skis in hand, trudging toward the mountains for a day of excitement and spills. Such an exhilarating sport! One feels tired, but so refreshed by the pristine mountain air.

For those who enjoy indoor sports, little is lacking. In one of the spacious hangars, a large smooth, hardwood floor in available upon request. Every evening screams and laughter can be heard as teams tangle in a fast, exciting game of basketball. Badminton and ping pong are played by those who prefer something a bit less strenuous. In the evening were one to hear melodic strains, they could emanate either from the dance in the recreation hall or from the skating rink. Both are well-supported events.

Probably the most rarely seen sign in the world is found here. "Stop, Look Out for Airplanes" is at an intersection off the runway. It is clearly seen and understood as the planes are very low when they cross the road for landing.

The airways provide the most popular and speedy mode of transportation. It is a thrill to board one of the larger planes and watch the wide-spanned wings gracefully rise skyward, seemingly defying the laws of gravity. The large planes are built for cargo; and seats are the "bucket" variety, built for one position only. Earthly things become as miniatures, one's ears ring, and the pulse beats faster as the giant bird rises like an eagle.

What is that queer-looking vehicle down the road? It appears to be a combination of car, wagon and amphibious tank. A jeep, you say? It is the most common ground conveyance in this part of the country. And here comes "Yukon Lil," the bus that takes the officers to their cozy hill-top club retreat, and others to town locations.

Walking the banks of the winding Lewis River one sees several boats, large and small. A large one named "The Bonanza

King" is badly weather-worn. It is in dry dock, a veteran of the Yukon. The Bonanza King was built during the Gold Rush to transport prospectors to the heart of the gold fields in Dawson City. It could not be made watertight and has since been in dry dock. During three months of the summer, several paddle steamers traverse the scenic banks of the Lewis River through Lake LeBarge, the settlements of Selkirk and Stewart, and to the frontier town of Dawson City.

Dog teams, when seen, are most often with Indians. One team is used by the Army Air Force mainly to reach wrecked planes which cannot be reached by air. A dog team may consist of 6 to 16 dogs. The huge husky dogs, with their glossy coats of fur, are symbolic of the Yukon. Little is missed by these pioneers of the trail, for their short pointed ears prick up at the slightest motion. If it meets with their approval, a tail wag is an indication; if not, a growl is forthcoming.

The most expensive railroad in the world runs from Whitehorse to Skagway. The Whitehorse and Yukon Railroad (wait patiently and you'll arrive) runs on a four-foot gauge. When the train has a heavy load, it might have as many as three engines attached to accomplish the job.

One large hangar is dubbed "Rendezvous on the Ramp." Contrary to its name, it is an aircraft maintenance facility. It also is the most beautiful office on the air base. One can look out onto the runways lined with various aircraft. Some are fighter planes, some cargo, and some utility planes equipped with pontoons or skis, depending on the season of the year. In the background, the snow-capped mountains glisten in the sun. Stained oak was used for the highly polished office floor, and the fact that it is built in a hangar makes it unique. The outside door of the office leads into the service bay area where planes are receiving engine changes, replacement of wheels with skis, oil changes, etc.

Some of the most colorful and interesting characters in the world are found in the Yukon. The native Indians are still quite primitive despite picking up on many western ways. They live in tents or shacks and are surrounded by numerous dogs, which are notoriously skinny. They wear bright-colored clothing, beaded buckskin parkas and high mukluks.

One also sees elderly bearded men, their faces lined with experience in hard winters. No doubt they could tell of the Gold Rush in Dawson City when they were prospectors. Young men in loud plaid wool shirts and coveralls work on the numerous buildings under construction or, with the skill of a sculptor, mold the earth into a well-built road. They are the builders of a land of promise.

The primary colors, however, are Air Force blue and Army khaki. Several thousand GIs and about 100 WACs serve here as an overseas unit. Occasionally homesick smiles are seen, but they are just a reflection of those around them. Numerous civilian girls from all parts of Canada and the United States are seen walking to and from their homelike barracks. Four girls share an apartment consisting of two bedrooms, a living room and a bathroom.

At mealtime the "chow hounds" throng to the mess halls. Civilians eat apart from the military, but the food is the same, perhaps with a little more garnishment.

The Royal Canadian Mounted Police, or "Mounties" as they are called, might be classified as almost natives to this territory. They were among the first sent to endure the cold, risk and even give their lives, that this isolated terrain might be governed by law.

One of the most interesting buildings on the air base is the Army chapel. Here people of all faiths come to worship. The altar candles illuminate the stained glass windows in the background. The windows were originally intended for a log church in Bennett during the Gold Rush. Before they arrived, however, the church had been vacated because the prospectors had left. They were then brought to Whitehorse and stored in a barn where they remained for 40 years. Where they will go from here is conjecture, but for the moment they add dignity and beauty to an Army chapel in the Yukon.

The Aurora Borealis or Northern Lights are spectacular the further north one goes. Looking to the horizon they fill the heavens with enchanting colors, first a streak of light, sweeping like lightning across the sky, then a dazzling arch that darts in several directions. All the colors of the rainbow merge in glistening rays of almost supernatural light. They appear close, and yet so far, as they fade from sight. The euphoric atmosphere lasts well into the morning. For those who go to work by moonlight, often the Northern Lights illuminate their paths more than do the stars. The days seem very short, because their return home is also by starlight.

As one flies northward, one sees a straight line on the land going on interminably into the horizon. It is the Alcan highway, which goes for miles and miles without a twist or turn.

A memorable feature of Fairbanks is that almost every other door leads to a bar. In the evening large and small neon signs, lighted noisy night clubs and the honking of incoming traffic remind one of suburban Canada or United States. As one GI puts it: "They call

Fairbanks the garden-spot of Alaska. I don't think I'd care for all these rocks in my garden." It is a picturesque town, however, and in its large department stores I found many items I had considered "out for the duration."

To Those Who Enter--you'll find an open gateway to an artist's paradise and a land of high adventure!

*****

VJ-Day was declared, and great were the celebrations on and off the base. Tears of joy and homesickness mingled freely. The jubilant air prevailed for several days. Almost immediately the military personnel were put on rotation orders. This meant that weekly, if not daily, some of my good friends left for home. It was depressing, realizing that in all probability I would never see these people again. As if the uncertainties of the day were not sufficient, Alice, my sister, stowed away on a transport plane with her fiance (who was on orders to return to Alabama). They were married at our Magrath home. It was a real cloak-and-dagger arrangement, with me playing a key role because of the strategic nature of my job relative to knowing which planes were due in and out, plus both of us knowing some of the pilots. It was exciting and scary at the same time, as I was sworn to secrecy to tell no one of her whereabouts. Of course, her immediate bosses phoned me and I had to feign ignorance. However, she phoned them as soon as the knot was tied. The real miracle was that she eventually got orders to return so that she could make an official exit and return to Alabama as a "spouse." She had been in Whitehorse over two years; I fulfilled my contract in 14 months.

I was terribly miffed that I was deprived the privilege of being her bridesmaid, but it gave opportunity for some introspective thinking as to the direction my life would take next.

Initially I thought I would go to Brigham Young University in Provo, Utah, but my savings were insufficient to sustain me a full year. My sister Virginia extended an invitation to live with her and her husband in Salt Lake City while I looked for permanent quarters. I secured employment at a roof manufacturing firm, where I was a secretary-payroll clerk. After three months I moved in with 14 girls, happily sharing a big house in Sugarhouse in the Emerson Ward. Many of them are still close friends.

I enjoyed my job; but at the close of another year, the sand in my shoes reminded me of other commitments I wanted to keep.

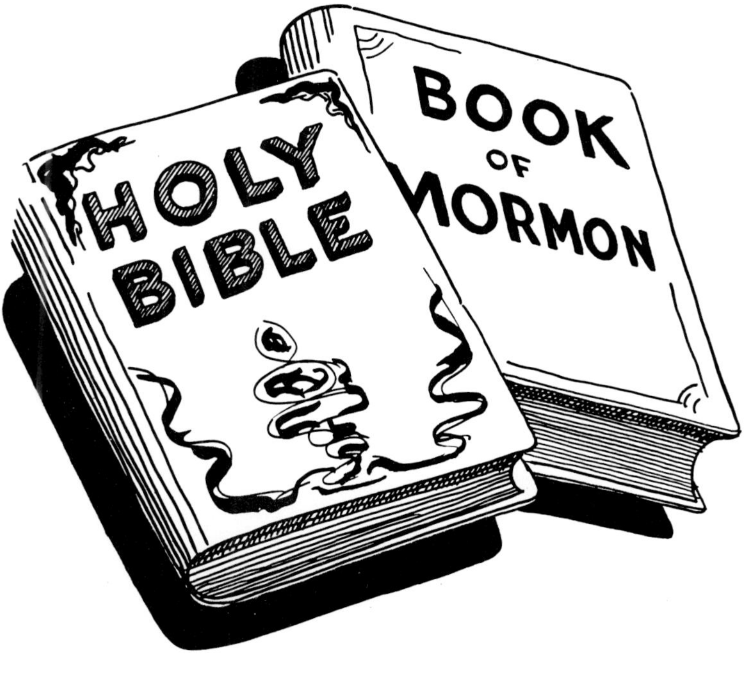
BOOK
OF
MORMON
HOLY
BIBLE

*H*ermine
in the
Mission Home

*M*issionary Picture
Hermine – 1946

CHAPTER III
THE GREEN YEARS

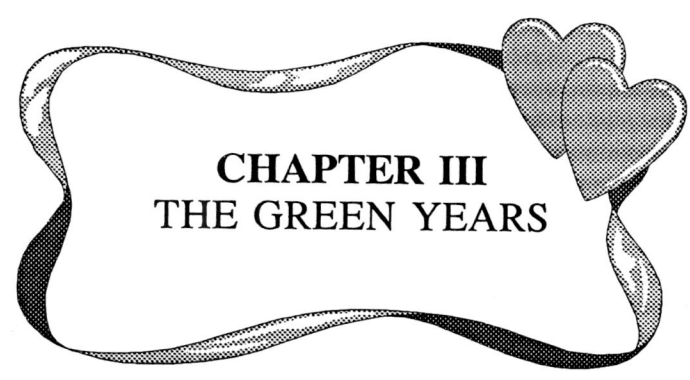

<u>Southern States Mission (1946-1948)</u>
Having reached the ripe old age of 19, I was anxious to serve a mission just as my parents and several of my brothers and sisters had done. However, at this particular time the required age for lady missionaries was 23. That seemed an eternity away! In crying my heart out to Mother one day, she suggested: "Why don't you pay a visit to my mission president, Charles A. Callis, and see what he thinks about it?"

Charles A. Callis was an apostle of the Church and a senior member of the Missionary Committee. He had been in our Canadian home previously while attending a conference. He was short and portly, about 75 years old, with deep piercing eyes that twinkled when he smiled. As we visited at his office, he became quite animated when I told him I was the daughter of Emilie Osterloh. Clearly, Mother was one of his favorites.

After a brief interview, he asked, "Now how old are you?"

"Nineteen," was my meek reply.

"Why, you're practically 23!" he said with a mischievous grin.

My spirits soared.

"I can't tell you where you'll be going, but wouldn't it be grand if you served where your mother and I served 50 years ago?" he added.

My call to the Southern States was in the mail within the following week. However, before I even opened the envelope, I knew where I was going!

With headquarters in Atlanta, Georgia, the Southern States Mission (1946) encompassed Georgia, Florida, Alabama, South Carolina and Mississippi. I labored in the first three states and had an inordinate number of companions. I wasn't certain if the president was afraid to leave me in one place too long for the damage I might do, or whether I was such a delightful personality he wanted me shared with as many as possible!

The week before Christmas six missionaries from Salt Lake City arrived in Atlanta, Georgia. My sister Alice was living in Anniston, Alabama, and arranged to have her sister-in-law bring her to Atlanta. We were very glad to see one another since it had been over two years since she married and moved south. I was in the mission home and had just returned from our meetings when Alice arrived. It was immediately apparent that the sister-in-law, Francis, smoked. Even without her lighting up, the aroma of cigarette smoke permeated the mission home like a cloud of dust. To my horror, she later lit a cigarette and smoked it to the nub before anyone said anything to her. By this time, of course, there came a knock on my door. It was my mission mother. With a very distraught look on her face, she demanded an explanation for the smell of smoke. I apologized profusely, and made all kinds of excuses; however, I felt like an innocent victim in the situation. I truly believed it was Alice's place to speak up in my behalf. Nevertheless, I knew for a certainty that I was off on the wrong foot. It came as no surprise that my first assignment was as far removed from Atlanta as possible: Waycross, Georgia.

Waycross, Georgia

My companion was Jean Norton of Salt Lake City. She was my senior by only two weeks; consequently, we had the privilege of "learning the ropes" together. We loved every minute of it. She was very ambitious and saw to it that we worked hard. The branch was small and dominated by two families. The branch president, past and present, were married to sisters. When one was released, a jealousy arose between the two men and their wives which resulted in a complete division of the branch. It was the first such incident I observed, but unfortunately, I found dissension quite typical in many small branches. However, we learned to love the Saints here and the good people of the South. Elder Claud Fernsten of California was our district president.

Savannah, Georgia

Four months later I was transferred to Savannah, Georgia, where I labored with Betty Hess of Ogden, Utah. She was a seasoned missionary and also knew her scriptures very well. I determined that I would follow her example. I put myself to the task of memorizing 350 scriptures with their chapter, verse and location in the Bible. Of course, it was an ongoing endeavor inasmuch as each lesson had many scriptures supporting it. We taught chiefly from the Bible since we were laboring in the Bible Belt and most people were well acquainted with it.

Dothan, Alabama

When I had been out seven months I was assigned as senior companion to a sister who had been out twice as long as I. We labored in Dothan, Alabama. This presented some challenging and serious problems. Had it not been for a wonderful district president, Keith Adamson of Highland, Utah, I don't know how I would have coped. He helped me in countless ways, but especially gave me courage to do the things I had been sent to do. With the Lord's help, the work went forward. It was such a treat when he and his companion came in "Little Lulu" and gave me a spiritual shot-in-the-arm. He remains one of my great friends today. He and his wife, Louise, accompanied my husband and me, forty years later, back to our old haunts in the mission field while on a Mississippi cruise.

Mobile, Alabama

Mobile, Alabama, was my next assignment, and my companion was Betty Lou Marshall. She was very petite, and we were often dubbed "Mutt and Jeff." She was from Garfield, Utah, and was a fun-loving, great missionary. We enjoyed singing duets together, sometimes in church, other times while tracting.

When Sister Marshall returned home, Sister Reva Mathie of Salt Lake City, Utah, was my companion. This companionship was short-lived and followed the pattern of all of my companionships, for her mission was nearing completion. We grew to love one another immediately, and had great times with fellow roommates, Carey Pearce of Gadsten, Alabama, and Nelda Kirkman of Idaho Falls, Idaho. We lived in a little dilapidated old servant's house on the rear of a large estate. Its lane was bordered with azaleas and other flowering shrubs which bloomed continuously. It was quite a romantic setting for four single girls. Mobile is on the Gulf of Mexico; thus, the climate is quite muggy and humid. My hair was a delightful strawberry blonde by now from being sun bleached and was quite curly. Further, I had the first tan of my life (even through silk stockings), and I did not peel. However, I suffered with the heat, as I have done all of my life.

*S*ister Briggs – Mobile, Alabama
– 1946 –

*Hermine Briggs, Lester Henderson
and Evelyn Northgrave,
All Southern States Missionaries
from Magrath, 1946–1948*

Mobile had the advantage of a new chapel. It was a great blessing because it meant we could have investigators come to a place we were proud of, and where there was a small but strong congregation. Mobile was a fruitful field for our labors. We taught many discussions and saw several choice people come into the waters of baptism.

It was not uncommon at this time to hold street meetings every Saturday. It was the greatest challenge of my missionary experience. We fasted the entire day before our presentations in the local town square. It was a very humbling experience, complete with hecklers, heat and hostility. Once in a while we held a handful of prospects spellbound as they wondered about this youthful little group making such bold statements.

I don't know of specific converts who were thus contacted, but the testimonies of the participants were certainly strengthened. I especially remember an elder from Rawlins, Wyoming, who had a severe speech impediment. It was a great challenge for him to speak at a street meeting. We fasted and prayed that he would be able to speak and be understood. As he bore his testimony, our hearts and minds rooted for him. He spoke fluently and unhesitatingly, with great power. From that time forward he never stammered again. Talk about the prayers of the faithful being answered!

Miami, Florida

My next transfer was to Miami, Florida, where my companion was Frances Harley of Charleston, South Carolina. She was a true "southern belle," complete with southern accent. We had a delightful time together, and were the first lady missionaries to work in Miami. Unfortunately, we were both financially embarrassed at the same time. Living costs in Miami were double those in our previous assignments, and the members were not yet used to inviting "LMs" to dinner. So for a solid week, we ate nothing but potatoes and onions in as many forms as we could imagine. In fast meeting on our first Sunday, Sister Harley, much to my embarrassment, bore moving testimony of our deprivations. It bore fruit quickly. We soon had many dinner invitations.

I must mention that I arrived in Miami on the tail of a hurricane. Warnings were out to all people in the area, especially those driving. Homeowners were told to "batten down the hatches." This meant to board up big windows and stay off the streets. It rained and blew for the best part of four days. When we finally emerged we found giant palm trees uprooted, neon signs blown down, and debris-strewn streets. The devastation was something I had not seen before, nor could have ever imagined. Even coastal highways were washed away. This was also the first time I became aware that hurricanes have "eyes," meaning the center of the motion, and are given names, all female names at this time in hurricane history.

We were fortunate to be safe in the home of Branch President Barfield. The Barfields were very good to us during this time. Among other things, Sister Barfield made fresh coconut pies for her new-found waifs. She had the children gather fresh coconuts that had fallen from the trees. I grated them for her, and she put it in the pies. They were very rich, but very good!

Elders Nielson and Howells were also in Miami. They were not sure we were on the same team! But they soon realized we were out for the same purpose they were, and we became good friends. It took a measure of time for this to happen, however. They also turned one of their investigators, Sister Lucy Peele, over to us to teach. We loved her and she responded positively. She was eventually baptized, and we had the privilege a few years later of helping her come west to go through the Salt Lake Temple. She was indeed an elect lady.

Miami is an interesting city, with many Hispanics and Jews. The climate is tropical and the scenery breathtaking. Tourism is the number one industry, and much of the population is comprised of "snow birds," people who are there only for the winter. Therefore, one meets people from all over the world while tracting. Few of them are interested in anything other than having a great holiday. The Jewish people, however, are very hospitable and willing to engage in conversation about our mutual polygamous roots!

Ft. Lauderdale, Florida

Soon Sister Harley and I were transferred to Ft. Lauderdale, which is up the coast about 80 miles. Our district president was Anthon Ernstrom of Sacramento, California. This city is less commercial than Miami, and we settled in for some serious proselyting. Here we found avocado trees producing fruit as large as grapefruit. The novelty of it attracted us, and we frequently were seen carting them home for our nightly meal. They were delicious and often were blown from the trees that lined the sidewalks in the orchard areas. On one occasion we approached a door with an overly ripe avocado in hand. A lady appeared at the door. Just as one of us was about to identify who we were, the other dropped the fruit on her doorstep. Kerplop and splash! While she was not amused, we got the giggles. Unfortunately, we finally managed to tell her we were missionaries. She was not impressed. A convert we did not make!

While in Ft. Lauderdale we survived several hurricanes, also. On two or three occasions we literally took our shoes off and walked down the streets with water up to our knees to keep an appointment. Unfortunately when it rains heavily in Florida, there is no place for the runoff except the ocean. The water table is so high, drainage is impossible; so the water stands on the ground. One of the major hazards, however, is that many snakes indigenous to the area come out for a swim. I was more than hesitant to walk through the water barefoot. Many homes and shacks were also snake-infested after a storm. I saw my first big moccasin snake while here. In this instance the water had receded, and the snake was sunbathing across the width of a country road. It had a head about the size of a volleyball and was more than ten feet long. I didn't want to see another one.

At a conference attended by President Meeks, I told him I had heard from Evelyn Northgrave (Naylor) from Magrath. She was laboring in Winter Haven, Florida, and had had a rather difficult mission. With only six months left, she was anxious to leave on a positive note. She asked if I would consider being her companion. Of course the decision was not mine. Pres. Meeks listened for a few minutes, and then asked, "Do you think you two could do any good together?" I assured him that we would work hard and give it our best. Two weeks later I was transferred to Winter Haven to labor with Evelyn. In the same district was Lester Henderson, also of Magrath, Alberta. He and I attended high school together. What a small world where three country bumpkins were together in the same mission so far removed for our northern roots! The three of us shared the news from home and had great visits. He was an outstanding elder.

<u>Winter Haven, Florida</u>

Evelyn and I worked hard. We walked miles and miles around the many picturesque lakes in the vicinity. We were instrumental in teaching the Gospel to a single Greek girl, and two sisters, Hancina and Arina Olsen. We loved working with the Sainsburys, a couple from Salt Lake City, who provided us with transportation to our distant teaching assignments. Our district president, Harold R. Germaine, who left a young bride at home, was a spiritual giant. Most of the elders at this time were recently released from the military and were a bit older than the norm. They brought an added maturity to their calling and were tremendous proselyters.

After Evelyn was released, I had a few days of being alone. It was my first such experience since being a missionary, and I found it devastating. At length Sister Helen Fredrickson of Roosevelt, Utah, arrived as my companion. She was in her late thirties and had spent most of her time in the Mission Office. We were together until I was released.

The highlight of my mission was when about 400 of us met in Atlanta for an all-mission conference. We had one day of sports activities, one day of workshops conducted by our mission president and his assistants, and one day of testimonies wherein everyone present had opportunity to express himself. It was a great spiritual feast and an opportunity to renew old friendships and make new ones-- eternal friendships. Pres. Meeks was a spiritual giant and a man of great compassion and understanding. Further, he was a great preacher of the "pulpit-pounding" variety. He moved his listeners like the good old traveling evangelists used to do. He was a former Southern States missionary as well, and served under President LeGrande Richards, now an apostle of the Church. Sister Meeks was a dear, sweet lady, but she was not as dynamic a person as was her husband.

Before I left the field, I also served under President and Sister Albert Choules of Idaho Falls. He was nearing the 77-year-old mark, but what a powerhouse! His only failing was that he could not remember names, though he always knew your face. Sister Choules was so cute. She stood at his elbow and said: "You remember Sister Briggs in Miami." He would reply, "Oh yes, Sister Briggs, of course!" We dearly loved these dedicated people who gave so freely of themselves even at this stage of their lives. They were an inspiration to us.

My mission was a soul-stretching experience for many reasons: (1) learning to live with and love new companions constantly; (2) studying and memorizing the scriptures requisite to teaching the 25-35 lesson plan; (3) learning to understand and love a culture foreign to me, the beautiful people of the South, with their colorful characteristic manner of speech, and (4) giving full-time service to our Father in Heaven because it is imperative to live very close to the Spirit in order for one's efforts to see fruition. It was a humbling experience and one I shall ever cherish.

I also had the good fortune to meet two people in Atlanta who remembered my "beautiful mother." She attended Brigham Young University after her mission, and I was soon to follow her lead.

MY TESTIMONY

Through study, prayer and patience
And obedience to His will,
My life has found a priceless gem.
May it remain, forever, still
   My testimony.

There is within my being
This burning, bright and clear,
Though visible to no one else,
I always feel it near.
   It is my testimony.

Since finding this great possession,
My way of life, God's laws,
Are far more beautiful to me
With truer meaning, because
   I have a testimony.

Though the world may reel with turmoil,
And my days be filled with strife,
May I keep this within my being,
My guide toward eternal life.
   My testimony.

  When I returned from my mission in 1948, Daddy let me know how pleased he was with my growth in the Gospel. He took several occasions to tell me in detail how he appreciated the things I had done with my life and how important all of his children were to him. He was, in very truth, a family man. Further, he let me know that his expectations of me were far from being fulfilled, and of course, he expected that I would marry well and give him grandchildren. Each time I returned home from that time forward, he would listen to my litany of activities, and the bottom line was always the same: "But isn't there someone you know who is now or is becoming very special to you?" I was truthful and told him that perhaps my eternal companion had been killed in the War in Heaven! He and I shared the same kind of humor and he always left the subject on a positive note, indicating that the men now-a-days are not as smart as they were in his day! I identified with his appraisal and loved him more for his genuine interest.

    * * * *

THE NIGHT PROWLER

It was 1948. I was living at the Prince of Wales Hotel in Waterton Park and working as Secretary to Mr. Harvey Boswell, hotel manager. I heard that Apostle Benson was going to preside at a stake conference on the next Sunday in Cardston. I had to be there! My cousin, Lexi Wood, lived in Cardston. We had enjoyed a close relationship, so I phoned her and asked if I could "sleep over" after the Saturday night dance at Waterton. She agreed, but added a few instructions: "I may have someone sleeping in the front room on the hide-a-bed. You go in Joanne's room and sleep with her. I will leave the back door open."

The Saturday night dance was great and, despite a downpour, was well attended. My objective for the evening was to "win and woo" someone who wanted to take me home, but who lived in Cardston. I can't recall his name, and he was not a good dancer, but no mind--he was a wealthy young buck who drove a big, beautiful, new car! I assumed he was not LDS as he had not heard of Apostle Benson.

It rained all the way to Cardston. I instructed him as to where Lexi lived. We drove in the driveway, and since it was still a downpour, I said my hasty "thank you" and dashed toward the back door as fast as my high heels would let me. I entered the kitchen without turning on a light, and made straight for the bathroom and prepared for bed.

Inasmuch as I came directly from the dance, I had only the clothes on my back and my makeup in my purse. I scrounged around for a few bobby pins to secure my long red tresses during the night. I stripped my clothes down to my underwear, and stealthily made my way towards Joanne's room. As I passed through the kitchen, however, I heard the voice of a woman. I hesitated as she gave me a cheery "Hello!" I responded, thinking this was the "hide-a-bed guest," and continued on toward the bedroom, believing the 2:30 a.m. hour was no time to visit with strangers.

She stood her ground and, seemingly wanting to talk, queried: "Aren't you Emma Lou's sister?" I answered in the affirmative. She smiled a broad smile and said, "Then you probably want to go to Lexi's. She lives next door."

I was aghast! In an instant I became painfully aware of my near-nakedness (still no light turned on, thank goodness!) and the fact that I had broken into someone's home! I apologized as best I could, and prepared a hasty retreat. She told me that the floor plans of both houses were identical, so without light I could easily feel "at home." Depending further on the late night cover, I donned heels, suit jacket and raced next door. Sleep was slow to come as I quietly chuckled to myself and mused about the ridiculous and embarrassing experience I had.

The next morning I met my surprise host family at Conference. Eph and Verna Jensen chided me in good humor, and I turned beet red. So much for my "house-breaking" career. I believe I tried to return the bobby pins, the only booty I had stolen.

I had the undivided attention at the staff dining room that night at the Prince as I told of my experience. However, they were slow to believe my tale--they thought I made it up!

* * * *

BYU AND ME

I realized that my education was incomplete, and many of my friends were at that time pursuing degrees at Brigham Young University. I worked at the canning factory in Magrath all summer for 40 cents an hour, and arrived in Provo with little more than faith. Daddy gave me $55.00 for my first quarter's tuition and said, "That is all." I checked into a co-op house owned by the University and secured employment as a secretary to Oliver Smith, head of the Journalism Department. Here I earned 65 cents an hour and, due to my expertise with financial juggling, somehow eked out a living my freshman year while carrying a full student load and working four to six hours a day.

While attending BYU in September, 1949, I received word of my father's death. He had been working on the farm with Ernie building a new pond. He was on the big tractor and somehow got the two rear wheels astride the pond's bank, causing the tractor to overturn into the excavation and pinning him beneath. He died almost instantly. Of course, the shock was tremendous and especially hard on Ernie. Mother felt she had to be strong for Ernie's sake, so set a great example for us all. Daddy's funeral was as large as any ever held in Magrath. An old Indian, Chief Body, drove his team and wagon all night to attend the funeral. Of Daddy he said, "He was the best friend I ever had." Countless are the individuals known and unknown who echo that proclamation, for Daddy made a friend of all. He was quick to recognize the needs of the widows in town: a ride to a special event, or an invitation for a group of them out to the farm for a chicken feed. Mother was always equal to the task and supported his reaching out because it was second nature to her also.

He was people-oriented and enjoyed conversing with individuals from all walks of life. His advice was sought by many. He valued his friends, relatives and family. The years do not diminish my loss, but make me aware of how great our reunion will be. I am grateful for the twenty-two years wherein he blessed my life.

A full schedule of studies helped ease the pain. I loved learning; I loved the dynamics of campus life. I was stimulated by my peers and the dedicated professors whom I met in class. I got high on Tuesday and Thursday assemblies when we listened to General Authorities or heads of state of nations of the world. The Lyceum Program brought musicians and artists of renown to broaden my cultural horizons. Spring and fall made me heady with the beauty of the campus. I loved Karl G. Maeser for his monumental contribution to understanding how an LDS education must differ from the world's.

I spent three great years working as secretary to Dr. Harold Glen Clark, Director of the Extension Division and Alumni Affairs, while attending the university part time. I lived with a houseful of returned missionaries whose friendships I cherish.

* * * *

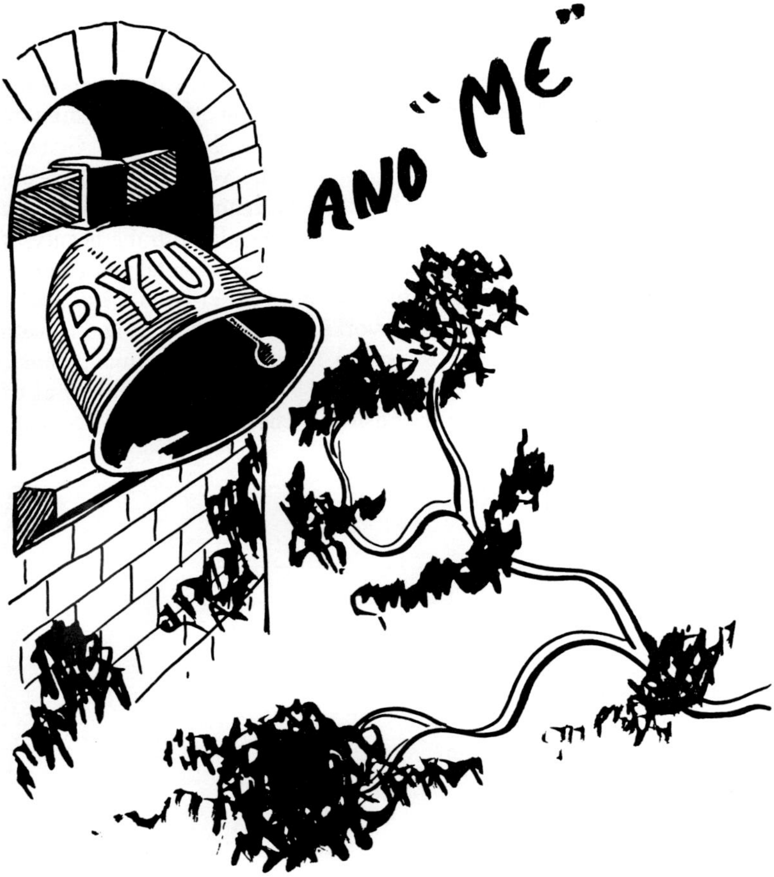
BYU
AND "ME"

My Parents – 1948

My Sisters – 1948 Back: *Emma Lou, Beth & Virginia,* Front: *Alice and Hermine*

My Brothers – 1948   Back: Don, Ernest
Front: James, Fred

*D*ream Girl of Delta Phi?

DREAM GIRL?

Every college campus has its share of queens. There seems to be one for every major social event. This practice adds a competitive spirit and generates enthusiastic support for the activity. The greater the number of competitors, the broader the publicity. On BYU campus one of the most heavily contested pageants each spring was for the title "Dream Girl of Delta Phi," sponsored by the male returned missionaries.

To say that I was an "unlikely" candidate was a statement of fact. However, due to the urging of my new-found boyfriend, Cal, and my numerous roommates, I was persuaded to compete.

Sister Beth wrote a little ditty of introduction for Cal's presentation. I bought a lovely black dress with three tiers of scallops and some pretty black suede sandals. All details were in readiness except how to get Cinderella to the ball. Cal's only mode of transportation was a bicycle. I could not see myself riding sidesaddle in my finery. Beth came to our rescue a second time by suggesting we borrow their family car, a black Plymouth sedan. Cal was pleased to accept the offer.

The long-anticipated yet dreaded day finally came. We drove to the circle of the Maeser building without incident. My hands were clammy cold and Cal's nonchalanace was a bit superficial. However, the contest turned out to be a pleasant experience. Twenty-eight hopefuls were introduced. Each one made short statements relative to "her" reign. The vote was secret, and just as well. (It was a consolation to know Cal voted for me!)

The trip to return the car soon became the focal point of the late evening. Cal turned the key, but only a sputtering sound resulted. He thought he had flooded the engine so we waited a while before trying it again. Several attempts produced the same disgusting results. We were parked alongside a wide footpath. Cal conjectured that if we used the footpath which headed down the hill, we might get the car started by compression. We pushed the car around the Maeser circle to make a run at it. We gave the black monster several opportunities to start but it resisted all our feeble attempts. Halfway down the long path Cal suggested we park the car and return early in the morning with some help for its removal. My concern at this point was being ticketed by campus police for having a vehicle on a much-traveled sidewalk. With few options remaining at the late hour, we walked to our respective apartments. By the time we reached my place, I had blisters on both heels and felt like I had run the Boston Marathon instead of competed for a queen title.

As agreed, the next morning Cal and I met at the car at 6 a.m. Still, it refused to budge! I was dressed appropriately for my office, which was in the Maeser building. I was wearing a skirt with a sporty 8" slit in front and back. Cal suggested that he push the car while walking beside it, once more trying the compression angle. As he did so, the car veered to the right, right where I was standing! I found myself directly in front of the car, trying to hold it on course rather than run me over. Despite my attempt, I was knocked to the ground and landed in spread-eagle fashion in the wet, humus soil surrounding the shrubs. Cal pulled the emergency brake on and rushed to my aid. However, by that time I was on my feet and assessing my personal damage. I was not only covered with mud, but my black skirt was slit to the waist, front and back! He took one look at me and quickly declared, "You had better go home!" I knew that. A sense of humor brought timid smiles to both of us. While Cal ran the opposite direction in embarrassment, I wasted no time heading homeward, but told him I would call campus police and request their help. I was reluctant to see anyone, but several students stopped to ask if I needed help. I assured them: "No, I am beyond help!"

By the time I got cleaned up and was once again ready for the office, the car had been removed. Cal reported the car started the minute they put some gas in it. We discovered my brother-in-law had loaned us a car with an empty gas tank. As to my romance with Cal, it, too, ran out of gas. It was not a relationship made in heaven. It withered at the first experience with adversity.

* * * *

Education was great, but I was faced with the real necessity of supporting myself. The lust for gold took me to work at Geneva Steel in Orem, Utah. My 150 wpm shorthand achievement was put to good use in taking verbatim minutes of meetings with the company versus the union. I stayed a year but soon realized the long hours and stressful nature of the job were overwhelming despite the advanced salary.

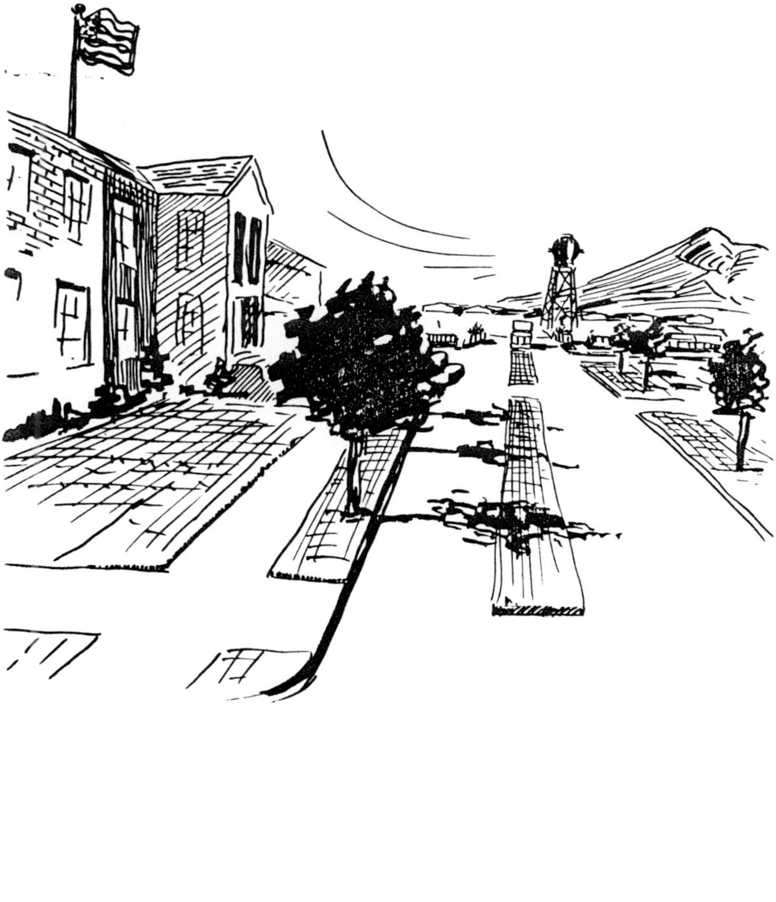

*H*ermine at
A-5 Navyway
Washington Terrace
Ogden

*T*he Briggs Girls – 1950   Beth, Mother, Alice, Virginia,
Hermine and Emma ou, in Ogden, Utah

SECOND STREET MINUTEMAN

Volume I   OGDEN, UTAH, MAY 7, 1952   Number 3

EUROPEAN TRIP IS NICE, but—

By Cliff Thompson

A trip of a lifetime ended last week for Hermine Briggs, a secretary in the Signal Supply Section.

As a member of an educational tour sponsored by Brigham Young University with an itinerary that included seven European countries and the British Isles, Miss Briggs got a first hand glimpse at some of the landmarks of time that to most of us will come no closer than the history books.

From the pages of legend stepped the Romantic Isle of Capri, the Gondolas of Venice, Rome's seven hills, the mysterious black forest and the storied Zuider Zee.

Embarking from New York City on a Holland-American liner early in June the group of 36 student enjoyed a pleasant cruise to Le Havre, France. After spending a whirlwind 6 days in Paris, the group boarded a chartered bus that took them thousands of miles through the French and Italian Riviera, the mountains and forests of Switzerland, Austria and Germany and the picturesque lowland countries.

"It was a wonderful experience in learning tolerance and friendliness," Miss Briggs said. "People in all countries were courteous and treated us as guests, even though 34 girls in peddle pushers and levis often taxed their imagination. Evidently such costumes are worn only to bed, except in France.

"France gives the tourist an impression of international politics, wines, women and song, and they almost pride themselves in living up to this reputation. However, it is largely an agricultural country and their love for the soil is evident in the fact that every inch of ground is productive.

"In France we saw our first communist propaganda by way of billboards and banners denouncing American policy and frequently roads would be painted 'Ridgeway Go Home.'"

All roads do lead to Rome, Miss Briggs said, but the Italian road makers seem to have taken the ancient cart trails and applied a hard surface leaving them as narrow and winding as they were in the times of Columbus. The best roads in Europe were found in Germany where Hitler's Autobahn gives the traveler the ultimate in superhighways.

Little evidence of war was seen in France. Mortar damaged mine traps and fortresses still stand in Italy while bombshelters and frames of large buildings are all that remain in some sectors of heavily bombed Germany. Reconstruction is slow but gradually such landmarks are being erased.

"The first buildings rebuilt in German towns are the churches and opera house," she reported. "One small town was hit so hard that instead of rebuilding, the townsite was moved."

Infamous Dachau, where 100,000 prisoners died in gas chambers, was visited. "The Germans have made Dachau a museum," Miss Briggs said, "and seem to be genuinely ashamed of it."

She said Holland and Switzerland impress the visitors as the cleanest countries in the world. In Holland shop owners scrub the sidewalks around their shops every morning. "Can't you just see a business man of Washington Boulevard down on his hands and knees with a pail of water and a scrub brush."

Hermine Briggs

Don't Get Seasick

It's "Bon Voyage" for Hermine Briggs, Signal Supply Steno. The likeable redhead has accepted an invitation from the BYU Modern Language Department to travel through the countries of Europe. She leaves May 30th and the agenda calls for a two day tour of Washington, D.C., a nine day ocean voyage, and two and a half months of sightseeing through France, Germany, Switzerland, Austria, Italy, Belgium, Holland, Denmark and British Isles.

Miss Briggs, a Canadian citizen from Magrath, Alberta, Canada attended BYU prior to working at Utah General Depot. She majored in Sociology and concentrated her efforts toward learning French and Spanish. Although she submitted her application for the European tour, she felt it would never become a reality. To her pleasant delight, she was mistaken.

Beware of those romantic Italians and Frenchmen, Hermine!

The storied Zuider Zee is giving way to the demands for land to produce food, but is still enchanting with its quaint ferry boats commuting from village to village.

"England, without its language barrier proved to be one of the most beautiful and historical countries of our visit. Especially interesting was Westminster Abbey, London Bridge, Stratford-on-Avon, Buckingham Palace and countless other landmarks. Every Britisher is busy talking or working on a project relative to the queen's coronation.

The only dampening feature of the trip was an Atlantic gale that rocked their ship in a storm-tossed lullaby for most of the return voyage. "I think I know now the feelings of our returning service men, for never before had the Statue of Liberty seemed so beautiful."

HEART STRINGS   121

UTAH GENERAL DEPOT, OGDEN, UTAH

Having been a civil servant before, I pursued opportunities in that field. I landed a job at Second Street, Utah General Depot, Ogden, Utah, as secretary to the Signal Supply Officer (military) and the civilian administrative assistant. Marge DeBoer was my first woman boss and was very good to me and appreciative of my contribution. She even allowed me to take the summer off for a BYU European Tour without forfeiting my job. However, I had to promise to remain in the position for another year, which I was glad to do.

While working at the Depot the first year, I lived with my sister Alice and her growing family of six in a two-bedroom house. We enjoyed much "togetherness" and I learned anew the many virtues and talents of this older sister. The following year I lived in Salt Lake City and commuted while living with a missionary companion, Iva Lou Peterson. But BYU had not seen the last of this country girl.

BYU--AGAIN

In 1953, Iva Lou accepted a position in the Physical Education Department at BYU. She encouraged me to join her and to continue on as her roommate. Upon inquiring at BYU Placement Bureau, I was informed that there was a critical need for administrative secretaries. Four openings were offered me: (1) secretary to Ernest L. Wilkinson, president; (2) secretary to Harvey L. Taylor, vice president; (3) secretary to William E. Berrett, vice president and also administrator of the Seminaries and Institutes of the Church; and (4) Wesley P. Lloyd, dean of students.

I had previously taken a Church History class from William E. Berrett, and he impressed me with his humility and knowledge. I found the selection process an easy one. I stated an interest in his interview only. Thus began my longest and certainly my most productive employment, which extended into a six-year saga.

Initially there was only President Berrett and me, plus two supervisors, Joy Dunyon and A. Theodore Tuttle. Joy was replaced by Boyd K. Packer, an innovative young seminary principal from Brigham City. With the rapid growth of the seminaries and institutes of the Church, and Deseret Clubs, it soon became necessary to hire a staff of from five to fifteen girls to assist. I was not only secretary, but office manager as well. I loved my job. Often I declared that I'd report to work every day whether or not I was paid. (I am glad I was never put to the test!) I was made to feel that mine was a unique contribution that went beyond the mechanics of "getting the work out." They relied upon my creative abilities and taxed them to the limit when we'd brainstorm a convention theme and ways to implement it, work on a particular lesson presentation, or prepare a special talk. We all grew in our shared experience. I also had ample opportunity to write and edit and enjoyed seeing my efforts in print in a monthly publication which was distributed to every teacher throughout the system, as well as the General Authorities. The publication, Pinpoints, was a digest of current writings devoted to teaching techniques, classroom and counseling skills, human relations, etc., printed in magazines, journals and periodicals. The seminary teachers reviewed the articles and sent them to the office for editing before being republished. It was a fascinating part of my job description. Writing an editorial each month was challenging, as I tried to incorporate the LDS philosophy of religious education. (See appendix.)

During this assignment the Improvement Era published my contribution, "Unto Every Man. . . ." I was also a paid monthly contributor to the Era's "Last Word" which was a collection of humorous anecdotes printed on the last page.

President Berrett was a great administrator and was dearly loved by me as well as the teachers and staff. He was always approachable, and one of the kindest men I have ever met. He gave me sufficient rope to hang us all!

Ted and Boyd were my confidants. They coached me through my courtship with "Mr. Right," and often our sessions ended with a smile as they helped me put things into proper perspective. Both were blessed with a great sense of humor, and we shared many good times together. I loved their wives, Marne and Donna, and on occasion even tended their children. In the case of the Tuttles, I stayed with the children frequently so Marne could accompany Ted to conventions.

The pace of working for three high-powered executives was "stimulating" to say the least. One of them was either coming or going, which necessitated meeting numerous deadlines. I had to be "Johnny-on-the-spot." Still, we were successful in maintaining a pleasant, even fun, working relationship shared by all who worked in the office. But with the onset of summer and all three of the bosses preparing to leave simultaneously, I knew it was a "fishing trip" couched in a "convention" as they made their way toward the Snake River. I penned a few lines called "Super-Vision" detailing my knowledge of their "reel" plan knowing they were "tying many flies" on this "convention" deal. I further asked forgiveness for this particular thinker, who knew it would be a great convention, complete with "hook, line and sinker." President Berrett's response came in the form of a memo addressed to all secretaries:

DONT'S FOR SECRETARIES

1. Never be too inquisitive of the goings and comings of your boss.
2. When there is a choice in guessing where your boss is, between a place of business and a place of pleasure, give him the benefit of the doubt.
3. In your poetry, never confuse temples with lakes, and big ones with little ones.
4. Never ramble; you might get lost.
5. Never try to out-guess your boss. He may change his mind.
6. Don't leave the office; somebody has to do the work.

/s/ William E. Berrett

What an awesome threesome these administrators represented! It was a choice experience to feel their spiritual strength. It was not surprising to me that both supervisors became General Authorities. President Berrett was heard to lament: "I feel as if I'm running a prep school for general authorities."

While employed with the Church Department of Education, I was called as a member of the MIA General Board under the leadership of Sister Bertha S. Reeder, Emily S. Bennett, and LaRue Longden. My first assignment was to the Speech and Drama Committee. Shortly thereafter, I was assigned to the Sports-Camp Committee to fill the vacancy left by my roommate, Iva Lou, who deserted the ranks for marriage.

As a board member I wrote frequent editorials, a camp manual (the first issued by the Church), and skits for June Conference presentation. I also attended conventions throughout the Western States wherein representatives from several stakes received instruction. It was a challenging but most rewarding experience. My creative abilities were fully utilized. I found myself accomplishing heretofore impossible feats, i.e., June Conference two-and three-day presentations dealing with camping and sports that were geared to enhance the spiritual and physical development of maturing youth. Each committee was comprised of several well prepared and capable men and women. Moana Ballif Bennett was chairman of Speech and Drama; Betty Killpack, chairman of Sports and Camp.

With each passing year I realize more fully the value of this experience. To rub shoulders with such great men and women, and to know that these friendships are eternal, certainly humbled me and magnified my soul.

* * * *

ODD-MAN-OUT

Our European group was preparing to go to Vienna, Austria. Everyone was excited to visit that famous city. As we approached it, however, we were made aware that it was a city divided among the Allied powers. One had to enter via the country of his citizenship, viz.: the Americans entered the American sector, the British subjects entered the British sector, the Russians entered the Russian sector, etc. Since I was a British subject with Canadian citizenship, I alone was to enter the British sector. The bus took all Americans of the group through the American sector. I was devastated! First, I did not have money to make a journey alone. Secondly, I knew I would get lost and never find the group again since my German was non-existent. The last city in Austria before entering the zones was Linz. There were missionaries there whom we contacted and the suggestion was that this "problem" student be kept at a member's home until the group's return. Happily I was taken to the home of Maria and Tony Vogl, a recent convert family. They had three children under the age of eight, two boys and a girl. None of them spoke English and I spoke no German, so we resorted to sign language. We sang every hymn in the book, each in his own language, and by the time that exercise was over, we had laughed enough that we were quite comfortable with each other. But the funniest thing was when Maria asked what we raised on our Canadian farm and I replied: "Herr Weinerschnitzel!" which was to convey cattle or steers. She got the message and we enjoyed the laugh! The family was so sweet to me and the children, especially, found me quite an oddity. Makeup had not yet returned to Germany, so each time I put it on they crowded 'round to watch the process. Since this was done in the bathroom, it made allowance for little else to take place there! It was a bit embarrassing at times. They had no bathtub, so arrangements were made with an LDS army captain who lived in a hotel to use his bath while he was on duty at the army base. A bit unusual, granted, but my, it felt good to wash hair and body and soak for a time, all without an audience of children.

I was in Linz three days, and the Vogl family and I were quite bonded by the time the bus group returned. We kept touch for many years and renewed our friendship on a recent trip to Europe. They have continued strong in the faith, with Brother Vogl in the stake presidency and Maria on the Stake Primary Board. Their daughter is married to the current bishop. Ironically, we were again en route to Vienna with my children, Briggs and April, when we stopped at Linz to visit the Vogls. They were out in the country in a beautiful ranch-type home. We were absolutely exhausted, so we opted to remain there for some R & R in lieu of going to Vienna! Again, we remained three days and left the storied city awaiting our next trip to Europe! It is nice to leave something to "go back for." I am sure Vienna is worthy of a visit.

The foregoing scenario is prelude to explaining the reason I returned with a determination to change my citizenship. I promptly enrolled in a citizenship class at the local high school in Provo. The class was conducted in the evening and was attended by approximately two dozen immigrants mostly from Scandinavia. I was the only English-speaking person. The course was essentially geared to American history and the functions of the various branches of government. We had a text which was well outlined and written by the State Department for the purpose of preparing immigrants for citizenship examination. I thoroughly enjoyed the course, mostly because I was the teacher's pet. I knew most of the answers, having had American history in college, plus having lived in the country for several years. It was a six-week course for two hours once a week. We all became good friends and looked forward to our graduation. We planned a giant smorgasbord in the Scandinavian fashion to celebrate.

We were instructed that we had to have a character witness accompany us to the examination. Cherie Smith Pardoe took time off her teaching job to be present with me. There was a male examiner and a middle-aged female examiner. While the man examined the 23 Scandinavians, the woman examined me for two hours in what was a grueling experience. I admit I got hung up on some of the functions of the government, but only after I felt I was harassed by her "trap-type" questions. Her barracuda-style attitude only added fuel to my already flaming frustration. When the interrogation was completed, she called in my character witness.

"How long have you known Miss Briggs?" she asked.

"For about five years," Cherie replied.

"How closely have you been associated?"

"Oh, I suppose we have seen one another every three or four days."

The interrogator apparently thought she could trap Cherie and said, "How is that possible when she has been out of the country two or three times for extended periods?"

"I went with her," Cherie retorted.

In an unbelieving tone of voice, the interrogator snapped, "Remember, you are under oath!"

Cherie nodded, saying she was well aware that she was, but that she had indeed accompanied me to Europe and Mexico.

At long last the examination ended. I returned to the group, red-faced and frustrated. They could not imagine what had happened to me since in the same time interval all 23 of them had been interviewed by the male interrogator! I have often wondered why I was so lucky to be put through the refiner's fire, while very little was required of the others applying for the same citizenship. Regardless, we all rejoiced around the wonderful smorgasbord. I do not remember at what point I took the Pledge of Allegiance, but I am certain that in view of my extensive interrogation, I was the one most relieved to arrive at that point! And I have never regretted having done so, as I am proud to be a citizen of this great country. At least now I can stay with the "group" rather than be separated as the "odd-man-out."

*H*ermine
– 1952 –

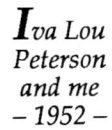

*I*va Lou
Peterson
and me
– 1952 –

My
First Car
1954
Green
Chevrolet

Jim and I
Ran it's
Wheels Off!

"*H*ave Suitcase
— Will Travel."

Hermine
Showing Off
Her Decals
from Europe

HEART STRINGS 129

Back from Europe
— 1953 —

At My Desk
in Pres. Berrett's Office
BYU, Provo, Utah
— 1954 —

My Last
Bachelor Apartment
547 East 6th North
Provo, Utah

Beverly Knowlton,
Hermine Briggs
and Cherie Pardoe
— all Single!

130 HEART STRINGS

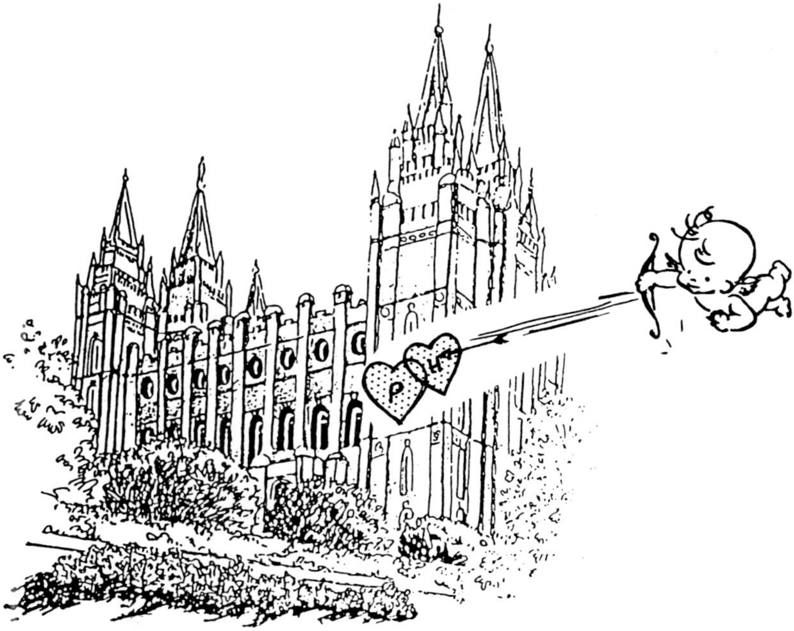
P
H

CHAPTER IV
IS MR. HORMAN MR. RIGHT?

"WHEN YOU WISH UPON A STAR--hope for a blind date"

Dear Diary:

    Have had about three dates with a tall, dark and handsome teacher from Wyoming. Each date becomes a little more "meaningful" and What's His Name has asked me for Homecoming. Gladly I accept, but that is ten days away, though I expect no serious interference. . . .

September 1, 1957
    Had a blind date tonight
    With one Phares Horman
    Saw slides of Europe at Whitfields
    Enjoyed them--and HE IS A MORMON!

P.S. I like his big brown eyes.

September 20, 1957
    I had a dinner date tonight
    With Phares--like his smile.
    'Twas delicious chicken
    Served us "southern style."

P.S. He admired my white gloves!

September 27, 1957
    He's getting to be a habit
    (You'll not hear me complain!)
    We enjoyed the dance and music
    We saw in "Pajama Game."

October 4, 1957
    'Twas dinner and a football game
    In Provo this crisp night.
    The roomies all invited dates
    'Twas kind of a happy sight.

P.S. He was 20 minutes late and the rolls got quite brown. But I think he was impressed with the dinner as a whole. We had a delicious roast with all the trimmings. Really enjoyed just chatting and having him explain what was going on in the "huddle." After burning popcorn at the house, we took the long way back to Salt Lake City so I could go on an MIA Convention the following day.

October 7-10, 1957

Golly, I have been sick!
With the Asian flu or worse--
Temperature reached 104 degrees
Jenna Vee acted as nurse.

We talked about life and love,
But even in delirium dreams
This person "Phares Horman"
Seems to dominate the scenes.

My strength just "up and left me"
Until I heard the elders say,
"You'll be up in no time
Perhaps by Saturday."

P.S. I must get better. I have a Saturday date for dinner at his home, and he has given me new reason for being.

October 12, 1957

My first meeting with his family
Was pleasant--I love them all.
I had a silent partner, though
So serious, dark, and tall. . . .

P.S. He was really quite detached from the scene as he came home and found me talking to his parents. I could not understand his aloofness until it became apparent that he had not told them about me and our plans. I was hurt. I had second thoughts about What's His Name. However, Phares kissed me on the forehead when he took me to the door. I fell apart at the seams. Cried, prayed, and confided in Cherie 'til 4:30.

October 13, 1957   We had a delicious dinner
With friends, Cherie and Frank,
They like him, and I tried my best
To hide my "sleepless" prank.

He drove me back to Provo
Via Don's and Arlyne's place,
<u>To see me with a boyfriend</u>
Brought new color to their face!

Attended church in Second Ward,
The Bishop's talk was great.
"If you're to judge a person's worth
Don't leave it all to fate."

P.S.   Seems as if the Bishop's talk was especially for us, as we discussed so many of the ideas he expressed.

October 16, 1957   We met after General Board
'Twas hard and a long, long wait.
We missed Dee's roadshow
Cause we were just too late!

P.S.   He was waiting for me in front of the wrong building at 47 E. S. Temple. We drove to Snelgrove's for an ice cream cone. The way he looked at me tonight, I can tell he is falling in love, I hope.

October 18, 1957   We saw a show tonight, I think. . .
It's name I don't recall.
We had a big chat thereafter.
I was most surprised I didn't bawl!

He asked me how I felt
And I had to confess,
The constant lack of sleep
Was a point of some distress.

The cause of insomnia I tried to define.
Our romance just "rung a new tone."
And his first kiss reassured me tonight
I wasn't just dreaming alone!

P.S. We prayed together tonight for the first time. I can't remember what he said except that he expressed so well everything that was in my heart.

October 23, 1957
Board meeting was incidental
To the "real issues," you see.
While parked at 40 North Main
He avowed he loved me!

P.S. I could hardly believe my ears--but was so thankful that we both said it so freely for the first time--to each other. I do love him, so very much.

October 24, 1957
I almost scared the boy to death
When I called him at the "U"
To make sure that his declaration
Of love for me was true!

P.S. I really came to the city on an office errand, but was thankful for it. I left him my Treasures of Truth book, and together we read my patriarchal blessing. He was neither overwhelmed nor underwhelmed, and I'm so glad. What's His Name is becoming very attentive, no doubt in response to the new glow I'm wearing. It's hard to tell him it's caused by someone else!

October 25, 1957
More important than the show,
We agreed that we are ready
To quit playing the field
And start a-going steady.

P.S. Tomorrow is Homecoming at BYU--and we both have dates with someone else--our last, no doubt. He's going to a party with Betty and I'll be with What's His Name all day!

October 27, 1957
Today we dined at Fred and Dee's,
His first and hardest test.
If he can take the "FAB'S"
I won't worry about the rest!

P.S.   He liked them and thinks the kids are cute. He drove me to Provo where I sang in a trio in church, "Prayer Perfect." I believe he inspired my very best unscared performance.

November 1, 1957

> I met him sorta breathlessly
> As he knocked upon my door.
> We enjoyed the Tuttle's leg o'lamb,
> Then talked and planned some more.
>
> I played him my new theme song
> And confessed to him that I
> Am a fan of "South Pacific"
> "In love with a wonderful guy."

P.S.   He brought his patriarchal blessing for me to read. It's amazing how similar the terminology is to mine. It contains many beautiful and challenging promises.

November 3, 1957

> The Hackneys played our hosts today,
> Turkey and trimmings were great.
> The kids were unusually well behaved.
> I think Beth suspects my fate!
>
> He drove me back to Provo
> In a blizzard 'most the way,
> Still we went the long way home
> We had so much to say. . . .

P.S.   After our parting prayer, he gave me a box of Valora's chocolates.

November 4, 1957

> I met the bishop after class.
> 'Twas good to hear his views
> On life and love and other things,
> Though none of it was news--
>
> He reminded me of many things,
> I had "normal" feelings too.
> "He must be quite a lad to
> Put a ripple on such as you."

P.S. I feel that for the first time I have met a fellow who can lead me spiritually as well as in other ways. I feel secure in turning the wheel over to him and know that he will try to be a "good driver." Believe me, this is a new confession, another first in our relationship. Dr. Charles Taylor, my bishop, really has my interest at heart. He is a gem!

November 6, 1957
I related the gist of the bishop's advice,
He thought his psychology through.
"If he approves, there's really no need
To take a less positive view!"

P.S. My testimony was really strengthened through this experience. I so wanted him to understand the situation as I did. More than ever, I am a firm believer in the efficacy of fasting and prayer.

November 8, 1957
Had dinner with the Mercers,
Took in a show, and then
Had a good chat and drove back
To Salt Lake City again.

The hour was early, a.m. that is!
When we parked in front of Dee's.
About the same time he proposed
Here came the highway police!!!

P.S. Dee called them since the car in front of her house worried her. By now we should be used to such a reaction. The police seem to dog our footsteps, every time we stop to talk. It happened in the Church parking lot in front of his home, and now at my sister-in-law, Dee's. In each case we were merely talking over serious plans and our conduct was above reproach. I don't understand how they have time to "move us on" when there are so many others out there who need the prod. It makes one wonder if people sometimes get married just so they can have some quality time alone! Dee was embarrassed, as we were. I gave him the little poem he inspired.

DIAGNOSIS

I've a most peculiar malady
Do hope the case is chronic,
My waking hours are peaceful,
My sleeping hours symphonic.
I've been to see a specialist
Skilled in love's sweet arts,
But he's now confined his practice
To anchoring Cupid's darts.
His therapy is simple,
Lots of tender, loving care
Administered to his patient,
Whose symptoms he can share.
Because he understands her case
And is glad that he too, knows,
The malady so oft defined
"Heart--on tip-toes."

November 13, 1957

Our Board "pre-meeting" today
Was one of those rare affairs.
He seriously informed me
He won't have a wife who swears!

P.S. 'Tis a puzzlement--I must be saying something which sounds like something awful--'cause I really don't swear. I was hurt by his accusation, but glad he shares my views on the matter. What I cannot understand is how he figures a "swearing woman" is called to the General Board! In due time I decided that my expletive, "Oh Shoot," is the offensive phrase. Why not call a spade a spade and bury the whole subject?

November 15, 1957

When the Preference Ball was over
And after the pizza feed,
We made our big announcement
And drove to Salt Lake, slow speed!

P.S. He says the nicest things--he thought I was beautiful in my green nylon chiffon formal--and he always wanted a beautiful wife.

November 16, 1957   Tonight we saw "Around the World"
                     'Twas good, and costly too.
                     We discussed rings and furniture
                     Before saying goodnight at two.

P.S.   Saw an old boyfriend in the lobby during intermission--also
       Joy Dunyon. Both of them looked the situation over. They
       approved, no doubt!

November 20, 1957   This day was just one big surprise.
                     At last--I got my ring.
                     It's beautiful, round cut,
                     And just a splendid thing!

                     My announcement to the Board
                     Was hardly a surprise.
                     "We knew it was forthcoming
                     By the love-light in your eyes!"

                     Mother arrived this afternoon,
                     A welcome sight to me!
                     Alarmed Phares when I said,
                     "Meet your mother-in-law-to-be!"

P.S.   Oh, I was so glad to see her. I know plans are going to
        move more smoothly with her as engineer. She likes him,
        and I just know he's going to be her favorite son-in-law!
P.P.S. Barbara (Bentley) didn't even wake up when I went in and
        tried to tell her I had a ring! I was really disappointed--it is
        so beautiful!

November 26, 1957   From now until December 20th
                     Will seem twenty years away.
                     So much to do, so little time,
                     Before our wedding day.

                     Showers at Cherie's, Evelyn's,
                     Berrett's, Barbara's, and Merle's,
                     In Ogden, in Alpine, at Marion's
                     I'm so indebted to these girls!

November 28, 1957   Thanksgiving day means more, somehow,
                     When shared with one's special guy.
                     We addressed a thousand announcements
                     Or did the count just seem that high?

                     I resorted to a sponge to lick the stamps.
                     Know a good cure for writer's cramps?

P.S.   Thanksgiving dinner was delicious and I enjoyed getting to know the Hormans better. We looked for houses to rent, but won't think of living in anything we can afford!

December 2-18   I've burned a lot of gas this month
                     Despite my new Plymouth car.
                     The distance from Provo to Salt Lake
                     I find is much too far!

P.S.   Especially when I am making the trip two to three times a week for showers, parties, General Board, etc. We especially enjoyed the Board Christmas Party on the 18th. Met Brother John Longden who has consented to marry us.

December 19, 1957   We went through the temple tonight.
                     The spirit was beautiful, and we
                     Walked hand in hand from room to room
                     A happenstance rarity!

P.S.   It was a real thrill. Phares looked so cherub-like in his new white clothes, yet so handsome, sweet, and clean. I know I'm a very lucky girl. If we go to the temple together, I guess we're almost "half" married! Was glad that Mother, Beth and Dad Horman were able to go through with us.

December 20, 1957   Both families, and many friends
                     From work and General Board,
                     Came to see us married
                     In the temple of the Lord.

                     Words just seem inadequate,
                     And can't even say in part
                     The gratitude, the prayers, the dreams,
                     That swell within my heart.

P.S. Brother John Longden, Assistant to the Council of the Twelve,
performed a beautiful ceremony. There were no tears--everyone was so happy. We almost got the giggles as we contemplated answering, "Yumpin' Yimminy, Yes!," instead of the traditional and formal, "I do."

> Humbly I approach this great new life,
> Secure in his love for me;
> Thrilled that we can build a home
> "For time and eternity."

This is just the beginning of something very wonderful for both of us. I am so proud that we were smart enough to see the real person within who was in need of tender, loving care such as only we can give each other. I am grateful, too, that we both realized very early in our courtship the need to take our Heavenly Father into our partnership. It has helped bring us close to Him and to each other, and has added a spiritual note to our relationship which has kept it beautiful. God grant us the wisdom to ever keep it so!

*P*hares T. Horman, Jr.
alias "Mr. Wonderful"
– 1957 –

Hermine Briggs, Phares T. Horman To Wed

Of widespread interest is announcement of the engagement of Miss Hermine Briggs and Phares T. Horman Jr.

Miss Briggs, who has been residing at 48 W. 8th North in Provo, is a daughter of Mrs. Emelia S. Briggs, Magrath, Alberta, Canada.

Mr. Horman is a son of Mr. and Mrs. Phares T. Horman, 1968-15th East, Salt Lake City.

The young couple will exchange nuptial vows in a ceremony to be performed in the Salt Lake Temple Dec. 20. The same evening a reception will honor them at the Olympus High School Seminary, 4080-2300 East.

Miss Briggs has filled an LDS mission in the Southern States. She has been a student and staff member at Brigham Young University.

The prospective bridegroom is currently attending the University of Utah, where he is affiliated with Delta Phi. He served an LDS mission in France.

Salt Lake City will be the future home of the bridal couple.

BETROTHED—Miss Hermine Briggs is engaged to Phares T. Horman Jr. They will wed Dec. 20.

Our Engagement Announcement

*P*hares and Hermine, December 20, 1957
"A Beautiful Wedding Day"

"Mrs. Phares T. Horman, Jr."

a PEEK in the SHOE

CHAPTER V
A PEEK IN THE SHOE

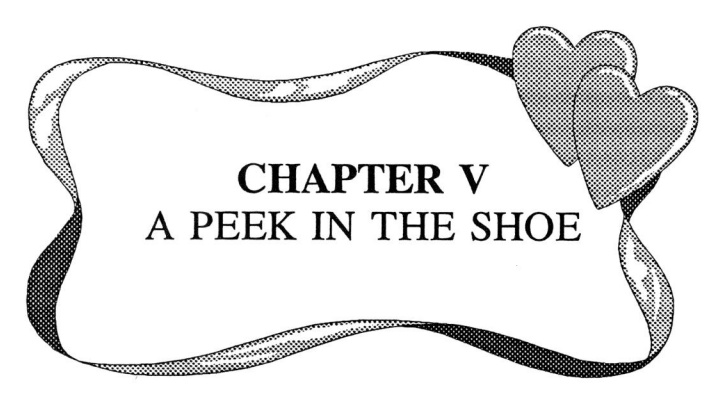

The shift from office manager to wife, mother and nursemaid normally is not like trying to jump the Grand Canyon! But proportionately speaking, at 31 the comparisons seemed legitimate. Regardless of one's age and education besides reading all the current how to books on such a transition, nothing prepared me for the myriad surprises along the way.

The hectic, hilarious and happy years devoted to the nesting process tumbled atop one another. Heather made her cheerful entrance in our home in September 1958. Twins, Susan and Karen, surprised us in September 1959. Rebecca joined the September train in 1960. What a bevy of beautiful little girls! My December anniversary and oft-repeated September delivery caused me to reflect that I was "all for peace on earth, but this goodwill toward men has got to go!"

With four children under two years of age, I was often asked: "What do you do in your spare time?"

My reply was terse and true: "I brush my teeth--very quickly."

I became quite philosophical in my self-imposed seven-year confinement. My entire house was child-proof, a virtual playpen. "How can you stand a steady diet of all these children?" asked my mother-in-law.

I replied, "We built our home so they would have a place to grow. If they are not happy here, we are negligent in our duty." A platitude, perhaps, but I believed it.

Despite the numerous demands put upon us as parents, we grew with the challenges. These were the years of building a bigger house as well as Phares' progressing in his engineering career and becoming licensed. Perhaps a broader Peek in the Shoe is provided through excerpts from our annual Christmas letters.

1960--The Briggs family reunion in Salt Lake City brought relatives from far and near and our Christmas letter was a picture of the Briggs' and their spouses, plus a short greeting:

> Christmas is a time for remembering
> The time of our Savior's birth.
> When angels sang "Good will to men,"
> And Peace upon the earth.
> Christmas is a time of remembering
> The old friends tried and true.
> Christmas is for sending greetings
> To wonderful folks like you.

1961 - Grandma Horman went to the hospital for gall bladder surgery. She didn't recover as expected. We lost her to cancer in about six weeks. She was only 58. It was a terrible shock to us. She was so excited with our children and they loved her dearly. I personally feel her loss keenly as she was a wonderful mother-in-law. Also, I grew up not knowing a grandmother, and so wanted my children to know this special relationship.

During the short interim I had only one child, Heather followed me everywhere and watched my every move. She especially loved watching me put on makeup. One day I was having a bad time getting eyebrows to look the same, so administered cleansing cream and started over again. She watched with great interest, and then asked, "Mommy, did you color outside the lines?"

Since Phares does not eat chocolate, I avoid cooking anything of that flavor. As he was working late one night, I decided to satisfy my own chocolate obsession by baking a chocolate cake. I took it out of the oven and served it to the children on a napkin. Heather eyed it carefully before asking: "Mom, did it burn?"

1962--At long last the hole we dug 4 1/2 years ago finally developed into something more promising. We thought sure we'd be settled by mid-summer, but waiting has increased my understanding of the classics. Ever wonder why it took so long to build the pyramids? Or why they were finished without plumbing? (l) Surely a typical husband had something to do with engineering the job, and (2) a few thousand years were spent waiting for the plumbers to show up. The problem would not have been so acute had we not discovered the race was on between very slow workmen and the two-legged bird, who came with not just one surprise package, but two! I thought the news of forthcoming twins would light a fire under someone, but it was soon evident that I was the only one on the hot seat. But bless the hearts of non-union carpenters, painters and friends who burned midnight oil and saw the job through so that I could return from the hospital to three bedrooms and a basement instead of our "wall-to-wall-cribs" abode of the past four years.

The house is really quite handsome. It faces west and has a balcony which affords a great view of the city and its gorgeous sunsets. It is red brick, a split-level, with a wood-trimmed garage overhang. Our two-car garage no doubt will accommodate only one car and one boat, however! Both the back patio and the front balcony are accessible through sliding doors. Its numerous windows and white interior make the house very light.

January 17th we got our beautiful babies--a little boy, named Phares Briggs and called Briggs, and a little girl named Shelley. We were delighted to have one of each kind this time. Phares bragged so much about "his boy," I believe it was a week after their birth that he was fully aware that a little girl also came in the package!

They weighed in at seven pounds each. I was as broad as I was tall this round! Once again we can happily report that "our cup runneth over, as doth the diaper pail."

Becky is a 1-1/2-years old. Being sandwiched between two sets of twins is like double indemnity. Talk about being the middle child! Whenever visitors arrive, one of the three older siblings is bound to ask: "Would you like to see our babies?" They always do! And, of course, the emphasis is usually on which ones are twins.

Becky chafes at this ritual, but her true feelings surfaced the day Granny Hackney came to visit. Becky answered the door, and Granny brushed right past Becky without so much as a word, and mounting the stairs, asked, "Now show me those twins!" Becky's little face was the picture of anguish at being ignored. She followed up the stairs, rounded up the twins, stood in front of them with her little hands on her hips, and shouted, "AND I'M A SINGLE!"

1963--My lamentation of a year ago was "I do hope that this marriage lasts long enough to enjoy this new home." Well, it did, and now I have added, "If only things will hang together until we get the lawn in."

"The Near Perfect Child"

Heather Horman

– 1959 –

*T*wo Bundles of Joy!
Karen and Susan – 1959

HEART STRINGS 153

*P*roud Mom and Grandparents – 1959
Hermine, Karen, Grandpa Horman, Susan,
Grandma Horman, Grandma Briggs and Becky

A Growing Concern – 1961
Susan, Heather, Karen and Becky

Tricycle Built for Two!
Twins Susan and Karen

Heather, Susan and Karen, 1959
384 Scott Avenue, Salt Lake City

The children continue to delight and amaze us! Heather turned five at last, and is in kindergarten. Susan and Karen (4) think they should know all that she does, and do quite well. Becky (3) feels a little like an accessory-to-the-fact, or after-the-fact as the case may be. It is not easy being between two sets of twins, but she copes quite well. Shelley and Briggs are changing so fast, almost walking. Briggs' hair resembles a Fuller brush as it stands straight up like nothing you've ever seen. He has big brown eyes which give him a look of total astonishment. (We were surprised to get him too!) Shelley is a little smartie and imitates everything she sees and hears.

Our front door opens to a small landing and stairs leading to the front room and kitchen. If the door is left open, the draft is felt instantly throughout the house. It was a cold day and the door was obviously open. I called downstairs: "Shut the door! Were you born in a barn?" A small little voice replied: "No, but Jesus was."

I was getting dressed and little Susan sat beside me on the bed. Running her hands over my knee she happened on a small mole. "What is that, Mommy?" she queried.
"That is a mole," I replied.
"Where did you get it? At the Cottonwood Mall?" (pronounced "mole")

At Family Home Evening the discussion had been on "living close to Heavenly Father." By way of review I posed the question: "Just what do we do to get close to Heavenly Father?"

Five year-old Karen's little hand shot up, and quick as a wink she replied: "Build a house next to his."

When the children were reluctant to eat their vegetables, I frequently reminded them that the green ones made their eyes sparkle. The results were always instantaneous when they ate a mouthful. Susan, five years old, made an astute observation when she declared: "Cows have sparkly eyes."

We took the older four to Yellowstone Park this summer and then on up to Canada. They haven't finished talking about the bears and Grandpa's boat and the fun they had at Uncle Ernie's farm. Upon seeing her cousin milk the cow, Susan looked underneath the cow, almost touching her head to the barn floor, and asked with a pained expression: "Does it hurt?" Whenever we get in the car they inquire "if this is the road to Grandma's." I hope they retain some of these precious memories.

1964--I suppose you might term the year a normal one for the Hormans. April came to us on April 2nd. We're glad she chose that date because we were all out of girl names! She is just about the cutest, prettiest, and best little baby we have had. She slept through the night in the hospital and has been doing so ever since we brought her home. She was 8 lbs. 9 oz., so she had a good start!

After a siege of thesis typing during spring and summer, I carried out my frequently-made threat of being so cross I could fly! I bundled baby April up and bought a ticket on Western Airlines for Magrath, Alberta. We returned to Salt Lake City just in time to welcome Sandra Fielding from England. After much negotiating, we sponsored her coming here to act as a nanny for the coming year. She is much more help than the unwed mother we have had heretofore, and seems as happy being here as we are to have her. She is 18, redheaded, and a two-year convert to the Church.

The children are at a delightful age and show early signs of a sense of humor. At Christmas time, we had a couple of inflatable reindeer on the balcony. The wind knocked them over and I asked Becky to put them upright. The air had leaked out of one of them so that its head flopped over. Said Becky: "I can't Mama. This one died."

On another occasion, when Susan refused to eat her beans (still won't touch them, to this day!) she added: "And I don't want to hear anything about all the starving children in China."

We were having a picnic with Aunt Beth and Uncle Gordon. It was delicious, with corn-on-the-cob, barbecued hamburgers, etc. However, the celery stalks were full-length with the tops intact. Three year-old Briggs surveyed the problem, then asked: "Aunt Beth, why do you like flowers on your celery?"

1965--With three in school we've joined the ranks of the perplexed on how to keep up with lunch money; hems that need letting down or putting up, or just putting in; shoes that were new six weeks ago now in tatters; new susy-longlegs with the knees torn out--but all keep life interesting. We kept Becky back this year for reasons other than the above, honestly! Besides the social problems of sharing kindergarten with the twins, she's a pretty good baby tender for the last three, and thoroughly enjoys bossing the job.

Briggs Family, 1960
Back Row: Emma Lou, Alice, Hermine, Beth, Virginia
Front Row: Fred, Ernest, Mother, Don and Jim (Left to right)

158 HEART STRINGS

Our Dream Home
3481 South 3530 East, Salt Lake City
"The House that Phares Built"

The Horman Nine – 1962

Easter Finery – 1966
Heather, Susan, Karen and Becky

What a Cargo!
Poor Phares with Offspring Atop! – 1987

*C*hristmas
at Grandpa's
– 1966 –
The Horman
Seven

A Visit From Santa – 1964

162 HEART STRINGS

Christmas Nightgowns – 1968
Creations by Hermine

The Busy Parents – 1965

The "Mountainnaires Quartet" Hermine Horman, Libby Lambert, Connie Madsen and Lorraine Wilkinson

Twins #2, Briggs and Shelley, are at the magical age of three. Briggs is all boy, and that means top lung capacity. One jester put it perfectly when he said: "Feelings of insecurity? Not him! It's the neighbors!" Shelley is as feminine as he is all tiger, so they are a delightful twosome. And our little April, how we all dote on her! Despite our efforts to keep her a baby, she's rapidly learning the art of self-defense so essential for survival in the Horman household.

My quartet, dubbed "The Mountainnaires," had a busy year crowned with the glory of winning in the Stake Quartet Festival and participating in the regional competition. While we didn't win, it was a good experience and opened many doors for future bookings, some of which even pay real money. The children learn the songs almost before we do and have performed with us on occasion. They are quite stage struck at this point, but the performance that brings down the house is to see Briggs line up with the girls and sing with great gusto, "I Enjoy Being a Girl."

I made three visits to the hospital this year, with no baby to show for any of them. That is history! One visit was for stripping my varicose veins; two were to redeem some of the hearing of my right ear. Now that I'm hearing most of what goes on in my household, I expect to have a nervous breakdown!

Took the family to Yellowstone Park and Flaming Gorge. Phares and I spent a few days in California, leaving Sandra with the children. Upon arriving home we were summoned to Ogden where my eldest sister Alice was in the last stages of cancer. She passed away September 7th, after a heroic five-year fight.

The lessons of this year are manifold. This is the hour to cherish--to live fully--to express love and gratitude for one's friends and loved ones.

> 1966-- Christmas is not just a "December" thing,
> It's a whole year of remembering
> The priceless gift of God's own Son,
> The Prince of Peace, the Holy One.
> But at this season, we remember too,
> The joys and tears we've shared with you,
> And we're happy we can keep in touch
> With folks like you, who mean so much!

There was a song witten this year that aptly expresses my sentiment: "Stop the world, I want to get off!"

This was the year we packed all nine of us in the little red Comet and journeyed through the Northwest, and on up to Vancouver, through the breath-taking Rogers Pass, Banff, and to Magrath to visit Mother for ten days. And speaking of Mother, she hops from Canada to the U.S and from child to child just like the grandmother in "Bewitched." We're always happy to have her but find the children saying in their prayers, ". . .and bless Grandma, that she'll stay all night."

With regard to the trip through the Northwest, we carefully laid out the plan at Family Home Evening, complete with maps, showing the children the highway we would follow. Briggs got only one part of our plans indelibly in mind, and that was that we were going on a "trip." During the trip as the hours turned into days, all seven were heard to ask, "Are we there yet?" or "How much longer will it be?" But at least a dozen times a day Briggs would complain: "When are we going to go on a trip?" or "I thought we were going on a trip!" (I still wonder about his perception of a "trip.")

Also at this golden age of four, Briggs had his first conscious encounter with strawberry jam. It was full of luscious berries and he exclaimed: "Mom, did you know this has strawberries in it?"

Keeping the noise down to an acceptable decibel level with seven children in the car is always a challenge. One day Shelley complained long and loud that Briggs called her a "bad" name. With much trepidation I inquired as to what he had called her. "A hink-pink!" was her tearful response.

1967-- There was an old woman who lived in a shoe
She had so many children--but she knew what to do.

She found a big house on a half-acre spread,
Unable to convince hubby,
Won Uncle Sidney instead!

And hereon hangs a tale. . .but in the interest of time and the Christmas spirit, I won't tell all. Suffice it to say that I visited this big home every week all summer and watched the price go down from $36,000 to $27,000. It was set back in an orchard not far from where we live now, on a 3/4-acre plot, and it seemed like an ideal place for the family. You see, with the widening of Wasatch Boulevard they took out one entire street, which meant we were virtually sitting on the

Boulevard. It was just too hazardous for the children. Our neighbor girl (18 years old) was killed in the process of going to school while the widening construction was underway. Uncle Sidney Horman was called to evaluate the situation and said, "By all means, buy. That is the best real estate value in the Valley." By some miracle we swung the deal, with $1,000 down.

Phares enjoys his work at Mountain Fuel and still manages to keep a finger in the usual printer's ink and another one drawing plans for a four-plex now in process; still another finger dabbles in magic, and believe me, a magician he must be to keep one step ahead of our seven. He's done many half-hour shows and is really quite professional. He has threatened several times to make me disappear via sleight-of-hand but found I make a very lumpy elbow. Becky is proud of her magician Daddy and boasts to her friends that he is "magitch." She has other interesting words in her vocabulary. She also enjoys "pasketti."

Mother, Beth and I went on the Hill Cumorah Pageant tour, with stops in Washington, D.C., New York, and Toronto. This was Mother's first air flight and the night before taking off she was on the phone trying to get any one of a dozen friends to take her reservation. Since all of her children were buying her ticket, we had a vested interest in _her_ going, so in desperation Ernie finally said to her: "Mother, you remember how we treated that mare we took across the line when she was too scared to get in the trailer?"

"Yes, I remember," said Mother.

"Well, if you don't get on that plane as scheduled, we'll treat you just like we did that mare. We'll put a sack over your head, give you a shot of tranquilizer in the rear, and on you'll go." We heard no more resistance from our dear mother.

Mother was usually the life of the party despite her 78 years, or maybe because of them. We got along with her better after she got over just "paying the tax or the tip" and brought her wallet along instead! When we were on the fair site we rented a wheel chair for her. We saw twice as much as the rest of the travelers because the wheelchair was put at the first of every line. Beth and I vowed that whenever we traveled in the future, one of us would rent a chair!

Briggs and Shelley were the first to have chicken pox, breaking our family record of no childhood diseases. True to Horman fashion, the disease reached epidemic proportions within two weeks as the other five came down with it the day before Thanksgiving. We are thankful it didn't extend into the New Year. Shelley called them "chicken pops" while April contended they were "chick monks."

1969--Heather, 11, loves growing up. Karen, 10, freckles and fun. Susan, 10, twin teaser. Becky, 9, sensitive and fun. Shelley, 6, mischief with a dimple; Briggs, 6, minority group heard loud and clear; and April, 5, joy of our lives--these were the captions under their pictures this year.

All seven children attend Eastwood Elementary School. I'm trying to keep it quiet lest they appoint me PTA president by acclamation!

About July 4th it seemed imperative for me to have a change of scenery, so I literally flew the coop in a Piper Cub and 4-1/2 hours later landed on Canadian soil to spend the week with relatives. The return trip was the most! Due to stormy skies the pilot flew beneath the clouds. We were due to refuel at Helena, Montana, but because we had taken the "circuitous route," we couldn't find it! The gas registry hung precariously on EMPTY. The pilot promised that behind each yonder mountain lay the airfield. A dozen mountains later he was right, but our relief was short-lived, as the landing gear would not drop. He handed me the pilot's handbook and asked me to read instructions on "how to release landing gear manually." Fears mounted when I found he didn't understand some of the jargon used in the instructions which I was frantically screaming. We circled the field several times, painfully aware that time was of the essence. Each minute seemed an hour, but at length the landing gear dropped, and we came in for a soft landing after all.

Since it was Sunday there was no repair service available, so the pilot reported we'd have to fly with the gear down, which would cut air speed 15 mph. This was not disastrous except that coupled with thunderstorms which we had to fly around, we were three hours overdue on our flight plan. Arriving in Salt Lake City we were informed that a search party had been organized and would have taken off within ten minutes. Enough on mundane trivia in the life of one Salt Lake housewife.

Another first was the proclamation by the eldest four that dolls this Christmas would be their last one. Good news, perhaps, but the thought brings a lump in our throats. We wonder if we have adequately prepared them for maturity--or prepared our world to receive them.

Christmas at our house is a "big deal." However, I make an earnest effort to afford only one opportunity per season to have a private visit with Santa Claus. It was four-year-old April's first encounter with the jolly old elf. We were enroute to the Cottonwood

Mall and with seven staunch believers, the conversation was animated. Each one was eager to share his last such experience with April so she was properly primed.

After standing in a long line for some time, our turn finally came. Each child got on his lap, whispered in his ear, and was given a sucker for the exchange. April's enthusiasm faded as she watched each of the family members take their turn. By the time she was to climb aboard, she was very quiet and a bit sullen. No smiles and sparkling eyes as usual. No amount of pleading from the sidelines changed her expression. However, happy to have the event history, and with a sucker in each child's hand, I put the cherubs in our station wagon and headed home.

Trying to understand April's reluctance, I exclaimed: "Wasn't it fun to see Santa Claus?"

April replied: "Mom, I hate to tell you this, but that wasn't really Santa Claus."

"Wasn't really Santa Claus?" I asked, "What do you mean?"

"Well, I looked under his beard and saw the label that said, "'Made in Japan.'" (She could not read, but recognized that most of the labels at our house at that time obviously read "Made in Japan.")

April always was a wily little number, and wise beyond her years. That was both her first and last visit to see Santa Claus.

1970--Two special people have greatly altered status quo at the Horman Household this year. First, our baby, April, turned six, and therefore is in school a full day. Prior to attending she said: "Mom, I don't think I'll go to school this year. You'll get too lonesome." I replied: "Just try me!"

The other special person to impact our lives is Jeanne Aldrich, my 19 year-old niece (Alice's oldest daughter) who came to live with us. She was between jobs; so to provide transportation for her, we both hired on with ZCMI as clerks.

While so employed, ZCMI asked our family to present a Christmas program for the employees. It was a lot of fun and the kids came through like real troopers. Its theme was "The Magic of Christmas" and we used the following poem to introduce it:

> Christmas time is beautiful
> It's wonder and surprise.
> It's joyful anticipation
> Shining from happy eyes.

The Hormans feel 'specially blest
To see seven cherubic faces
Hang their stockings Christmas Eve
Assuming Santa's graces.

First came Heather, 12 years ago,
And before we were aware,
Here came Susan and Karen
Our first twin pair.

A year later came Becky,
Our household was in a tizzy!
But then came Shelley and Briggs,
My, that stork was busy!

Then along came April,
The last to add her joy
To the growing Horman Household--
Six girls and one feisty boy.

Having been away one evening, I returned home to seven angry children--all angry with their father. Heather (12) had been making cookies and the other six felt free to stick a finger in the dough for a taste as they passed through the kitchen. Heather jumped on her authoritative stool and drew an imaginary line between the kitchen and dining room and dared any of her siblings to "cross over." A shouting match ensued, and Phares, hearing the ruckus, came from downstairs. Each child in turn told about Heather's mandate, unfairness, etc. Poor Phares was quite bewildered, and didn't know which story to believe. In an attempt "to be fair to everyone," he bonked every one of them on the head. That is the point at which I entered, and I had to hear the sordid details from each one in turn. The last one to plead her case was five-year-old April, who was quite indignant. With hands on her little hips, she solemnly declared: "Mom, I hate to tell you this, but you married the wrong man!"

Another highlight was our annual backyard show under the marquee of "Around the World in Sixty Minutes." We did a number representative of 16 different countries, and were richly rewarded by a capacity (150) audience of loyal friends and relatives.

Adding to my title of jack of all trades and master of none, I put my name on the substitute teaching list. This I have thoroughly enjoyed. I must do a fair snow job because we all know my real major is having babies!

We enjoyed our annual pilgrimage to Canada for July 24th. I took a flying trip to Dallas, Texas, to visit brothers, Ernie and Jim, and families. Jeanne held down the fort.

1971--When thesis season subsided, we borrowed Dad Horman's camper, packed in our seven kids and Jeff, our nephew from Canada, just to make the buddy system work--and took off for Disneyland. The kids loved every minute of it and we didn't even lose a child, which is quite an accomplishment, even at church, let alone in an amusement park.

We took in MarineLand, Knott's Berry Farm, the beach, and spent a couple of hectic hours across the border in Tijuana. It was colorful and gave the kids a glimpse of how the other half lives.

We returned via Las Vegas and spent some time trying to teach the children the evils of gambling. It proved ineffective, however, as walking them through Circus Circus we dropped a few coins in the slot machine and the money just poured out. We had a regular cheering section behind the screen which proved a bit embarrassing!

I have been substitute teaching again this year, both in the district and the Seminary. I especially like teaching Seminary.

1972--We spent a fun summer in Canada visiting the haunts of my childhood. Phares remained home to study for an important engineering exam, and I thought I was doing us all a favor by taking the kids camping at Waterton for a month. We met my brothers and sisters there, intermittently, but Emma Lou and her three, and I and my seven, stayed on and on and on. We brought Mother up with us each weekend (at 84 years she still enjoys being where the action is). It was wonderful sharing the experience with her. We took our ukuleles, and were the most popular group at the kitchen every night where we had a new captive audience. We did a one-night stand at the big Prince of Wales Hotel, which was really fun for the kids. I dare say it was also something of note for the hotel patrons and management.

Our absence paid off because Phares passed the qualifying examination for his Utah State Engineering License.

In October I was asked to do a family program for the General YWMIA for November 28th. It proved to be quite a production and by far our greatest challenge to this point. Phares and I even sang solos--a first, and possibly a last, but it was always good for laughs and that is the only reason we dared do it. The worse it got, the funnier it was. The name of the song is "When the Kids Get Married," from I Do, I Do. At this writing we have done it eight times to a kazoo/ukulele accompaniment. We have two more performances on the agenda before the holidays are over. The kids are so used to it by now that they have no stage presence at all. They yawn all through it, and it is something of an ordeal for me to endure such behavior. I keep telling myself what good experience it is for the kids and then ask myself the question, "But do I need it?

1973--This year the Hormans had their greatest performance--at least our audiences were the greatest! We perfected our ukulele techniques, added some of Dad's magic, some new dance routines, a trio, quartet or two, and a script, and lo! We became a family show billed as "The Horman Ukulele Band" for a four-hour June Conference presentation. We have performed this particular program about 30 times.

We have a houseful of teenagers. Since they discovered boys or the boys discovered them, life has surely taken on a new dimension. Heather is in high school and is developing her artistic ability with distinction. Karen, Susan and Becky are in junior high. Karen is our pianist, Susan our "pep-clubber" and Becky tries to let neither school nor piano interfere with her fun. They are all great baby sitters; and if you value your life, you'll not intercept the stampeding herd as they run for the telephone.

The three youngest, Shelley, Briggs and April, are still a delight. Shelley is our "straight A" student and plays at the violin and piano. Briggs, our Little Leaguer, Cub Scout, plays at trumpet and piano. April, Secretary at Eastwood, practices violin and piano only when all other ideas fail.

Some of the magic of Christmas is missing this year since the children are all too wise, but they're smart enough to do a good pretend as they write their voluminous list to Santa. I must be a believer in miracles. Each year I am confident we'll never be ready for Christmas Eve, but somehow we always make it. So far we have always managed to fall into bed a little while before one of the early birds gets up.

1974--Suddenly the realization came that it has been ten years since our last family photo. Although this may not be earthshaking to some of you, it is to me! And while winding up the Viet Nam war was difficult, it was no more difficult than getting this group together! On Friday I announced the date and the hour and made the proper threats in case of default. Briggs (who hangs on to his baby teeth like there was no chance of a replacement), promptly lost two teeth the following day; April parted with one of her very last baby teeth on Sunday. At the zero hour, all posed for the photographer, I realized we were one child short. The report was that Shelley was shopping at the Mall, which proved to be true. Now I understand the reason for the ten-year interval between pictures. It takes that long to recover and forget.

You've heard "the only difference between men and boys (women and girls) is the cost of their toys." Phares' new toy is a beautiful 19-foot fiberglass Hydro-Swift boat which replaces the Old Ark. Her maiden voyage was on Lake Powell, where we all fried in the sun.

My new toy is a Mill and Mix which grinds wheat and mixes bread simultaneously. In the event of a power shut-off, it can be hooked up to a bicycle pedal. Perish the thought! We've enjoyed the difference in flavor of the freshly ground flour, but I confess it has been devastating to my waistline.

July 24th marked Magrath's 75th anniversary, my Mother's 86th birthday, and the Class of '45 Reunion. Since I was MC for the reunion, it was imperative that I spend two weeks in Magrath, somewhat like throwing Brer Rabbit in the briar patch. The town celebration was something! It was a three-day bash, complete with rodeo, huge parade, horse races, community barbecue, and a delightful program all filled with nostalgia. My three sisters, Beth, Virginia and Emma Lou, and I sang a quartet for the occasion. We made Kaftan dresses alike and enjoyed it to the hilt. I might add, we wore gorgeous fake long eyelashes for the performance. We heard we cut quite a swath! Six class reunions from various years brought countless folks back to the little home town, which was fairly bursting with people and fun activities. The Briggs clan alone increased the population by at least 35 when all of Mom's eight children and their respective entourages arrived to assault her little three-bedroom home. Tents and trailers occupied the front and back yard. Many yards were similarly utilized and made one think the lost Ten Tribes had been found and settled in Magrath.

The class reunions sponsored dances on two evenings. They were absolutely most exciting! Some of those present had changed so much, they didn't recognize me!

We had an open house for Mother's birthday. About 200 people came to her home, many of whom we had not seen for years. It was a grand time to remember.

The children loved vacationing in Canada with myriads of cousins. What a great-looking bunch they all are! We had innumerable family pictures taken to capture the moment.

In November we were shocked with the untimely death of Grandpa Horman's second wife, June. She was in the hospital and was inadvertently given a drug to which she had an allergy (so marked on her chart). She literally drowned in her own body fluids. She was only 53 years old. She was a choice person and we all miss her tremendously. She will be especially missed by the grandchildren, to

---

THE CHURCH OF JESUS CHRIST OF LATTER-DAY SAINTS
47 EAST SOUTH TEMPLE STREET
SALT LAKE CITY, UTAH 84111

SPENCER W. KIMBALL, PRESIDENT

December 12, 1974

Miss April Horman
Miss Shelley Horman
3600 East 3700 South
Salt Lake City, Utah 84109

Dear April and Shelley:

I was indeed sorry to learn from your recent letters that your grandmother passed away recently. From what you have told me, she must have been a wonderful woman and did much good in her life. For this you can be very proud of her and can best honor her by the way you live.

May the peace and comfort of our Heavenly Father be with you and your family during this time of sorrow. Please accept my love and blessings.

Faithfully yours,

[signature]

President

whom she taught piano lessons. Shelley and April were very distraught and wanted to pour out their hearts to President Spencer W. Kimball. I helped them write a letter to him. We all were very pleased that he took time to make a gracious reply, a letter they will always cherish.

1975--Surely any household of teenagers is a beehive of activity, but sometimes I feel that several swarms have come to our hive to nest. Phares and I sometimes get lost in the maze, and on occasion have to call a halt to scream, "Hey, remember us? We're your leaders!"

Many comment how fortunate I am to have so many girls, who "must be such good help in the home." The truth of the matter is they are so busy with their school and church activities, part-time jobs and occasional dating that when I really need some help, I call upon Briggs. He isn't quite old enough to be dating, though I am sure he gives the girls the eye. But he is smart enough to know that mother's car keys make his winter paper route a little more bearable, so he caters to his mother's requests for help. I often mutter to myself, "Yes, I know he needs the paper route experience, but do I?"

The big news this year is the purchase of a lovely home in Provo, Utah. We thought it a good investment for our children to provide them housing while attending BYU. Likely there will be three or four attending at a time, so our incentive was purely economic. The exciting part is that the home is the very one where I lived when I first went to Brigham Young University. Hopefully I can get rid of some of my early Halloween furnishings and get something new for our home.

Before we had time to recover from the financial shock of the house purchase, Heather and Becky were involved in an accident with the family car, a 1968 Ford station wagon. To make a long story short, we made another major purchase of a lifetime, a 1975 Ford van. It is a lovely two-tone job, blue and white with blue interior. What a delightful experience for all of us to go to church in the same car and still "not touch." We took it on its maiden voyage over Thanksgiving when we journeyed to Mesa, Arizona, to visit the Ernie Briggs family.

There have been several meetings of the clan occasioned by the weddings of Briggs grandchildren. I am getting a little firsthand experience in the art of wedding preparations. I don't foresee anything in the immediate future for my own, and sincerely hope they can each have a little college behind them before taking the plunge.

However, "just in case," I have been trying to make two quilts a year for their hope chests. It would be just my luck to have to mass-produce one quilt for each, all needed the same year (self-fulfilling prophecy?).

We have done some exciting printing projects this year, one of which was the Sylvester Low family history, which involved a branch of the family which originated in Scotland, emigrated to Utah, and some of whom moved on to Cardston.

The last project was the autobiography of Brother John Heidenreich, a former Congregational minister who 18 years ago converted to Mormonism, and most of the following period of time was a seminary principal at Skyline Seminary. It is an inspirational, moving story, which I edited, entitled <u>An Acorn to An Oak</u>, and is bound in handsome maroon leather with gold lettering, which is fitting for the story it contains. We took the books to him on our Arizona trip. He was very pleased. (See appendix.) These two manuscripts represent the highlight of my editing career.

1976--We sent our annual greetings at Thanksgiving this year, for reasons which will be explained.

> "It is my joy in life to find, at every turning of the road,
> The strong arm of a comrade kind, to help me onward with my load,
> And since I have no gold to give, and love alone must make amends,
> My daily prayer is, while I live, God make me worthy of my friends."
> --Anonymous

Emma Lou and I set up headquarters at Waterton Park, Alberta, in July. The Horman tent was pitched next to her tent trailer. Our kids and their moms thoroughly enjoyed the change of pace. We returned to Magrath on weekends to accompany Mother to church and/or bring her back with us. She loaded us up with freshly baked bread, cinnamon rolls, cookies, and other goodies she had prepared in our absence. Our last weekend in Waterton was special. We had a big turkey dinner, complete with all the trimmings, baked and served in the camp kitchen. We even had homemade ice cream! A number of the resident and visiting relatives came to see us, and we in turn furnished them a "sing song" that evening at Parkland Lodge (owned by cousins Bessie and Earl Hacking). What a great time we had, and how precious are the memories of those two weeks together. We planned to spend the last two or three days visiting Emma Lou in her new Calgary home. Enroute to Calgary, we had a terrible accident that cost Mother her life. While driving in a cloudburst, our new Ford van hydroplaned, dumping the car in the ditch. Hitting a culvert, we catapulted backward, end-over-end, and then overturned side-to-side. Mother had her seatbelt on but died instantly of a broken neck. Our son, Briggs, was thrown out and suffered a fractured collar bone, lacerations, and a broken arm. A niece, Dana Smith, and April were bruised but not seriously hurt. I was pinned between the seat and the steering wheel, with a crushed chest and fractured sternum. Facial injuries required seventeen stitches. Thanks to a passing motorist's CB radio, an ambulance was soon on the scene and took us to the Vulcan City Hospital outside of Calgary. The van was a total loss.

According to April's recollection, Briggs was certainly the man of the hour. In her article "Be Quiet and Pray" printed in The New Era, she records:

"Briggs, my 13-year-old brother, was thrown out the rear door of the van. He said that when he found me, I was screaming hysterically.

"Be quiet and pray!" he commanded, as he shook me to allay my shock. I calmed down. And I did pray. He stumbled to the highway and flagged down a car, even though his arm and collar bone were broken and his head was bleeding.

"Evidently my mother lost control of the van when it hydroplaned, a condition brought about by certain road conditions and excessive amounts of water. We crossed the road, skidded down an embankment, then continued forward until the wheels hit a culvert and we became airborne. We crashed into the dirt and rolled several times, then came to rest upright near a dirt road leading to a farmhouse. Mother was seriously injured with a crushed chest and a big gash on her forehead. I screamed at the sight of her on the grassy ditchbank. "It was hard not to panic, but each time the feeling came, I heard Briggs' advice to 'be quiet and pray,' and it had a calming effect on me.

"There were two girls in the car Briggs flagged down. They in turn stopped a car with a CB radio, and an ambulance was at the scene in short order, as we were just a few miles from the small town of Vulcan."

We were moved to the Magrath Hospital the following day. From this point on, the experiences were many and varied, all punctuated with tender emotions and gifts of love. I shall always remember the warm feeling I had then, and relive now, when I think of the wonderful people of that community who rallied round our family and made our experience less painful. Mother was prepared to go. I am sure she welcomed her reunion with our dear Daddy and others who had gone before. But how we miss her! The darkest hour of every day is mail time, knowing for sure there will be no more of her newsy letters. We also miss her frequent early-morning phone calls.

In due time, the broken hearts healed. Within a week of the accident we hurried back to Utah to enroll the kids in school. Life continues to move at a fast pace. Although many times I am heard shouting, "Stop the world, I want to get off," I realize that work is good therapy. There seems to be an abundance of that commodity wherever I go--for this I am also grateful. And I am grateful for the ability to still meet life's challenges with all of my faculties, or at least as many of them as I have had for many years. This is truly a season for thanksgiving. We are grateful for you and your concern for us.

* * * *

ON SEASONS AND REASONS. . . .

Gone are the days of looking forward to "Mother's coming." With the changing of the seasons came the changing of the reasons for Mother's migrations. When the frost was on her Canadian pumpkin, we knew that shortly she would, like the Canadian goose she called herself, head south. Perhaps she would stay in Utah until Thanksgiving, or at least until she had helped heap my shelves with the bounties of my fruit harvest. What patient, able, helping hands were hers, and how my children eagerly anticipated her visits!

By Christmastime, if a car had not whisked her away before, warmer climes beckoned her to Arizona and California for visits with Ernie and Jim's families. They too, looked forward to Mother's visits and evening games of Rook.

When a profusion of blossoms burst upon the Utah scene, we knew that Mother's itchy feet would lead her back to Utah and from hence to Magrath, where she had to "get my garden planted, and get my house and yard ready for my summer visitors." She also loved to return to the many dear friends she knew in Magrath. At times it even became imperative for some of us to take her home so that we could visit her!

Or maybe it wasn't just a change of season, but merely a change of reason that gave flight to her plans. Usually the reason involved an expressed or unexpressed need of one of her loved ones. Often it was the safe nesting of a grandchild or family which she felt needed her mothering right now; frequently a wedding was the happy occasion of her visit. But whatever the season, the reason was sufficient to justify the trip. No personal inconvenience or sacrifice was too great if she felt someone needed her help, her counsel, her love or all that she had!

The seasons have lost part of their beauty and charm. Then a still, small voice whispers that once again there will be an eternal reunion in another splendorous season for an infinitely glorious reason!

* * * *

1977--At the present time I am wracking my brain to think of places the girls might get summer jobs. None of them want employment to interfere with their plans for fun this summer, but I am determined that it will.

Jeff Smith, Curtis Briggs, and our son, Briggs, are planning to attend the Scout Jamboree in Washington, D.C.

Heather has been at BYU this year and has enjoyed having Justine Briggs, Jim's daughter, as her roommate. It hurts a little to think that they are no longer our little girls.

Contemplating our Christmas greeting, I pondered the traumatic events of the past year. I decided that I could say it all by reporting we have seven teenagers in the nest, give you our best wishes of the season, and leave it at that. The details, without sound effects, just would not do justice to the facts. However, tossing discretion to the wind, here I am again to make my annual report from the over-crowded, over-hysteric, over-reacting, over-sensitive, over-worn "Shoe."

Phares finished a beautiful hangar in Wood Cross, Utah for the Mountain Fuel aircraft. I took a three-day-a-week job with the LDS Department of Education. I do office work and keep six sets of books, traveling between six junior seminaries. I was always one to love to travel, and that is about as far as finances permit these days!

April is the last of six to get braces on her teeth. We have a sneaking suspicion our account alone materially aided the orthodontist to upgrade his digs to a nice location in our ward.

Heather opted to work in the Radiology Department at the University Hospital. Her spare time and money is spent perfecting her gourmet skills and trying it out on various members of the opposite sex. She is a beautiful blonde.

Karen and Susan are seniors at Skyline. Susan is going to school half days and learning cosmetology the other half. We hope it will help her through college to a kindergarten teaching position. She is tall, slim and our brown-eyed Susan.

Karen is taking health occupation classes to prepare for a nursing course next year. She plans to attend Ricks College in Rexburg, Idaho. She waitresses at the Hotel Utah. She is a vivacious redhead (hair almost to her knees) and so far, is our most petite, standing 5 ft. 5 1/2 inches.

Becky is our glamorous, long-haired blonde. She is a junior at Skyline and a Pep-Clubber. This activity takes up all her spare time and money.

Briggs and Shelley are excited with their jobs as seminary officers. Briggs grew eight inches in anticipation of this great honor, and has a whole drawer full of "floods." Shelley has taken on the stature of a lovely young lady especially since discarding her orthodontic braces.

Last but not least is April. She is 5' 7" and still growing. We just hope she knows when to "turn it off." She loves school and has discovered boys and vice versa. She plays the piano with a passion, which pleases us all. The nicest present she gave her Mom was a reprieve from a paper route, the first in four years!

We bought the kids a giant trampoline for Christmas. So far as we are concerned, it is the best investment we have made outside of the home. Our kids are becoming quite the gymnasts and love to perform. We had to resort to a sign which read: "No jumping between 5:00 and 6:30 p.m." to preserve some privacy from neighborhood children. One day the Visiting Teachers came during those hours and asked, "If we come in, do we have to jump?"

The first week of June, I had the opportunity to drive a car to San Diego, so I took Becky and April and we set out for a little vacation with the Jim Briggs' in San Marcos. No sooner had we arrived than we were met with the tragic news of an accident involving my brother Fred's son. Nineteen-year-old Chris was preparing to go on a mission. He was in an open jeep on the freeway, and was hit by a drunk driver and thrown out. He died the following day.

Another Magrath Parade: Briggs, Dana, April, Shelley, Karen, Becky, and Noelle (left to right)

Tenting at Grandma's in Magrath: Beth, Emma Lou, Betty, Lu, Aunt Leona Schow, Mother, Dee and Hermine –1975

Christmas – *1969*
April and Shelley with Favorite Dolls

182 HEART STRINGS

Singers All
Emma Lou, Beth and Me
at Patty's Wedding
in Mesa, Arizona

Lehman Caves – 1976
We Lost 'Nary a One!

HEART STRINGS 183

*B*irthday Cake for Sue, Karen and Becky
– 1968 –

*T*he Phares T. Horman Family
(Ringlet Parade) – 1968

*P*lum Blossoms at Easter – 1969

*G*randma Briggs with Some of Her Horman Progeny--1968

*G*reat Fun in the Magrath Parade

*W*aterton Park, Alberta

Hermine with the Clan
– 1968 –

186 HEART STRINGS

*B*asking in Our New Home – 1968
3600 East 3700 South, Salt Lake City, Utah 84109

*T*he Shoe
Tenants
—
Hormans
All

"Big Home for Big Family"

Up a Tree in California
– 1965 –

The Horman Nine – 1966

Ron and Joan Ririe, formerly of Magrath, recently of La Jolla, California, moved into our ward. It was delightful to become reacquainted with them. An added bonus is that they have two fine sons! Joan is in a wheelchair with a disease much like multiple sclerosis.

We spent Thanksgiving in Arizona again with Betty and Ernie Briggs in delightful balmy weather. It was great being with them and were reminded anew how very special family ties are and how important it is that we preserve them. Ernie has a couple of very promising thoroughbreds soon to race at Turf Paradise in Phoenix. I guess that is the best term for all race horses--"promising." I got so excited watching strangers' horses race, I can just imagine my performance if they were really "kin." One just might have to take me home in a basket.

I spent an exciting week in Connecticut (New Haven) attending a beautiful Greek wedding for my niece, Nancy, Virginia's daughter. I also visited NaDene Forsyth in Washington, D.C. I loved meeting old and new friends while there.

1978--Topping the list of activities for the year was our Briggs Family Reunion held at Waterton Park with eight brothers and sisters and their families. What a great time was had by all, both in games played and experiences shared. Even feeding the multitude was worthwhile in view of the tremendous outpouring of love enjoyed by first and second generations. I recommend it, whatever the sacrifice. Going back to Magrath and rubbing shoulders with some of the best people in the world warmed our hearts and let us know how blessed we are to have such choice friends.

The nest is still crowded. Heather is working as receptionist at University Hospital, and plans to attend Snow College in Ephraim, Utah after Christmas.

Susan finished cosmetology in September, and the following day enrolled at Dixie College in St. George, Utah.

Karen is at Ricks College in Rexburg, Idaho. She considered a nursing degree, but a high school chemistry course changed her mind.

Becky is a senior this year and divides her time between one Kevin Ririe and her school work and cosmetology. She works at the Regency Theater in her spare time.

Shelley is a sophomore and has become quite proficient on the flute. She also works at the Regency and puts every cent she makes on her back! She is a fashion consultant for us all, and we love having her around.

Briggs plays trombone, loves hiking, and recently was awarded his Eagle Scout. We were especially pleased with this endeavor. He is a great basketball and volleyball player, and his 6 foot height is no small advantage. From a mother's point of view, he is very handsome.

April keeps the social pot boiling. She has so many fingers in so many pies, each taking her in separate directions, that she needs a fulltime chauffeur. The phone rings constantly for her, and we're all trained to say: "April's Answering Service!" I tell all the girls that they must not get conceited about their looks, for without a good orthodontist the story could be different! But million-dollar smiles they all have!

Phares' hairline has receded a bit more and the white is becoming more dominant. He loves his sweatshirt which reads "Older is Better." As for yours truly, the most exciting thing I have done this year is go blonde. I heard blondes have more fun, so decided to put it to the test. Tune in next year to hear the exciting results.

1979--The month of June saw me, my daughter Karen, and my two sisters, Beth and Emma Lou, leave for an 18-day stint in Israel. It was magnificent to truly walk where Jesus walked and to feel the spirit of Biblical events "on location." Our Jewish-Mormon guide gave us unique insights into current happenings in the MidEast. It was a never-to-be-forgotten experience. I will spare you the details of my jet lag suffering, but I now know what the term means.

We especially enjoyed our annual camping experience in Canada and Southern Utah because of our newly acquired tent trailer (bought used from Joan Tangren). We call it "The Horman Hilton."

Heather attended Snow College. She loved her art and Institute classes and college life in general. She participated in the Cumorah Pageant in Palmyra, New York. She took two jobs to finance her trip. We are proud of her. In October came a mission call to Auckland, New Zealand. We are thrilled with her opportunity to serve.

Karen got two waitress jobs to finance her trip to Israel. Unfortunately, she didn't give sufficient attention to her passport until the zero hour. She received her passport, but only after six long-distance calls to San Francisco, the intercession of a benevolent third party, who sat on the steps of the Embassy until he got the passport, then flew to Salt Lake and presented it to Karen at 12:00 a.m., the morning we left! Suffice to say, grateful tears were shed by more people than just Karen.

Susan attended Dixie until spring term, then went to work to finance her BYU Semester Abroad (six months study in Israel). She was sufficiently determined that she secured a student loan to make up the deficit between her savings and tour costs. She had a rich growing experience, and we were blessed to have her there when the Orson Hyde Memorial Park was dedicated in Jerusalem. She sang with the BYU students on that occasion and met many local and Church dignitaries. She lived in a kibbutz the entire time, and spent two weeks working on a banana plantation. We welcome her home in December, just in time for Heather's farewell.

Becky graduated from Skyline and has been working at Regency Theater until she passes her State boards in cosmetology. She plans to work in Provo and perhaps attend a few fun classes at BYU. Her boyfriend, Kevin, is serving a mission in Albuquerque, New Mexico.

Shelley, Briggs and April are all at Skyline and having a great time. Briggs is involved in Church basketball and plays trombone in the concert and cadet bands. Shelley is on the flute and April on violin. Both are launched into modeling, acting and TV training. They are optimistic about acting-modeling careers. If determination, charisma and proper measurements count, watch for the "Horman Oscars" in the 80's! April was also thrilled to have an article, "Be Quiet and Pray," published in the September New Era. (See appendix.)

All three of the high schoolers were in The Music Man. Briggs had one of the singing leads, the Anvil Salesman, while the girls were in the chorus. Briggs finds it hard to be humble now that he's so famous! His working hours have been confined to McDonald's and helping care for a special friend who's in a wheelchair. He dreams of a Ferrari, but has a hard time coming up with enough money for a tankful! He's a handsome 6' 1" and looks down on us all most of the time!

April had her first job at Hogle Zoo but went on to more exciting things at Taco Time. She and Shelley surely keep my car busy!

Always one to try the impossible, I walked through a plate glass window at the high school recently. Two black eyes and a "nose job" didn't improve my appearance, but I realize the accident could have been worse. The absolute darkness inside and outside the building makes me think we're carrying this light conservation a bit far.

1980--Heather is on her New Zealand Mission. Her letters are thrilling as she recounts the joy of seeing others' lives change. It has certainly been a growing experience for her and us as well.

In June all eight of our family had opportunity to accompany another family, Kirk and Shirley Collins, to Hawaii for two weeks. We had condominium accommodations, rented a car, and did our own thing. It was a first for most of the group, so each day was crammed to the hilt with excitement that only Hawaii affords. Just taking in the beauty of our surroundings provided much pleasure. Of course, while everyone else was working on a beautiful tan, I was looking for a shady corner. I broke out in hives anyway, my usual reaction to the sun. For those who haven't had the opportunity, the trip is worthwhile if only to attend the Polynesian Cultural Center at Laie. Everything seemed anti-climactic after spending a day there. We were also able to attend a session in the Hawaiian Temple.

Karen graduated from Ricks in April with an associate degree in child development. We are proud of her.

Susan returned from Israel in December. She and Becky moved to our Provo home to attend some classes at BYU and work full time as cosmetologists. In July the three mentioned above were participants in the Cumorah Pageant in New York. It was a great experience for them and whetted their appetites for the real missionary experience. When Sue and Karen returned home, they immediately prepared for a mission call. We were thrilled to have them both called to Australia, one to Brisbane and the other to Sydney. It was memorable getting two away at a time.

Briggs and Shelley are seniors this year. Briggs made cheerleader, Madrigals, and a lead in Paint Your Wagon. Shelley was elected president of the girls' association, is on the Castleton's Teen Board, and does modeling. She is also a member of Concert Choir and works at Shiner's, a men's shop. Briggs is far too involved to work--at a time he needs it most! Suffice it to say, they are getting in their final licks at the fun, extra-curricular activities of high school.

April is a junior. She started working on a student exchange to Europe for next year. Quite unexpectedly she was given the opportunity to go this year and had two weeks to get ready. This was made possible only by a series of miracles, large and small, not the least of which were several benefactors among our good friends. She left November 5th for Ahrensburg, a suburb of Hamburg, Germany, where she attends school. Her German parents will send their daughter back with her next fall. She is excited with the total experience, and it will become even more meaningful as she becomes fluent in German. What opportunities our kids are having that were not even dreamed of in our day! Despite her enthusiasm, I detect some homesickness. I'd surely feel bad if there wasn't a little bit of that, since we miss her so much. The piano hasn't made a sound since she left and we all miss that. She has daily opportunity to explain why she doesn't smoke and drink. As a result she keeps a running list of referrals for the local missionaries. Says April: "I guess I've just started my ministry." We are proud of her and know that the missionaries appreciate her, too. I freely admit a severing of the umbilical cord with the older children, but find April still firmly attached.

I had to hurry home from my Canadian vacation in July to attend the Briggs Family Reunion in Salt Lake City. We lucked out by having three young mothers with five children under five stay with us. We had such a good time that no one wanted to leave, so they stayed on about ten days. The only thing that dispersed the clan was the unwelcome visit of a skunk who got caught in our window well. For some reason everyone immediately had more important business elsewhere. Honest Injun, I did not plant the varmint!

We bought a new Subaru which is called "Mom's car." I like the sound, but the reality is something else, with seven teen drivers.

We are pleased with the election results. I believe Reagan is a mighty good man, but he will be wading in muddy water for some time before he can make a difference in this country. We know that adherence to the principles taught by the Prince of Peace is our only assurance that peace can be a reality in our day. Pray that it might be so.

1981--April returned on July 20th from Germany, where she spent an exciting year. She had the opportunity to travel through many countries on the Continent and came home quite a seasoned traveler. She speaks German very well.

Her flight came in at Denver, so we made our Denver trip serve many purposes. First, we met her, second, we shopped for a wedding dress for Becky, and third, we had a good visit with our friends, the Mercers. Becky's missionary, Kevin Ririe, completed his Albuquerque mission and popped the question shortly thereafter. We knew we would have a busy summer preparing for a garden reception at home, August 21st, especially in view of the needs of our yard. And then the plot thickened. . . .

Heather returned from her New Zealand mission a couple of days before April returned from Germany. She had an unusually successful mission. She gave a good report and the following day left for the State of Washington where a young fellow by the name of Spurlock (Shylock?) wants to see if the glass slipper fits. It did, as our Cinderella returned home ten days later with plans for a September wedding! They met four years ago when Heather was at BYU. He recently returned from a mission to Japan.

Not only did we have two receptions to prepare for at home, but each one required an open house out of town. Becky and Kevin were given a lovely open house in Magrath, Alberta, by Kevin's mother's family, the Harkers. Again, it was like throwing Brer Rabbit in the briar patch for me to "have" to return to my old haunts.

As soon as we got Heather and Ken safely ensconced on their honeymoon, we made haste to arrive in Spokane in time for an open house given by the Spurlocks. It was a lovely affair. Never have two brides been so wined and dined and gifted as were these two. Both young men are outstanding and ambitious, and we love them like our own.

Susan and Karen write from Australia that they are enjoying some thrilling experiences. However, because of the beehive of activities they know they are missing, I detect a note of homesickness. They will return in May '82. It has been rewarding to share in their spiritual growth.

Briggs and Shelley graduated from high school. Shelley attended summer school at BYU, moving into our Provo home. Briggs spent the summer as a "mule skinner" at the Grand Canyon. The family enjoyed an all-day tour with him, and I even rode a mule the entire day. I may never be the same again, but I kept telling myself what a good time I was having! Briggs went to Dixie College in the fall.

By all calculations, April should be the only one home this year, but 'tis not so. She comes with an entourage. First her friend, Sara Scott, from California has lived with us since December of '80. She returned to stay the school year. Next came Annette Grassman from Germany. Dana Smith, my niece from Calgary, Alberta and daughter of Emma Lou and Gerry, decided she would like to graduate with April. I was pleased to make it a "foursome" of seniors. They have had a great experience in "dorm living" and whatever follows should be easy! Girls this age are delightful and fun, even if I find myself with four long dresses to make for concert choir. They keep our home lively, I can promise you that!

The news hot off the press is that Briggs has been called to serve a mission in Johannesburg, South Africa, where he will speak Afrikaans. He will leave January 21st. Though he will be sorely missed for two years, we are thrilled with this opportunity for him to grow and serve.

1982--When the kids were small, we described life at our house as "mealtime at the zoo." Using the same idea, the cry now is: "Help! All the animals are loose!"

When we most need our second wind and stamina for the marathon ahead, we realize that this month is our 25th, Silver Wedding, anniversary. When our Christmas letter tradition began at least that long ago, I had no idea that we would still be excited to report--much less that you would still be reading--but thanks for both favors. In discussing our 25 years together, we agreed that we have had many surprises and perhaps at times felt that we had settled for consolation prizes! Be that as it may, we decided that divorce is too good for either of us. We are now the product of the other's tutoring and therefore deserve each other. We're looking forward to the next 25 years and hope that we can reminisce with you again at that time. I read the other day where someone said "they stayed together for the children. She didn't want them and he wouldn't take them." Maybe there is some truth in that for all of us, at least for all who have just survived the trials of teenagers in a large family.

Last January I had surgery on my left knee to remove damaged cartilage. So now you are blessed to hear about my operation! It was called "microsurgery" and was done through three little punctures with a laser beam. How they choose to define it matters not; it is still "major" surgery so far as I am concerned. I claim it aged me "prematurely," but the pain prior to the operation left me no choice in the matter. I hope by the time I am a grandmother I am not too incompetent to be trusted holding a baby, at least sitting in a rocking chair. (Maybe just feeble enough they won't want me to baby-tend?) This year we will also try out the role of "grandparents." Heather and Ken Spurlock, living in Spokane, will have our first grandchild in February. Only those of you who are already grandparents can relate to our excitement. It is such a miracle that she survived to become a mother despite the incompetent hands who received her!

Susan and Karen returned from their Australian missions in May. We met them in Hawaii for a week of R&R and found they have grown and developed into lovely, mature women who have given commendable service in building the kingdom. Sue is a beautician working close by, while Karen is finishing her studies at BYU.

* * * *

A SERIOUS CHARGE

The odors and sounds unique to the maternity ward were especially stifling at 6:30 a.m. I was wide awake, despite the sedation given me preparatory to my 7:30 a.m. surgery. This was my fourth caesarian section. Procedures were becoming more familiar but the operation was not easier with practice, especially with the added worry of another multiple birth. Little did I know all that was in store for us with twins born and yet to be born. I had slept well, feeling secure in the knowledge that the four little ones at home and the details of leaving them had been handled efficiently. This sense of well-being was shattered with my husband's entrance.

"I didn't sleep a wink last night," he said.

"What's the matter, labor pains?" I quipped.

"No, but between your dumb sister, the police and a half dozen phone calls in the middle of the night. . . ." He continued a story so unbelievable, I was certain he was fabricating it in a ridiculous attempt to ease my motherly concerns.

I was scheduled to arrive at the hospital Wednesday afternoon. Our eldest and youngest daughters had been farmed out with relatives. For obvious reasons our two-year-old twin girls had not been eagerly spoken for.

On Sunday, a friend Helen, whom I had not seen for two years, paid me a visit and inquired, "Where are you sending these two?" I explained their "availability" and she volunteered to add them to her family of three boys, with the proviso that I also send their clothing and bicycles.

Late Wednesday morning my sister Alice from Ogden dropped in, and seeing the twins still home, asked who was taking them. I told her my husband was to deliver them to Helen in Bountiful that evening. She offered to save him the trip, which she did later in the evening.

Phares remembered my girlfriend's name, Helen Wood, but did not recall her husband's name. He searched through the many "Woods" in Bountiful, and by some magic method known only to him, chose one, gave my sister the address, and kissed his chubby cherubs farewell.

Upon arriving at the designated address, my sister was informed that the Woods had recently moved. She pursued this lead and found the new location was impressively spacious and obviously new. Answering her knock was a teenager who was babysitting while Mr. and Mrs. Wood attended a movie. She expressed no alarm at two "unknowns" being left in her charge, but efficiently made a space for bicycles and a large cardboard box containing their clothes. The drowsy twins were placed in the master bedroom.

Upon returning about midnight, Mr. and Mrs. Wood opened their bedroom door, and found two children, unfamiliar children, asleep in their bed. With utter astonishment they listened to the sketchy details related by the babytender, were informed of the bicycles and box of clothing, and deduced they were the victims of an absolute case of child abandonment! Nothing to do but call the police. The policeman agreed with their conclusion. It was a familiar pattern. He asked them to keep the children overnight, with the promise that the situation would be thoroughly investigated the first thing in the morning. The children would then be placed in a foster home.

Meanwhile, Mr. Wood awakened the children and quizzed them at length. By this time it was nearing 2 a.m. They were very cooperative, and told him their daddy was Phares Horman, a name easily mistaken for "Ferris Harman." The local directory listed one by that name, so he called him. No, the children were not his, but try "Horman." The first listing under that spelling was, by chance, my father-in-law, so he was the unhappy recipient of the next nocturnal phone call. Detailed explanations followed with obvious overtones of indignation. No, the twins were not his, but he had an idea where they belonged. He promised to contact the parents.

The next phone call pierced the stillness of the dark, near-empty house at 384 Scott Avenue. Phares jumped on its first ring. His father excitedly related his growing concern for the twins' welfare, against the intermittent protests of a somewhat confused parent. Bit by bit the bizarre puzzle took shape. Reactions of dismay, anger and disgust were shared, with the burden of the blame being placed on my "irresponsible" sister. A quick apologetic call to Mr. and Mrs. Wood cleared the air for the moment. They volunteered to keep the twins until morning.

But Phares was uneasy. He checked my personal telephone directory, scanned the "Ws," and to his chagrin found the name, address and phone number of Helen Wood in Bountiful. Her dreams were also ruthlessly interrupted and became a part of the fiasco. Sensing his extreme concern, she insisted on picking up the children immediately, despite the 2 a.m. hour. After tucking them under "proper" bedcovers a few minutes later, the twins fell quickly asleep. They were oblivious to the fact that they had, for all appearances, been "lost in the woods."

This was a fitting prologue to a yet-to-be delivery. My loud laughter had been heard only minutes before they wheeled me in for surgery. Some commented that they thought I'd already been given laughing gas. Fortune smiled. We finally got our boy, with a darling daughter, number five! Another double blessing for "unfit parents" so recently charged with "child abandonment."

* * * *

DOUBLE TROUBLE

Everyone is entitled to be an authority on at least one subject. With the birth of my second set of twins I felt confident that my area of expertise was about to be clearly defined. However added to my long list of "wrong agains," I place this erroneous theory.

The first twins (Susan and Karen) were fraternal girls, as different as night and day in appearance, and just as opposite in disposition. One was right-handed, the other left-handed. They were happy children and all went well until school beckoned. I asked that they remain together. I was advised against it for "very professional reasons." They were separated. The same scenario followed the second year, with this parent being more adamant. The results were the same: separation.

The third year I more or less gave up the fight and said nothing. Naturally, they were put in the same class! I was neither elated nor disappointed, as at this point in time and from year one, both were very independent of one another and had their own friends. However, it facilitated a saving in time and gasoline when their activities were shared. Suffice it to say, with five others needing similar attention, this time saver was a welcome reprieve.

Problems mounted in junior high when both vied for the same friends, pep club, student offices, etc. The competition became more keen as they entered high school. While very supportive of each other, one's victory could hardly be celebrated without throwing salt in the wound of the other's defeat. It was a no-win situation in the home and became very divisive to family relationships in general. These relationships did not normalize until, happily, some maturing occurred when we sent them to colleges 500 miles apart.

The second twins, Briggs and Shelley, were a boy-girl combination. Problems described with the two girls were non-existent here. Briggs and Shelley were good friends throughout their school years, and because they were not competing for the same offices, gave great support to each other as they tried for and won positions of leadership in plays, speech, music and student government. Many thought they were boyfriend-girlfriend, since they walked to school together, him carrying her books, and unless they knew the family, didn't suspect they were related, much less twins.

Research on fraternal twins indicates that they are more alike than their siblings. This proved true in the case of Susan and Karen in their choice of companions. Both married men unusually large, whose first names both start "Mar" (Marty and Marvin).

At this writing (1991) Shelley and Briggs resemble each other more in facial features than do Susan and Karen. Interestingly, both pairs of twins include one brunette and one redhead. In the first set the redhead has blue eyes, the brunette brown eyes; in the second set the coloring is reversed.

Apart from the obvious added discomfort in carrying twins, raising them was far from burdensome. They always had a playmate and seldom tired of one another. They were far less demanding of parental attention than were the "singles." They learned skills quickly from one another--all except Briggs and potty training!

I encouraged their individuality by dressing them differently, although on occasion they had matching styles in different colors. Frequently, however, I'd buy or make identical clothes for singles Heather and Becky so they could share the "twin look" just for fun!

In retrospect, I can truthfully say that once the initial shock of two babies wore off and double equipment was acquired, they were a delight to us all. By the time the second twin shrimp boat arrived, we met it with enthusiasm, in fact we hit the deck running. We were now veterans in the regimen required for two babies and agreed with the commercial that twins were "double your pleasure and double your fun."

* * * *

OF SCISSORS, STROLLERS AND SEARS. . . .

My vinyl baby buggy, a gift of Grandma Horman, was suffering from over-use. It served as transportation for the eldest four and then became their over-sized doll buggy. It was well worn and noticeably shabby. With the birth of another set of twins I thought it high time we upgraded the kiddy conveyance. I wanted to show off my new babies in a streamlined, state-of-the-art twin stroller. I found that twin strollers were hard to come by, both financially and through local availability. However, I typed a couple of theses, got my money and put in an order. It was a lovely looking side-by-side light green model. On its maiden voyage we went to a nearby Sears store.

I had some trepidation going to Sears because my last venture there was somewhat embarrassing. My expensive pinking shears were constantly dull because my children thought their zigzag cut was indispensable to their paper work. It only took a few cuts to render the scissors useless for any other kind of material. The problem was it cost $6-$10 to have them sharpened.

While reading the evening paper I found a Sears coupon for sharpening pinking shears for $3. It got my immediate attention. I cut it out and pinned it to the bulletin board. In a day or two I found it on the floor; back to the bulletin board. A few days later it was on the kitchen table; back to the bulletin board. Meanwhile, a week or so went by and it was nearing the expiration date. I took the precious coupon and placed it in my wallet, knowing I'd be in Sears within a few days. Sure enough--I found myself in the store with my ubiquitous shopping list to be crossed off. I hastily accomplished my task and was hurrying back to my car when I remembered the infamous coupon. I went to the proper department, opened my wallet and told the story of my inability to keep track of the coupon. I was so proud to have beaten the odds at our house! The clerk gave me her rapt attention and then asked: "Thanks for the coupon--but where are the scissors?"

My friend, Cherie Pardoe, accompanied me on the stroller tryout. She had her three little ones with her. I had four toddlers under three and the twins in the stroller. It was an ordeal just to get the seven little ones, all under 4 years of age, inside the store, but to get my new stroller with its precious cargo through a double set of doors was impossible. The stroller was far too wide, so we had to maneuver it sideways. Cherie got on one side of the carriage and pulled with great gusto. I was on the other side trying to get eight little wheels to slide the opposite direction for which they were made. Our grunts and groans were audible, as was an occasional epithet. Meanwhile out of the corner of my eye, I could see my four naturally inquisitive children disappearing in a busy department store. Cherie's were more timid and stayed on the other side of the door, crying for us to hurry. The twins in the stroller began to cry. Even they knew this was a game plan doomed to fail! More than one distraught clerk herded a couple of my children toward the mounting racket at the door. Customers coming in and going out were notably amused or mumbling something under their breath as they saw our small flock gathered inside the store and out. After much weeping, wailing and gnashing of teeth, we miraculously got the stroller through the inside door. The next challenge was to attempt to gather up our unruly crew and assault the store with our numbers. On second thought, however, we decided it was too much for either of us. We made our first smart move of the day. We did a U-turn as soon as space allowed and prepared to leave. Besides, by that time I'd forgotten what I went there to buy! So had Cherie. I began to wonder if Sears was giving me some kind of message.

It didn't take long for me to decide my well-worn buggy was far more manageable with one child at each end. The magnificent hard-earned stroller was sold the following week.

* * * *

SERENDIPITY

Dad Horman's big steelcraft boat, SARAH ANN II, was docked at Yellowstone Lake. Our family was invited to spend the weekend of July 4th with him and his girlfriend, June. We all loved the boating excursions that took us away from home and let us recline in the "lap of luxury" even for a day or two! It was equipped with a stove, frig, bathroom with shower, and sleeping accommodations for twelve, plus lots of room for the kids to play. Briggs and Shelley (4) were farmed out at our friends, the Bergstrom's; April (2) blessed Aunt Birdie Horman for the weekend. We packed our gear and the four eldest into our little red Comet stationwagon. All went well until outside Kemmerer, Wyoming, when the clatter in the radiator alerted us of pending disaster! Evidently the fan belt had broken and had flipped into the radiator. There was only one garage in Kemmerer and it was closed for the day. However, at a local bar we found the mechanic who agreed to work for us for time and a half! We were in no position to quibble. He quickly ascertained that they didn't have the right size belt, which would have to be sent from Salt Lake City. This was Saturday, and our hopes sagged along with our spirits. The radiator damage would have to be assessed after the fan belt replacement. The whole procedure took 4-6 hours.

While Phares was busy encouraging the mechanic, the four kids and I were sitting on a rock in a little grassy area, swatting mosquitoes large enough to need clearance to land! They were horrendous in quantity and size. Further, it was a very hot day; shade was non-existent. With each passing hour I saw us all change from light pink to crimson red. Between running herd on the kids, I was reading Michener's Centennial (1900 pages) which helped while away the hours. The kids were appropriately dressed in sunsuits, and their tender little bodies were covered with large welts which seemed even larger with the sunburn.

As sunlight diminished, it became apparent that we were not going to go anywhere until morning. While Phares stayed with the mechanic, I began to look for a place for the night. I approached the only motel on the highway. Outside was a large sign: "No Children Allowed." I thought for sure they were kidding so went boldly in with our hard luck story. They moved not an inch, and told me they didn't really want my business if the kids came in the package. I was indignant and let them know as much!

Before having a panic attack, I thought through our options. They were not numerous. Surely there is a branch of the Church here, I mused. Finding a telephone book, I hastily flipped the pages to the welcome entry, "Church of Jesus Christ of Latter-day Saints." I called the number and the bishop's wife answered. She put me in touch with the Relief Society President. She was sympathetic, but had a houseful of her own and couldn't accommodate more, but said she would check around. After waiting another hour or so, she finally phoned to say that if we would go to the chapel, we could put our sleeping bags in the aisles and spend the night there. The only problem was we had to wait for someone else to pick us up and take us there.

Upon arriving at the chapel we found a home renovated to meet the needs of the small branch membership. The bishop told us that the house had belonged to a family whose ranch had been inundated when the new dam was built. They donated the house to the Church. The story was too familiar--it sounded like one told me by a former BYU roommate, Kathryn McKay. She described the event to me the year before our trip. So it was with a kindred spirit that we prepared to bed down for the night, albeit in the sanctity of the chapel!

The sun rises early in July, so at the crack of dawn we were up and rolling our sleeping bags. We also bathed preparatory to getting ready for church services which convened at 9 a.m. This proved to be one of the easiest times ever in preparing to take the family to church. And there was no way we could be late! It was Fast Sunday, both by fact and circumstance. We all bore our testimonies as to the great insurance it is to have Church members to call in time of need. We also expressed how grateful we were to have a roof over our heads in a community where we were not welcome at the local motel. It turned into a real tear-jerker, and when it was over we had at least four invitations for dinner. The children's emotional appeal obviously warmed the hearts of the listeners. I admit, however, to being a little embarrassed. We slept at the chapel again that night.

We started out about 11 a.m., after spending over $100 in parts and labor for the car. We were more eager than ever for the sight of Sarah Ann II and beautiful Yellowstone Lake.

Grandpa informed us that the trout were biting at West Thumb, so the boat was steered in that direction. There were fishing poles enough for all aboard, so, dropping anchor, we prepared for the fishing encounter.

I have never before nor since seen such a spectacle! Grandpa baited the hooks with worms, and as fast as he could do so, someone brought in a fish and needed his help to take it off the hook! Within 45 minutes the dozen people on the boat, including the children, had their limit of eight trout each! The squealing and laughing and shouting of the children was a delight. The expression on my face must have been one of great satisfaction, as I am not a fisherman by reputation. But this was an experience where everyone won, and for sure it whetted our appetites for further fishing. No subsequent expedition has been as fruitful, however. It was a joy to get out the frying pan and fry fresh trout for lunch. While I was doing so, everyone continued to catch fish, bringing them in in rapid succession, so much so that the Forest Ranger came along and asked to search the boat for over-fishing. Fortunately by that time, we had devoured enough so that the fish in the frig was not in excess of our individual limit--so we averted trouble. But it was a good thing he did not x-ray our tummies!

(Incidentally, the bishop of the ward in Wyoming confirmed that we stayed in Kathryn McKay's former home.)

* * * *

KIDNAPPED?

Remember when you could buy a Dee's hamburger for 19 cents? Of course my children cannot remember, but I can. Those were rare events when I took all seven children with me, and we all ate lunch for $2.00 or $3.00, and that included root beer and fries!

Of course, we cut the hamburgers in two as no one could eat a whole one. My goodness, how times have changed!

Grandma Briggs usually came to Utah for the winter, and we loved having her stay with us until she "had to visit someone else in a warmer climate" for Christmas. It was during one of her Fall visits that we were driving near Dee's and she announced: "Stop, and I'll treat!" The little red Comet had very good brakes for such an invitation, so stop we did. I volunteered to get the treats if she would stay in the car with the children. I was no dummy--I knew my job was much easier than hers.

April was four and an independent little piece. Unbeknown to Grandma, she opened the car door and slipped away. There were many people milling around the parking lot, so it was easy to miss seeing one so small. I got the hamburgers and returned to the car, parceling them out to everyone, and we headed homeward.

As we piled out of the car, Grandma asked, "Where is April?"

I replied, "I left her with you."

Obviously April was not with us, and I was frantic. Hastily I got into the car and retraced our steps. No one had seen her at Dee's. A police car was summoned, and he said he would survey one side of 45th South going east while I took the other. There was a great deal of traffic this late afternoon, and I could not believe she had gone very far, but she had disappeared. I think there is little in the way of stress to equal a mother's fears when a child is lost. This was also the era of numerous kidnapping incidents across the nation. My mind ran the complete gamut of possibilities--all of them dreadful! Tears coursed down my face as each moment of the search proved futile. I wondered if perhaps the best alternative would be to remain at home and wait for the police to call me.

Upon returning home, I was surprised to see a police car pull in right behind me, with April at the wheel on the lap of a nice, kind-looking policeman. She was laughing and having a great time blowing the siren, making the lights flash and listening to the short-wave radio. I ran with enormous relief to the car. But all her smiles disappeared as she met me with the unhappy accusation: "Why did you leave me?"

My explanation centered on trying to put the onus on her for leaving the car, but she would have none of it. I clearly was the one at fault, and was quickly put on a guilt trip. What's a poor mother to do?

* * * *

....AND WE DID IT AGAIN!

It was our first trip to Disneyland. Talk about a group of "happy campers"--eleven of them, all packed into Grandpa Horman's camper. Taking Grandpa with us was part of the deal of taking the camper. We placed plywood on top of the stove and across the narrow aisle to make two more beds to accommodate us. At the gas stops, people stood in amazement to see how many kids piled out of one vehicle. With a Utah license plate they probably assumed that we were some of those "polygamous Mormons." Well, they had the last word right!

We were near Needles, California, on the edge of the Mojave Desert. Service stations were miles apart, so we decided to gas up there. As usual the girls took longer at the potty stop than did the boys. Missions accomplished, we clamored back into the camper, trading places from front to back. We had gone about six miles down the desolate highway when someone in front called: "Is Susan back there?"

"No, I thought she was up front with you," I replied.

All of a sudden I had a knot in the pit of my stomach. I knew we had left her at the gas station! We quickly turned around and each of us said a silent prayer for her safety. My great concern was supported by the memory that every atrocity committed against men, women and children seemed to see fruition on the Mojave Desert. It surely was the longest six-mile drive I ever experienced.

Soon we saw a lone little figure clad in a sunsuit, walking up the highway. What a relief! But Susan now tells me that instead of expressing joy in her safety, we chided her for not staying put, expecting her to know we would always come back for her. I suppose to an eight-year-old, finding the car seemed more appropriate.

We immediately instigated a buddy system so that we were responsible for each other. We didn't leave any location until everyone had his or her buddy present or accounted for. It was a great plan and was put to good use as we turned them loose at Disneyland during two different excursions. Try as we may, we always came home with the same number we left with! Disneyland fulfilled the expectations of the entire family. We enjoyed the company of our cousin, Jeff Smith of Calgary, and he was a great buddy for Briggs. Even Grandpa Horman had a good time!

* * * *

Briggs approached me one Sunday morning at 9:00 a.m. and announced that he had to give a talk in Church at 11:00 a.m. In view of the time factor I told him we'd better talk about something we already knew about. His suggestion was a retelling of the experience we had just had with Boomer.

LOST: "BOOMER"

We have two dogs, Dolly and Boomer. Dolly is the mother and Boomer is her pup. They wouldn't win a prize in any of the fancy dog shows and are a Heinz 57 variety, but as the saying goes, "We've grown accustomed to the wag." The neighbors hate them because of their barking, but the Hormans love them. It is Boomer that I want to tell you about.

He is a small dog, brown, standing about a foot high. He has soft, big brown eyes. He has a lame hind leg caused by getting too friendly with the dual wheels of a Sears truck when he was just a pup, so his credentials stand out in any group. The postman refuses to come up our driveway, as both dogs guard our lane jealously. Boomer is a yapper, and he barks at any new shadow that even skirts our property. He alerts the entire neighborhood of the day's dawning (a mixed blessing) as he challenges the milkman each morning to dare put milk in our box! Robbers might be frightened if barking helps, but were they to speak a kind word to him he would lick their hands and wag his tail. Yes, his bark is far worse than his bite.

While we all love Boomer, he is adored by April. She takes every opportunity to literally have him sleep with her, eat with her, and live with her. It is no accident that her clothes and bed are usually covered with dog hair.

Recently Susan drove to the University to pick up Heather. Boomer jumped in the car, and while this is not generally allowed, she took him along for the ride. She ran in the building to get Heather, and during that unguarded moment, Boomer jumped out the car window and disappeared. Two tired and frustrated sisters returned home that evening, after hunting Boomer for two hours all over the campus at the University of Utah. We all felt bad, but can you imagine April's grief? Her tears nearly solved the water shortage of the State!

The evening and the following day were spent searching, praying, phoning, and visiting all the dog pounds and Humane Societies in the city. Every third day they destroy the animals, so one of the family was making continuous rounds. One futile day followed

Boomer

Horman Family – 1974

HEART STRINGS 209

*S*pringtime at the Horman's
What handsome children! – 1974

another, until six days passed. April pledged her entire summer earnings to buy him back from the pound, but by this time we were sure he was a lost cause.

On the morning of the seventh day as Heather was getting out of her car to go to work, she saw a very dirty, very frightened, very skinny little animal cowering between two cars. Yes, it was Boomer! He was so frightened she could hardly catch him. When she did, she put him in the car and made rapid tracks for home. She was in tears as she phoned me at work. I was in tears as I said, "Yes, you can get April out of school to take care of him." Great was the rejoicing at our home that night as we welcomed home the "lost one." Dolly came out of her quiet corner of mourning and joined in the festivities. Boomer fairly had a nervous breakdown, he was so glad to be back home. Evidently he barked so much his voice was gone, as he could hardly make a sound! And while the Hormans rejoiced and figuratively killed the fatted calf, the neighbors mourned his return.

This event caused me to think about how our Heavenly Father feels when one of His children is lost. How great must be His sorrow because of the many who stray, taking years to find their way back. Bruised, frightened and kicked by the multitudes, they look with longing eyes for someone to "show them the way." Have you ever been that someone? If you have, you know the joy that comes with having "brought one soul to the Kingdom of the Father." It is a challenge and a promise to each of us.

Now I don't know if dogs go to "people heaven," but unless they do, I fear April will not want to go. For that reason alone, there must be room for both because we surely couldn't do without her! Through this experience I have learned a great deal about love--not just love for a dog, but the love that we should have for one another, our homes and family, and the great love that our Father in Heaven has for us. He wants us to return to His home. He doesn't want us to experience all of the hurt and pain Boomer experienced during that week. He has shown us the way and marked well the path for us to follow back to Him. He gave us His Gospel because of his great love for us. Let us follow the way He leads and show Him our great love for Him.

* * * *

*T*he Magic of it All
by the
"Phares of 'em All"

A Horman Family Presentation
June 30, 1970

---Itinerary---

SIAM . . . "Whenever I Feel Afraid" . . Children's Chorus

ITALY . . Reading - "Maid Marion" . . . . April

HAWAII . . Dance - "Pearly Shells" . . . Becky & Heather
                                          Susan & Karen

AUSTRIA . . Duet - "I Am Sixteen"
                                          Briggs & Shelley

GERMANY . . Five Piece Orchestra . . . . Children

JAPAN . . . . Magic Presentation . . . . Daddy

AFRICA . . Piano Selections - "Moon River" . . . Karen
                              "Shortnin' Bread" . . Susan

MEXICO . . Uke Duet & Chorus - "La Cucaracha" . Heather
           "We Will Dance Around Sombrero" . . . Susan

CANADA . . . "I've Got That Mormon Spirit" . . Chorus

IRELAND . . Mom's Quartet - "River Shannon" - Libby
            Lambert, Connie Madsen, Lorraine Wilkinson

SWEDEN . . Tap Dance - "I'm A Little Dancer" . . . .
                                          April & Shelley

RUSSIA . . Magic Presentation . . . . Daddy

ENGLAND . . "Let's Fly a Kite" . . Children's Chorus

OUTER SPACE . Uke Duet "Small, Small World" . . . .
                                          Susan & Heather

MOON . . . . Piano Solo - "Born Free" . . . Heather

U.S.A. . . "This Land is Your Land" . Children's Chorus
           "God Bless America" . . . . and Audience
                        * * * *

Lights, Sound, Recording . . Daddy
Static, Interference, Noise . . Children
Costumes, Props, Prompter . . Mommy
Producers . . . . Hermine and Phares

The Horman Family presents
AROUND the WORLD in 60 MINUTES

June 30 6:30 PM

10¢ ADMISSION each
25¢ FAMILY RATE

3600 East 3700 South
Turn east at: 3680 Monza Drive

HEART STRINGS 213

*P*hares doing "magitch"

*G*reat Little Troupers!!
Shelley, Briggs and April

The Hormans in Mexico (with Jeff Smith)

*The Horman Ukulele Band
June Conference – 1970*

*O*ther
*Family Show
Performances*

216 HEART STRINGS

Disneyland, California
– 1971 –

*Hermine
and
Phares*

—

*Sun Valley
Idaho*
– 1972 –

The
Horman
*Traveler*s

*A*rches National Monument
– 1970

*J*acob's Lake, Arizona – 1973

*L*ake Powell – 1976
April, Becky, Shelley & Heather

HEART STRINGS 219

IT ALL BEGAN WHEN. . . .

I admit that where my children are concerned I find it hard to be objective, unbiased or realistic. At the onset of family, which hit like an epidemic, I expected the world to agree that my offspring were the cutest, smartest and most adorable cherubs ever sent to earth. It was because of these firm convictions that I wanted to share this truth with everyone I could cajole, manipulate or drag to the backyard family show!

It began with "A Peek in the Shoe" which gave expression to poems, songs (popular or Primary), baton twirling, modern dance or even a "diaper derby" putting Briggs and Shelley in a crawling contest on the lawn (since they did not yet walk).

A year or so later, April's birth gave us the makings of a girl's sextette. By the time she was two years old she soloed right on key, "Honey for Your Hotcakes." The following year she was able to carry the lead while I sang alto to "Edelweiss."

Daddy was the magician who carried the show to completion, while my quartet added some fun, four-part harmony. Our first attempt at "bringing in the neighborhood" saw us perform before about 50 loyal friends and relatives. The following year we added free popcorn to a growing repertoire and attracted an even larger crowd! It also helped that Harry Poll, "Mr. Sound" in the Salt Lake Valley, provided us with a microphone free of charge. We knew for sure, we had almost arrived! Some even conjectured that the Osmonds had better sharpen up as the competition was on its way!

Of course it was my task to choose a theme, write the script to give continuity to the performance, and teach the children their parts, be it singing, dancing or whatever. In preparation for their learning, however, records or sheet music had to be purchased. Phares then recorded the music for practice.

Practice--that's another story. Many a time I threatened to quit unless the whining and bickering stopped. It never did, but somehow the "show went on." It was a tremendous amount of work for already busy Mom. However, with each successful performance, I saw them grow in confidence and a desire to do it bigger and better next time. It really posed a challenge for me, as my ideas and teaching expertise were soon fully exploited.

Perhaps the best addition to our production came with Phares and I attending adult education classes to learn to play the ukulele. We purchased instruments for each of the kids and I arranged music for chording. We were dubbed "The Horman Family Ukulele Band" when we performed for four hours at a memorable June Conference. I sewed seven beautiful pastel patchwork long skirts, worn with white peasant blouses. We thought we were the finest tigers in the jungle!

Each time we performed, new invitations came. When one of the "stars" got a bit heady, he/she was reminded that it wasn't that we were so good, it was because our price was right!

The highlight of our six years performing was when we provided a program for the wives of the General Authorities and a full hour show for the MIA General Board members past and present. Our theme was "Sweet Talk." Other programs were combinations of, or confined to, themes such as "It's a Small, Small World," "A Peek in the Shoe," and "Around the World in Sixty Minutes" plus a Christmas program called "The Magic of Christmas."

About the time the kids reached junior high, none of us were sufficiently motivated to consider the effort to practice worthwhile. By this time they were taking lessons on the piano, violin, flute, trombone and trumpet. Still, I knew the family show had accomplished its objective--to give the children sufficient confidence so they were not afraid to try new challenges no matter what they might be.

Upon entering high school, it was fun to see them vie for studentbody offices, speech competition, plays and musicals. They often won parts, not because they were the most talented, but because they weren't afraid to try. When Briggs won the anvil salesman in The Music Man, he made my day when he declared: "You know where it all began, Mom--in our backyard family show."

College provided ample opportunity for a continuation of their creative expression. Susan, Briggs and April were in "Counterpoint" at Dixie College, a group of traveling performing artists. All three received partial scholarships in music. Briggs landed the big one, the lead as Professor Harold Hill, in The Music Man. April did a smashing performance as the Princess in The Princess and the Pea. Susan and April both tried out and won Miss Dixie Spirit. Sue went into the contest for Miss Utah, where she belted out an impressive, "I Got Rhythm."

Though all the children have not sought, nor had the same opportunities in the performing arts, all have "performed their parts" in characteristically impressive fashion.

At this writing I confess that I'm still very biased in my praise of their accomplishments. I find a natural carryover with their very beautiful, smart, adorable children--MY GRANDCHILDREN! If you don't have any children, come sit with me for a spell. I'll tell you all about the time my kids. . . .

* * * *

THINGS ARE SELDOM AS THEY SEEM

It was a cold January day and our golden-tressed Heather had a long-anticipated date with David Holcomb, a recently returned missionary from Germany. They went to Provo to a dance and returned about 1:30 a.m. Saturday night. They were not too quiet turning on the gas log and stereo, so I got up to shut my bedroom door. An hour went by and I heard the sound of a stuck car in the driveway. Reporting the same to Phares, he grunted an unenthusiastic groan and turned to resume his slumber. At length the commotion ceased, and presuming the car was "unstuck," I got up. I paraded in my nightgown down the hall to turn the front room light off. When I got to the front room entrance, I saw Dave standing facing the fire, with his back to me. I beat a hasty retreat back to my bedroom. On reporting the encounter to Phares, he yawned and said, "I'd proceed with caution, if I were you."

Next I heard the outside door slam a couple more times, another car motor start and I thought, "For sure he's gone now." Taking Phares' advice, I proceeded with caution, opened the door and found all was quiet on the home front. By this time I was so wide awake, I decided to confront Heather and find out how her date went before she had a chance to go to sleep.

Without turning on a light, I marched down the hall, down the stairs and walked into her room. Arms folded, exposing my night gown's worn-out elbows, I said:

"You little twerp. You've kept me awake half the night. The least you could do is come in and tell me what kind of date you had. Did you have a good time?"

A male voice timidly sounded, "Ah. . . ah. . . yes, I had a great time!"

Instantly I knew I was talking with the wolf rather than Goldilocks and I blurted: "Where is Heather?"

He quickly replied, "I don't know, but she's not here, HONEST!"

At this time Heather emerged from Becky's room across the hall and asked:

"Good grief, what's going on?"

I would have fallen through a hole had there been one. I quickly exited "Dave's" room with the admonition to "sleep tight!" Then I joined Heather in Becky's room, and we rolled with laughter.

Heather explained that she had left a note on the kitchen table giving Dave's whereabouts since he had successfully got two cars stuck in the driveway, completely blocking our exit. Since I neither went to the kitchen nor turned on a light in the house, this information did not surface until too late to save us all embarrassment. But then the excuses weren't all that was too late!

* * * *

A BIRD IN THE FIREPLACE

"Mom, come quick! There's a bird in the fireplace!" called Briggs from the front room. I was downstairs doing laundry, and ran upstairs to find a full-grown robin peering quizzically out the glass-enclosed fireplace. Obviously he had either fallen down or flown down the chimney and was in a place of no return.

We explored the few possibilities before us in setting him free, but none of them seemed feasible. Finally Briggs reached down in the laundry basket and pulled out a large waterbed sheet. "Now if you will hold it up as high as you can so he can't fly out in the hall, we will open the sliding glass door to the patio, and out he'll go!" he stated. Well, I believed him and did as I was told, but the bird was not as cooperative. Briggs opened the fireplace door, and Mr. Robin swooped to where the sheet sagged most and flew into the sky-lit hallway. In defense of my not holding the sheet properly, I contended, "Well, I knew he was not a very smart robin or he wouldn't have been in the fireplace."

So we moved our area of operation to the hall. At this point the robin was perched precariously on one of my several oil paintings. I had visions of trying to get the art work restored after his making a deposit on same, but--no time for such thoughts! Briggs hastened down the hall, closing all bedroom and kitchen doors. I was again summoned to hold the sheet over the archway, this time protecting the living room. Then Briggs opened the front door.

In as graceful a dive as a bird ever made, he swooped down from his perch and flew out the front door. We both clapped for joy in our successful attempt to help the frightened bird to freedom.

Briggs frequently involves me in problem solving of an unusual nature. This was one of our more successful attempts.

* * * *

UNIQUE COMPANY

I don't often feel the need to compare myself to animals of the barnyard, but one such comparison cannot escape me. When I had my first pair of twins (Susan and Karen), the pediatrician declared they were not the same age. Their development was so different, he affirmed they were 4-6 weeks apart in conception. Fortunately, they were delivered by caesarian section or they would not have been born at the same time. He further explained that while this phenomenon is unusual, it is unique only to fraternal twins. He really made me feel special.

Lying in my hospital bed in a euphoric state typical of post delivery, my mind unwittingly took me back to the farm. As I reflected on the unique conception and delivery of our twins, I vividly recalled a sow giving birth to two litters of pigs in short succession. Mother and Daddy were living in town in the Hillier home, newly purchased. Betty and Ernie were living at the farm, but had gone to Saskatchewan for a few days. Daddy drove to the farm daily, doing the chores in Ernie's absence. He returned to town one evening looking quite dejected. A sow had farrowed, but rejected her eight pigs, even to purposely lying on one. "They will all die because they must be nurtured immediately," Daddy said. He threw the dead one back in the manger along with the remaining piglets.

I felt a personal obligation to try to save them. I realized the economic loss they represented. They must be saved and I resolved to do so. I ran to the drug store and purchased two large nipples to fit a large pop bottle. Donning Daddy's bib overalls, I headed for the farm, against protests that my efforts would be for naught. I diluted some cow's milk about half with water, put in a little sugar, warmed it, and proceeded to feed each little pig in turn. By midday they were ravenously hungry and sucked with great gusto! Until this time I was unaware of the razor-sharp teeth they came equipped with--as my fingers were sore and bleeding. The purchase of rubber gloves initially would have been wise.

As I finished feeding each one, I put it in another manger so I would not feed the same one twice. To my dismay, after feeding seven, I still had one to feed, which meant that the one presumed dead had revived and was biting my fingers. I was encouraged and drove back to town, eager to report my success story. Daddy was pleased and said, "I never thought I'd have a daughter fill my pants as well as you do!" (Some sort of a left-handed compliment!)

We returned in the evening and repeated my bottle feeding. Intermittently we tried to get the sow to suckle the little ones, but she was adamant. She laid on another little pig and this one died. Daddy picked it up by its curly white tail and threw it out of the barn, lamenting, "I guess they'll all die anyway."

Each such comment only strengthened my determination that they would survive. I stayed at the farm that night to give them a midnight feeding. (I later learned that all new-borns nurse every three hours if they have a cooperative mother.) This painful procedure was repeated for three days and I was beginning to feel like a farmyard Florence Nightingale.

On the morning of the fourth day, Daddy returned with the news that another sow had farrowed, with nine pigs. We both seized upon the possibility of her taking the seven orphans. We put them together and were delighted when each piglet went eagerly for a spiggot apparently monogrammed for him. The sow grunted approval, and seemed genuinely proud of her instant proliferation. We were as happy as the surrogate mother.

This story might have ended here, but for two unusual happenings--first, within the week the original sow had another litter of 11 pigs. She claimed them as she had milk to nurture them. Daddy explained that infrequently a double conception takes place, resulting in two separate births. The sow could not suckle her first litter because the milk-producing hormones could not kick in until the uterus was empty of its cargo, hence her rejection of the first litter.

I thought about the birth of my twins and that of a lovely old brood sow with a double litter. I chafed a bit at my comparison to a sow, but was too thrilled and excited with my good fortune to object to identification with such unique company.

* * * *

HOW TO SAVE SANITY THOUGH CAMPING

I have always been a martyr to the cause of camping. It is a rigorous test of endurance from beginning to end. It is a first rate sporting proposition--woods vs. campers, with the odds heavily in favor of the woods. I have tried to justify forsaking my lovely home to enjoy the so-called camping vacation. Forget it, it's impossible. Either that or my attention span is alarmingly short. I have to keep reminding myself of the fun I am having and what a joy it is to get away from it all deduced to mean all the comforts of home. And as for really getting away from it all, we take it all with us of necessity (meaning the family and all their trappings).

I realize that a child's attitudes about life in general are largely influenced by those of his mother. This knowledge was no source of comfort as the children grew old enough for the camping experience. Still, I am convinced that every child needs the soul-growth and development camping affords. It just happens that I feel my soul has had sufficient growth to last a lifetime. Further, were the "growth of camping" limited to one's soul, that would be fine, but when I spent most of my hours in food preparation, growth is evident elsewhere as well.

Our camping caravan bears strong resemblance to a band of moving migrant workers. I disagree with one author who asserts that camping can be uncomplicated. "The common tendency," he maintains, "is to carry too much equipment. Just carry the essentials." How can a family of nine camp with less than enough essentials to fill a moving van?

We tried the tent route, complete with portables. This misadventure took us to Flaming Gorge. We had a portable stove that was incapable of sufficient heat to fry an egg except where there was no wind. Show me the campground, especially at Flaming Gorge, where there is no wind! We survived on a diet of cold cereal the entire weekend. We had a portable gas lamp that cast grotesque shadows with only one eye, as one invariably broke before we completed the pumping ordeal. It took hours to get the children settled down after seeing its scary shadows.

The portable john met its demise as the six-year-old tripped on a cactus, puncturing the plastic bag while enroute to "higher ground." Her screams were heard in the neighboring State park! We also carried the portable basin-tub-dishpan combination on which the ice had to be broken before that refreshing and memorable washup. With my flannel nightgown frozen stiff from the vapors emitted by our crew sleeping in a 30-degree tent, I found it difficult to greet the dawn with a smile, much less with a hot drink. Yes, we've been the tent route, and hopefully, it too has passed away.

My emotional barometer neared explosion as each weekend approached. So Phares enjoys hiking in snow hip-deep and carrying a soggy pack to the mountain crest. He doesn't seem to mind cold, wet feet and frozen socks. But I do! I have cold feet all summer, perhaps in anticipation of the upcoming camping ordeal. This year, however, just before the familiar impasse, I hit upon a pregnant idea, and for a change it had no reference to me personally.

"Honey," I cooed, "if you will provide me with some of the comforts of home away from home, I'll not deprive you of your wilderness needs, complete with good company, good food, good air, etc., etc."

"Just what are you getting at?" he queried. "You've got every portable in the camping catalog."

"That's my point exactly. I am holding out for built-ins," I replied.

He flashed an understanding grin, as we had been over this ground before. "Oh, you want one of those new-fangled expensive campers?"

"You bet I do. But I feel the expense will be more than offset by the saving realized in comfort, convenience, and the time saved in making and breaking camp or chasing 'No Vacancy' signs," I countered.

He was quick to grasp the money-saving aspect, and added: "Yes, and even the relatives are glad to see us come when we bring our own guest room."

I agreed, and reminded him of how much easier we had accommodated some of our friends with a family when the children had a camper in which to sleep.

"It takes so much pressure off the house and the housewife," I added.

My arguments were convincing. That was the first miracle. Before the next camping season we were the proud owners of a large truck-camper, complete with built-ins from stem to stern: built-in cupboards, built-in beds, built-in stove, built-in oven, built-in shower, built-in sink, built-in electric lights, built-in gas furnace, built-in refrigerator, and last but not least, a built-in john. Now as each weekend approaches, I find myself anticipating fun and relaxation instead of a laborious ordeal. We keep the camper fairly well packed and stocked so that we can answer the call of the wild at a moment's notice.

Ironically, my husband doesn't agree with those who think I drive a hard bargain. He has found that dividends accrue to all of us in countless ways--in sharing some of the great experiences of life together, in nature, in family unity, and a togetherness not otherwise possible when we had to rough it his way. Now those who enjoy his rugged individualism can still do so, while the rest of us are happy doing "our thing in our own way."

When hubby returns to camp, he finds a happy atmosphere where busy little minds and hands have been occupied popping corn, picking pine nuts and wild berries, or feeding a squirrel. Tangible rewards are also measured in the aroma of a hot meal in preparation. (All women know that the way to a man's heart is through his stomach!) Now he thinks the camper was the best idea HE EVER HAD! As for me, I've finished reading <u>Lady Chatterley's Lover</u>. But that's not all--I have almost written a book entitled <u>How to Save Sanity Though Camping</u>.

* * * *

"GOD, I HATE YOU!"
by Hermine Horman as told by Jerry Pruyne

Do you have a favorite chair? Or a special place you return to again and again when you want to retreat from the world?

I do. I have an old-fashioned rocking chair which seems to transport me where e'er I will. In its straight arms I sense the freedom of childhood, the growth of maturity, and the answers to the frustrations of the present and future.

I savor my chair-time; and tonight as I watched the frost etch lacy designs on my window, my mind returned to the poignant scene I now recall.

"David! Boyd! Come home! It's time for lunch."

No response.

My wife solicited my aid in rounding up the boys.

"David! Boyd! Answer me! Stop teasing! Where are you?"

The intensity of our voices mounted with each unanswered call. David and Boyd, three and four years old, had been playing in the yard at our home on 6th Avenue next to the Manister River in Manister, Michigan. They had not been out of my sight ten minutes when they disappeared. An hour of frantic searching revealed no children. Panic set in. Better call the police.

Within thirty minutes a battalion of Boy Scouts, policemen, firemen, and friends were combing the area. About 4 p.m. the lieutenant reported, "Better call the State Police and have them bring Saber, the German shepherd."

Saber arrived, pulling hard on his leash. He charged up the stairs to the boys' bedroom and jumped on their beds. The trainer rubbed Saber's nose with the boys' pajamas.

"Off with the leash!" commanded the dog trainer, and the big dog scrambled headlong down the stairs. "Go get 'em, Saber!" he called, as the dog bolted out the door.

Saber was methodical. He sniffed the house and yard before running across the street to a small wooded area, then made a sharp turn to the south.

"Oh, no! Not the river!" I screamed, as I ran after the yelping dog. He didn't stop until he was right on the river bank where we both identified four little footprints walking out onto the ice about a hundred feet. The mute evidence was there. A gaping hole, the very jaws of hell--cold, black, swirling water!

Drowned? Dead? Two little innocent boys? These thoughts jammed my brain and froze my speech. I turned to avoid the awful scene and ran headlong into my brother and father. "Oh, how I hate God!" I screamed as I raced past them.

How long I ran I do not know. I do know that when I finally collapsed from exhaustion, I had covered a twenty-mile distance and was at the home of an old English teacher. She had been kind to me years ago. But there was no solace here.

The following morning I went back to the river. State police skin divers were about their grizzly task. Each minute was more painful than the last, as I watched men in wet suits ply the mirky waters. Periodically I cursed, "Oh God, I hate you!"

Three hours of probing. Finally one shouted, "Score one!"

Not a little boy, a child, but a number. Not my own flesh and blood, soft and warm, with a question on his lips--but a hard, stiff little form was lifted into the waiting boat. A statue with right hand outstretched and fingers clenched. It was David, and his frozen form told the tragedy. Boyd, the more adventuresome of the two, apparently went first and broke through the ice. David followed, reaching out to save him. Both went under and death was quick in the freezing waters.

A few agonizing minutes later came the second call, "Score two!"

Grief swallowed me and I cursed, "Oh God, how I hate you!"

The days which followed were a blur. I moved in and out of reality as funeral arrangements were made. I remember little of what was said during the service, except the minister's parting words, "This is God's will. We are not to understand."

NOT TO UNDERSTAND! I had to understand! These were no words of comfort. A vindictive God who would kill innocent children was no friend of mine now or ever, and I told the minister so.

Crises often solidify marriages, but not mine. I was so saturated with bitterness that relationships of any kind were impossible. I alienated people wherever I went. I remained on a collision course. My anger spilled over into every facet of my life. I pulverized the driver who made an illegal left turn in front of me, after forcing him off the road. I battered the face of a 6'6" skier whose skis jabbed me in the ribs while waiting to board a plane. My assault and battery charges mounted, as did my debts to avoid sentencing. Anger and violence stalked my footsteps. Vengeance grew more difficult as I continued kicking against the pricks.

I chose the usual means of worldly escape. Still the pain remained. I cried every time I relived the awful scene. I continued cursing God and blaming him for ruining my life and my chance for happiness. Years of total frustration followed; and although I remarried and moved from my native environs, peace did not come.

Upon returning home from work one evening, I encountered two young men approaching my door. They announced themselves as missionaries of the Church of Jesus Christ of Latter-day Saints. I abused them verbally before taking one of them by the nap of the neck and ordering him off my property with the threat, "And don't let me see you in this neighborhood again, or I'll bash your brains in!" They left the premises quickly.

The incident, typical of all of my days, was soon forgotten. The following week, as my wife and I were about to sit down for the evening meal, the doorbell rang. I answered it and, much to my astonishment, there stood the same pair of young men I had ordered off the property a week ago! Before I had a chance to administer my well-worn epithets, one of them looked me straight in the eye and said very sincerely, "I know you don't want to hear what we have to say, but we have a very important message for you from our Savior, Jesus Christ. HE wants you to hear it!"

The brazen yet humble tone in his voice caught me off guard, and I listened. I gave vent to my anger and spilled out my bitterness. They listened, and they understood. They talked to me of "free agency," a new term in my vast store of misunderstanding. My heart responded. And thus began my quest for truth.

I was like a man possessed, so eager was I for each weekly visit. My soul hungered for the answers to the questions: Who am

I? Where did I come from? Why am I here? And after death, what? Methodically they opened the eyes of my understanding through the scriptures. My longing, aching heart began to heal.

This profound principle of free agency explained a lot of heretofore unanswered questions. I felt that my little boys died prematurely because, perhaps, <u>they chose</u> a shortened life span in order to have the privilege of earth life. What a beautiful concept! They were not victims of a vindictive God who mercilessly saw them drowned. They were a party to His plan long before they became my David and Boyd. This was merely a step forward in their eternal progression. The magnitude of this principle made a great impact upon me.

Today, tears still well in my eyes when I think of them. But they are not tears borne of anger or hate. They are tears of love and understanding. This single principle transformed my life, and I joined the ranks of the believers.

* * * *

Sisters –
Emma Lou, Virginia, Beth and Hermine,
At Mother's 85th Birthday Party and Magrath's 75th

*M*other's 85th Birthday – 1975
Emilie Sophia Osterloh Briggs

With daughters

*A*nd Sons

*Heather's
High School
Graduation
– 1977 –*

*Karen, Kevin Ririe, Susan
High School Grads – 1978*

*P*roud of our Eagle Scout – 1977
Eric Gilzean, Briggs, James Bischoff,
and Chick Hillier

*B*ecky's
Graduation
– 1979 –

*H*ermine in Israeli costume – 1979

Massada, Israel – 1979
Emma Lou, Hermine and Beth

A nightgown Christmas – 1980
karen, Susan, Shelley, Hermine
and April

*B*ecky and Kevin
Announce Marriage
– 1981 –

*B*ecky in wedding dress

HEART STRINGS 239

Heather
Looking to a Mission
– 1979 –

*Heather and Ken
Announce Marriage
– 1981 –*

Heather in Wedding Dress

HEART STRINGS 241

*S*helley and Briggs Graduate
from Skyline--1981

Shelley and Briggs Graduation – 1981
Premission for Briggs to South Africa

Susan and Karren--Premission

*A*pril – Our
*Skyline Graduate
and
Sterling Scholar*

*S*kyline Graduates – 1982
April, Cousin Dana Smith, Sarah Scott

CHAPTER VI
A TIME OF HARVEST

Phares worked eighteen years for Mountain Fuel Supply, the local gas company. In addition, we moonlighted for thirty years from a print shop in our basement. He did the printing and I the typing. Countless theses, family histories and wedding invitations emanated from "Distinctive Printing." We had on-the-job training for maintenance and repair of a 1250 Multilith press, a process camera and a binder. We operated a complete print shop which helped keep the wolf from our door and this mother in the home. Nonetheless, it was a mixed blessing! I oft declared that when my time came to die, I'd have one more thesis to type before I could go.

When Mountain Fuel followed a national trend to retire personnel at 55, we were both devastated. Not only did we need the steady income for our maturing family, but twenty-four hours of togetherness was too much for two so young!

Fortunately, we had the print shop to fall back on, and the emerging role of grandparenting held new promises and challenges as we approached this milestone.

College, Cupid, and Church commitments kept us humble.

1982--Shelley had a wonderful experience in Israel for six months, returning home last July after touring the continent. She was fortunate to find a teller's job at the local First Security Bank. It's nice there is someone in the family who has funds at her fingertips!

Briggs writes from Johannesburg that he is a member of the Mormonaires, a quartet of elders. They have caused quite a stir locally as they take their music proselyting to schools, hospitals, malls, or wherever they can find people to listen to them and their message. It has been a joyful experience for all concerned, but especially for me to see some of my old quartet music utilized again. He is having an outstanding mission and has been blessed with great companions and two much-loved mission presidents, Wood and Margetts.

*W*hew! We Finally Made it to Disneyland Alone!

First Grandson Featuring Jacob Spurlock, at Spokane, Wahington

Grandpa and Grandma Horman with First Granddaughter, Alisha Ririe

*M*arty and Karren
Announce

*O*ur Karen Bride

250 HEART STRINGS

*P*hilippine
Bound
Shelley
with
Briggs

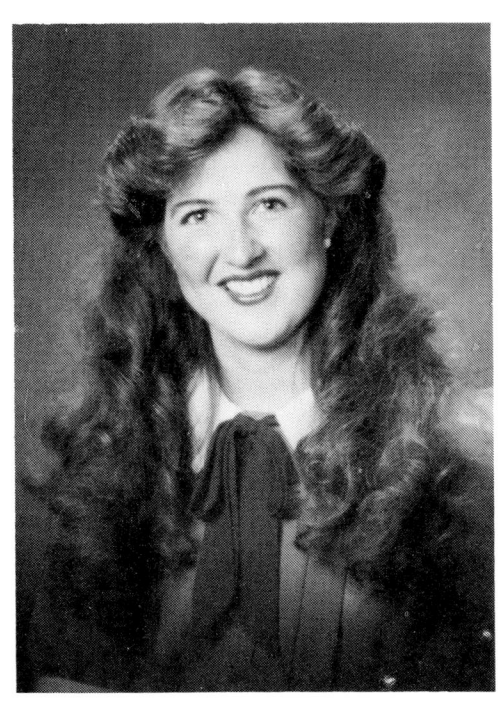

*S*helley,
Sister
Missionary

*Clowns Susan and Hermine
at Dixie College
Mother's Week*

*D*ixie-ites
April, Susan, "Bish Putnam" and Briggs

*D*ixie Homecoming Pageant
Queen Susan, Malea Mathis and April

HEART STRINGS 253

Queen Susan – Homecoming Celebration

Professor Harold Hill in Music Man
Alias Briggs Horman

*H*orman Family – 1985 (Left to right)
Back Row: April, Becky, Briggs, Shelley
Front Row: Heather, Phares, Hermine and Susan

April and her live-in associates graduated from Skyline. They have all gone their separate ways and are doing great and noble things. She opted to work Fall Quarter to help line the larder for her study abroad with BYU in Israel. She was a Sterling Scholar last year in languages, sang with the Concert Choir and Madrigals, and was also on the Seminary Council.

After having seven live wires attend Skyline, it aged me a decade to see school start this year without an ounce of input on my part! And Skyline seems to be doing just fine, which is even more disconcerting!

1983--While Karen was at BYU this year we found her spending an increasing amount of time going and coming to Salt Lake with one Marty Phelps. Of course it was platonic. But nonetheless, Cupid hit his mark, and June 7th saw us busily engaged in their wedding. (See Self Fulfilling Prophecy.)

This year I feel as if I rubbed Aladdin's lamp and took off on his magic carpet! It has only been two months since our fabulous trip abroad and daily I have to pinch myself to be sure that it was not just a figment of my imagination.

Briggs completed his mission in South Africa in July. He served the last six months as assistant to President Margetts. Simultaneously, April finished her study abroad with BYU in Israel. We arranged for her to meet us in Johannesburg. The four of us toured South Africa for three weeks. We rented a car (and they drive on the left side there) and drove over 2,000 miles going from Johannesburg up the south coast to Oudshoorn, Port Elizabeth, East London, Wildernesstuin, Transkei and Durban.

First stop was Kruger Park, which surpassed our wildest imagination! We saw elephants, lions, giraffes, baboons, hippos, jackals, wildebeasts, water buffalo, many kinds of deer, warthogs, zebras, crocodiles, etc. It was incredible seeing them in their native environment. And the ant hills resemble miniature condos, with turrets and chimneys. The ants are enormous, and thus able to complete such construction projects.

Victoria Falls in Zimbabwe (formerly Rhodesia) was almost worth the entire trip. It is so vast and the water falls so deep it creates a rain forest on the opposite side of the crevasse. Other falls in the world are dwarfed by this spectacle.

South Africa is breathtaking! I had no preconceived idea of it, other than bare natives, and we did see a few of those. The scenery is gorgeous, but Africa suffered six years of drought, so one can only imagine its beauty had they had sufficient rain. Its cities are ultra-modern, but one drives hundreds of miles with very few settlements in between.

The spacious modern stores are a study in black and white. They capitalize on the obvious and store windows had both black and white mannequins in black and white stylish clothing. Their merchandising certainly had eye appeal.

The blacks are not allowed to live in the cities but live in their own communities some miles removed from the metropolitan centers. They are bused in for their daytime jobs and returned to their homes at night--hence very few blacks are seen except going to or returning from their places of employment. Since they are by far the majority, their problems are much more complex than we can realize. The strict government-imposed <u>apartheid</u> policy of segregation compounds and gives continuity to the abolition of equal rights. Our would be solutions are not feasible in such a complex society.

* * * *

CULTURE SHOCK

<u>Johannesburg, South Africa</u>

We arrived in this beautiful city in the evening of Saturday, July 12, 1985. Scarcely had we found our luggage, met our son, Briggs, and been billeted into the mission home, when a warm, bright Sunday burst upon us. Briggs informed us that we were going to attend our meetings in the all-black township of Soweto. We were excited and full of anticipation.

In the distance a heavy cloud of smog hung over the community where only wood and coal are used for fuel. And even though it was July, it was their winter season. After a drive of about a half an hour, we arrived and entered a schoolhouse-type building. It appeared as if the lights had been shut off and the blinds drawn, it was so dark inside. As our eyes adjusted to the environment, it became apparent that none of the above was true, but the hall was half-filled with black people, and I mean BLACK people! Blacks sat on one side of the aisle, a handful of whites on the other. Only eyes and teeth were discernible of those on the stand. Two youths gave talks and occasionally I could understand a word or two. I asked Briggs what dialect they spoke. He smiled and said, "English." But oh, what a different version--English with an African accent, coupled with a dozen or so native dialects. After listening to their English for a couple of weeks, I finally had my ears tuned to understand most of what was said. However, it was a unique experience, unlike listening to English-English, Australian or New Zealand English, or any other English I ever heard. Culture shock was beginning to set in.

Our second meeting was Relief Society where the sister in charge wore a woolen blanket wrapped around her for a skirt, a red sweater with long sleeves and a woolen turban on her head. She had about six gold teeth. They pull the good ones and put gold in their place because it is a status symbol. The skeletal structure of many black people is entirely different from whites. Our spines are virtually straight with a slight curve at the base. However, theirs has a definite curve which produces tremendously large derrieres, making the ladies appear as if they are wearing bustles. The lady president had such a "bustle" and weighed upwards of 200 pounds. She was in no way different from the other 20 sisters who occupied the classroom. There was one other white lady present. As I looked around the room I felt overwhelming culture shock and wondered momentarily what in the world I was doing here. Being only a day removed from Salt Lake City was my great disadvantage! As I listened to this dear sister speak and carefully explain gospel principles, I was touched. Midway in the lesson the priesthood next door started singing "Israel, Israel, God is Calling" in four parts with the most beautiful descant I had ever heard. I thought sure I was hearing an angelic choir, albeit the rhythm was slightly different than I was accustomed to hearing. It was breathtaking! The blacks have an uncanny sense of harmony and find it actually difficult to sing in unison. We then settled into the lesson which was executed with feeling and great conviction. I later learned that this lady was a member for only three years, held three masters' degrees, and spoke 13 languages fluently. I was humbled by her presence and intellect.

We met an 18 year-old man whom Briggs baptized a few weeks earlier. He looked impressive in a suit, shirt, tie and shoes, sizes too big, donated by homebound elders. He proudly held his scriptures, also a donation of the elders who taught and baptized him.

After the meetings the blacks lined the sidewalks, waiting to say goodbye to us. They would not extend their hands first, but waited for us to do so. They were so childlike and humble, and acted as if we were doing them a great favor by shaking their hands. When we extended our hands, the sisters hugged us. It was an experience I shall never forget and it changed my life in a positive way. Sisterhood is beautiful and is a blessing to all of us wherever we meet. I was humbled by this congregation and especially by this special sister who taught the Relief Society lesson.

* * * *

We spent the next five weeks in Europe, tramping through Germany, Austria, Switzerland, Denmark, Sweden, Norway, France and England. Each country has a charm of its own but all seemed to share lush forest scenery and alpine retreats. Our experience in Europe was delightful, except in France where Phares lost $350 to a very adept pickpocket, and my passport was stolen. (See related stories.)

One learns to travel light or suffer the consequences. When I returned home and packed my bags away, I thought my arms would involuntarily fly upward without the burden to which they had become accustomed! I developed shoulder, arm, and leg muscles I hadn't used since the days back on the farm!

One reason this trip was possible was because Phares was retired from Mountain Fuel on his 55th birthday in April. Retirement certainly did not fit our time schedule and did not coincide with the completion of raising our family. We still had four to educate, send on missions and marry off--but retire we did. Phares keeps busy with his rentals and home computer. I anticipate working at the Legislature again this year, and perhaps he will too. I cannot bear the thought of him lying in bed with the soaps while I slave away at the office.

* * * *

BULAWAYO TO ZIMBABWE

We were on our way to see one of the seven wonders of the world--VICTORIA FALLS.[4] We arrived at the airport with our many bags. When we passed through to show our tickets, the man in charge asked if April did not have luggage to check. "Just my hand luggage is all," she replied with a smile. He looked at her giant

---

[4]"Victoria Falls was discovered by David Livingston in 1855 and named for Queen Victoria. The Falls lie between Rhodesia (Zimbabwe) and Zambia, about halfway between the mouth and the source of the Zambesi River. At the Falls' location the river is about a mile wide and drops suddenly into a deep, narrow chasm. A canyon about 40 miles long permits the water to flow out. The height of the Falls varies from 256 feet at the right bank to 355 feet in the center."--<u>Worldbook Encyclopedia</u>.

The mist and spray created by the Falls can be seen for several miles. This cloud and the constant roar causes the natives to call it "Smoke that thunders." It is used for hydro-electric purposes, though its potential is virtually unharnessed. The vines and trees in the rain forest remind me of the kind Tarzan and Jane used--many rope-like vines and roots in great fern forests. The view from any angle is breath-taking and certainly it is worthy of the description one of the seven natural wonders of the world.

backpack and further inquired, "Are you bringing your own parachute?" We laughed and nodded our heads affirmatively.

At this point in time, April was indeed a seasoned traveler. She studied in Israel for six months and traveled Europe with two other girls. After traveling alone for a month in Europe she joined us in Johannesburg. She had seen all the grief connected with lost or misplaced luggage, and had definite ideas about what was essential or just nice to have along. She was strictly a carrier of the essentials at this point in time.

We walked down the tarmac to the waiting plane. One look and we all thought a parachute was a good idea! It was a twin engine turbo jet with two props. It seated about 20-30 people. The cabin was not pressurized and the two-hour flight felt much like a sauna or steam bath. It was quite an experience flying over the huge game parks, seeing the umbrella-type trees from the topside. We began to realize the vast wasteland that makes up much of South Africa. We were happy to check into our air-conditioned motel.

Everyone who goes to Africa returns with wood-carved heads of natives. We were "typical" and found our "el cheapo" digital watches fine bargaining chips. I met a young man who actually carved the handsome man and wife team I so prize. He was happy with my watch, albeit a woman's watch. I also paid him $15 for the pair. We both felt we had quite a bargain.

> Moral: Always travel with a big hanky. You never know when you might need to bail out.

* * * *

LOOK BEFORE YOU LEAP

<u>Stockholm, Sweden</u>

While in Stockholm we were the guests of Christer and Karin Osterlund, uncle and aunt of Ann Osborg, Briggs' penpal of the past two years. Since Christer's wife was in Malmo, he took us to a wonderful smorgasbord dinner. He suggested that inasmuch as we would be leaving the following day, we should take a ferry into some of the beautiful fjords. This would not normally be a Sunday activity, but in view of our tight itinerary, it seemed practical. We took his advice, boarded the ferry and basked in the sunshine and the luscious scenery of that great land.

Upon returning, the ferry went into one of a series of locks in the boat channel. Ironically, it was adjacent to the tram station closest to Christer's home. He suggested that we get off the ferry and walk across the street to the train, saving about an hour instead of going the long way. It was a fine idea because at the time the ferry was on the same level as the dock. Briggs and April hopped out like the teenagers they were! Phares and I hesitated, and with each minute the ferry sunk lower in the water. As it did so, I became more and more apprehensive about jumping out, since there was no ladder or toe-hold for me to hoist myself up. Finally all voices on the dock shouted, "Mother, hurry and jump!"

Before I knew what was happening, I found myself scurrying up the side of the ferry in a most unladylike stance wearing my Sunday-best dress, hose, and sandals. Phares was pushing from the rear! I was later told that a stranger passing by also got into the act and gave a great heave to my bottomside. Needless to say, I spread-eagled myself on the dock. I tried desperately to salvage some vestige of propriety in the process, but to no avail. Phares followed after me shortly, and endeavored to assuage my waning dignity.

I felt like I had been through the refiner's fire. However, this turned out to be only the beginning! We were trapped in a graveled yard enclosed by a six-foot fence from which there was no escape. We made several runs up the steep gravel inclines with the hope of scurrying over the fence. All I accomplished was scratches, bruises, runs in my socks, and blisters on my heels.

Christer was embarrassed, as he thought we could merely walk out of the yard. Evidently he had not tried it. Well, we climbed all over that yard for nearly 45 minutes in the heat of the day before we were finally successful in our escape. I personally looked like I could have charged someone with assault and battery! None of us were fit to board the train by the time we got to it. I seriously doubt that we saved five minutes in our attempt to short-cut the system.

    Moral: Look before you leap. It might be
              only the beginning of something
              worse!

* * * *

*B*riggs at Victoria Falls, S. A.

*P*hares in Retirement
Shoveling a Bit of Snow

*Briggs Standing on Ostrich Eggs
Oudtshoorn, South Africa*

*Briggs, Hermine and April
Holding up a Banyan Tree in
Capetown, South Africa*

*P*achyderm in Kruger Park, South Africa

*T*he Eighth Wonder of the World, Berlin

*P*hares, Briggs, April in Copenhagen

*P*hares, Hermine and April in Oslo

HEART STRINGS 267

April, Hermine and Phares in East Berlin

*A*pril, Hermine and Phares Enroute to England

The "Other" Way to See Europe!

*P*hares and Briggs at the Matterhorn, Switzerland

PERSONAL REVELATION

Stockholm, Sweden

One of the most delightful and anticipated events of the trip was to meet each Sunday with the Saints in a different ward in the Church. As we entered each lovely chapel we were met by someone inquiring if we spoke the local language, and if not, we were assigned someone who would interpret in English for us. We arrived a few minutes early in Stockholm, and a dear sister was immediately assigned to me. She told me of another sister who was "the backbone of the ward." She related this story:

Early in the 1940's when the German purge of the Jews was just beginning, a family in Hungary was endeavoring to escape. Grandparents, parents and two little girls made up their group. One day the grandfather took the 10 year-old girl aside and gave her a "patriarchal blessing" telling her that likely she would be the sole survivor of the family. He impressed her with the fact that she would be personally responsible to see that their family name was kept in remembrance.

The war waged on, and all her family was captured and taken to Auschwitz, the dreaded concentration camp where thousands of Jews lost their lives. True to her grandfather's prophecy, this little girl was the sole survivor, despite the fact that they used her as a guinea pig, trying all kinds of experiments on her body, the last of which was to inject gasoline into the bloodstream. One can only imagine what that would do when such contamination reached the brain. Undoubtedly it affected her whole body in a devastating way, but she did survive in very fragile health.

In the course of the next few years, she met and married a Danishman who served in Hitler's army. I personally feel that because of his remorse for the atrocities he knew Hitler committed, he felt somehow exonerated by marrying one who had suffered so deeply. He was a member of the Church and brought her into the waters of baptism. In view of her health, it was something of a miracle that they were able to have six daughters, all of whom were married in the Swiss Temple. Further, she became an avid genealogist and has been true to her promise that her family name will "ever be in remembrance" in the way only temple work affords.

Naturally I was anxious to meet this remarkable lady. As soon as she entered the building, she was pointed out to me. She looked just about the way one would expect--light brown hair in a straight dutch cut, brown horn-rimmed glasses over the most intense brown eyes I have ever seen. I found myself almost staring at her, so magnetic was her presence. The meeting ended, and I hurried to make my way to her. However, I was disappointed to see her and her husband go out the side door. In my anxiety, I called to the missionaries to call her back and tell her I wanted to meet her. They did so and when she returned, there we stood--neither of us able to speak the language of the other. Finally in desperation I pleaded, "Just tell her that I love her." The elder did so. Instantaneously she broke into tears as did I, and we clung to one another and wept. I then told her that I hoped that her story was recorded at least for her posterity, if not for everyone. She answered that it had been written. She turned and went out the door.

I was left with a mountain of emotion--most of which I did not understand. Why were there so many tears for someone whom I had never met? With tremendous power and conviction came the answer: "You have just felt the pure love of Christ." I was further moved and rejoiced in the revelation of what it might be like to live in His presence surrounded by people who share such love. I have never been the same since. It changed my perspective and I determined to live so that such a privilege might be mine. I cherish this experience and share it as the spirit dictates, especially in recounting the "specialness" of sisterhood in the world-wide Church.

* * * *

A LONG, LONG NIGHT

<u>Stockholm to Hamburg</u>

If there is anything efficient in Europe, it is the rail system. You can set your watch by the arrivals and departures. Even a non-seasoned traveler can "get around" because trains and tracks are clearly marked and announced in adequate time to transfer baggage. However, we carried all our luggage with us, which, though a burdensome task, removed some of the risks inherent in traveling abroad. We paid about $150 each for a Euro-rail pass which allowed us to ride all over Europe for the entire summer, had we opted to do so.

However, anything so positive must always have a downside; and there was no exception here. The downside came one night on the train and it almost did me in.

We were assigned the lower bunks in our compartment. In early evening two hikers came in with us and occupied the top bunks.

Cleanliness turned out to be a major issue for these two. It soon became apparent they had not changed their socks throughout a summer of hiking. The air turned blue with the stench of stinky feet. We spent a miserable night trying to figure out how to tactfully tell them to either put their feet out the window or do us a favor and keep their boots on! That certainly was the longest night of the two-month trip. By the time we got off the train, we wondered if we still carried the ugly scent.

> Moral: You can't choose train bedfellows any more than you can your relatives. Or "we might all die unless you die with your boots on."

* * * *

THE MAGICIAN SUFFERS SOME SLEIGHT-OF-HAND

<u>Paris, France</u>
We were walking down Pig Ale on a Saturday afternoon. The throngs were oppressive as was the heat of the day. Phares was excited to be back in his mission field. He had just cashed several traveler's checks in anticipation of paying our hotel bill and carrying us through the next ten days in London. Hence his water-buffalo wallet from South Africa bulged with bills and Swiss francs left over from visiting that country.

We passed an ice cream street vendor and decided we needed an ice cream cone. Our "financier" opened his wallet to pay. There were countless people around who observed his apparent wealth. Scarcely had we started on our way before he was "attacked." April had just said, "This would be an ideal place to get pick-pocketed," and sure enough, it was! Briggs and I were both elbowed away from his side by the sidewalk crowd. Briggs went ahead with April and I dropped behind Phares. Immediately I saw a Frenchman brushing something off Phares' right shoulder and speaking excitedly in French. Evidently he was apologizing profusely for someone who spit on Phares, a way to mark a target. While distracting Phares, someone from behind relieved him of all his worldly cash, including the much-coveted water-buffalo wallet. It happened so fast we scarcely knew what was going on except that all three of us instinctively knew that Phares was in trouble.

Phares and Briggs ran to the police station to report the theft. They found a sign on the door, "Out for lunch," which was indicative of police concern for the petty thievery that thrives in that part of the city. When they returned, Phares, thoroughly frustrated and traumatized by the event, was still holding his ice cream cone while it dripped down over his fingers to his wrist! We encouraged him to eat it and save the mess, but he threw it away, saying his appetite for ice cream was ruined! I suppose so, having lost about $500 to the cunning hands of professional pickpockets. I can't imagine they needed it one whit more than we did.

  Moral: When you feel a hand in your
     pocket, make sure it is your own!

* * * *

LET NOT YOUR YEARNING EXCEED YOUR EARNING

<u>Paris, France</u>
  While Phares and Briggs did some sight-seeing, April and I opted to get some R&R in our hotel room. April had sprained her ankle in a sprint across train tracks with Briggs, who was mailing a letter to his "dearly beloved." Seeing the train slowly move away, they did some fancy footwork, which resulted in April's painful sprain. Her ankle was very swollen and sore. My ankles were swollen "just because." I was worn out with six weeks of trying to keep up with the racing crew who accompanied me.

  We started talking about the family at home, and a sudden pang of homesickness overtook my better judgment and I found myself placing a long distance call to Susan back home in Utah. She was holding down the fort all alone and I thought she needed to hear from her mother! So after checking the details with the operator, we let the call go through. We had a lovely visit and got caught up on all the news.

  All went well until check-out time when they told us there was an $85 charge for long distance service! All the arguing in the world didn't change things, so we paid the bill and went on our way much the wiser.

  Moral: Pay phones are much cheaper.

* * * *

A STOLEN PASSPORT

Austria to Paris

We took the night train from Salzburg and were to arrive in Paris at 6:45 a.m. As is the custom when riding the Euro-Rail, passports are collected the night before disembarking and returned early the next morning. I kept all passports in my purse and handed them to the conductor. The next morning at 5:30 a.m., the porter came down the aisle calling "Passports." It was still dark, but I took them from his hand and put them in my purse held close to my body. We got off at 6:45, found a hotel a couple of blocks away, and were checking in. They asked for our passports. I produced them--all but one reading "Hermine B. Horman." I knew immediately that he had not returned mine, as there was no way it could have been lost in the interim. Since there is a frightening black market in Europe on stolen passports, I was frantic to say the least!

Fortunately we had made reservations on the train, knew our compartment number, car number and the name of the conductor. Armed with this information, Phares and Briggs presented themselves at the complaint office and demanded the particular conductor be confronted with the theft. Since Phares spoke French, he made his case quite emphatic and heads started to roll. They tried to tell him that this particular train had already left for Italy, the conductor having gone home for the weekend. However, with the evidence we had, they knew they had to invent better excuses, because we didn't buy the ones they were using. Finally, they asked that we call back in a couple of hours, and they would see what they could find. We returned at the designated hour and, miracle of miracles, they returned my passport. They loudly lamented the fact that no one EVER finds a passport, that we were just lucky. Yes, we were lucky--lucky to have a man with us who knew the language and confronted them with a crime they could not deny.

> Moral: Better YOU get lost than your passport. You are easier to find and can't be sold on the black market.

* * * *

1983--continued

We were blessed with our first grandchild this year. Jacob, a darling bright, sweet and beautiful little boy, entered the family and completely won our hearts. Heather and Ken Spurlock were the fabricators and did a terrific job. We are sorry they live so far away; on the other hand because they live in Washington, we get to visit them en masse for Thanksgiving, and that is always special. Ray and Marion Spurlock are wonderful hosts.

Briggs and Shelley are attending the University of Utah. However, Shelley just received a call to serve a welfare-proselyting mission in the Philippine-Cebu Mission, leaving in February. We do tend to send our kids to the furthest corners of the earth.

April is attending BYU on the block program. Susan is back at Dixie College. She loves the environment of a small college. She is the Relief Society president, is in the performing arts with dance and music, and received a partial scholarship through that department.

Becky and Kevin Ririe are on the production line awaiting a new heir. Kevin also completed a 100-mile marathon in September. After that we wondered if there would be any heirs in the Ririe family!

A note to those of you anticipating traveling. Secure a copy of Frommer's Touring Europe on $20 a Day and live by it. Use the phone numbers provided for lodging in private homes. I can promise you some of the richest experiences of your sojourn. We had great success with the inexpensive billeting and made some choice friends in the process.

1985--I gave birth to A Century of Mormon Cookery. (See Surprise Entrepreneur.)

Susan, Briggs and April all attended Dixie. They had a wonderful time together and were all active in the performing arts. April had the lead in The Princess and the Pea. The local newspaper declared the college certainly must have "imported the lead." She and Susan tied for the honor of being named "Miss Dixie Spirit" at Homecoming. The title had never been given to two people before. Spring quarter Briggs had the lead in The Music Man as Professor Harold Hill. He was awesome. Meantime, Susan was AWS president and participated in the musicals. She was named Miss Dixie and Miss Washington County, which qualified her as a candidate for Miss Utah. We had an exciting spring and summer with these pageants. We kept the road warm between Salt Lake City and St. George just watching them "do their thing" and us doing ours--popping our buttons. We left our tent trailer down there so we had a "condo" to stay in on our frequent visits. But their fun and games led to things more serious, and here is where the plot thickens.

ON MAY 3RD, APRIL AND SIEG WIDMER (from my hometown) were united in marriage in the Jordan River Temple. They are living in Lethbridge, Alberta where he is employed by Woolco in the managerial training program.

ON AUGUST 10TH, BRIGGS TOOK HIS BRIDE, WENDY STOKES, of Roy, Utah to the Salt Lake Temple. Briggs is working at First Security Bank as a teller and Wendy is a secretary to the manager of Key Bank. Briggs attends the University of Utah.

ON OCTOBER 26TH, SUSAN AND MARVIN RAY were married in the Jordan River Temple. Marv's "outstanding in his own field" in that he is 6'7". In addition to other great attributes, we are most impressed with the fact that he operates his own automotive repair shop in Logan. (The Horman cars alone could keep him in business!)

Each of the wedding stories would make an interesting chapter in a novel, but it might not be believable. There was international intrigue in Sieg and April's love story, complete with mending a broken engagement of three years ago. Briggs and Wendy solidified their plans while on a musical tour through the Northwest, and announced their engagement to a packed house. Sue and Marv met on a blind date arranged by his mother who gets her hair done by sister Becky. The exciting, juicy details that run in between will have to wait for that novel. It may have to wait for the Millennium!

Shelley returned from the Philippines. She had a wonderful experience and really felt she made a substantial contribution to upgrading the living conditions among the people with whom she worked, as well as teaching the gospel to many. She is studying health education and plans to attend BYU next year, where she will be employed at the Missionary Training Center, her first love.

I tend Alisha (Becky and Kevin's little girl) while Becky works at Hair Handlers. Alisha is a darling. She has gorgeous curly auburn hair. Grand-parenting is to my liking and is a total surprise in that I am so emotionally involved.

We realize that we got our kids all at once, but does it necessarily follow that they leave the nest the same way? I am not prepared for an empty nest, especially at my age! But we are grateful that they have all found great and noble companions and are proud of their mutual good taste.

May 1986 abound with as many great blessings for you and yours.

* * * *

*A*pril and Sieg
Announce
Their Wedding

*O*ur April Bride

HEART STRINGS 279

Briggs and Wendy Announce

Briggs and Wendy's Wedding

*M*arv and Susan's
Announcement

*O*ur Susan Bride

HEART STRINGS 281

Korea and Hong Kong – 1987
Special Friends – Back Row: Cherie Pardoe
Bob Mercer, Rita, Beverly Mercer, Emma Lou Smith
Hermine, Irene Whitfield, et al.

1987--Three trips to Magrath this year were unprecedented. Any excuse will usually do, but we always have the best one--visiting April and Sieg and Morgan. They are living in my mother's little house. What a joy it is to have a tenant who cares about it, improves upon it, and makes it possible for us to visit the home so dear to us all. They had waist-high sweet peas blooming around the house well into November. It was a labor of love when three of us Briggs kids put a new coat of paint on the home this summer.

We have enjoyed hosting a dozen or so Japanese students (one at a time) while they are in Salt Lake attending English classes. They are so formal upon arrival, but we hug each other when they leave. One stayed over the Christmas holidays and I put him right to work, helping me dip chocolates, etc. He was keenly interested in our customs as they do not celebrate Christmas. We also give them the missionary tour of Temple Square, a Japanese Book of Mormon, and tapes of the Tabernacle Choir.

I worked extremely hard this year on <u>Mormon Cookery</u>. We printed 5,000 in our home and inundated ourselves with paper! It was a mammoth undertaking. We did all the production completely to the finished product. Fortunately, there seems to be a ready market for the books wherever we go.

In November I had opportunity to visit Korea, Hong Kong and Hawaii. It was an impromptu visit made with six former college friends with whom I had traveled before. We had a ball for ten days! We Christmas shopped at incredibly low prices in Korea and enjoyed the luxury of eel-skin shoes made to measure overnight and an ultra suede coat tailored in the same time frame. We also made some interesting contacts regarding the cookbook, and sold two accounts in Honolulu.

We found the Koreans to be very friendly and warm. The Chinese in Hong Kong are similar but different. They have a little more business acuity and reserve. Both countries are delightfully clean, which is a monumental accomplishment in view of the masses on their streets.

Do you remember the autograph books we had when we were kids? In mine someone wrote: "First comes love, then comes marriage, then comes Hermine with the baby carriage." It is true for most of us, and I see history repeating itself in my children. The last letter reported the romances and marriages of four of our kids. Now we report on our wonderful grandchildren, but feature only the most recent arrivals with a picture. We rejoice that they all arrived sound of limb and lung, and to happy, anxious parents. I assure you that

Grandma and Grandpa have ample opportunity to appease their parenting instincts.

To date: Heather and Ken have three great little boys: Jacob, Tyler and Nicholas. Karen and Marty expect their first in May. Susan and Marv just welcomed our littlest giant, 9 lb. 3-1/2 oz. Brandon. Becky and Kevin have 3-year-old Alisha and year-old Brady. Briggs and Wendy have year-old Brittney. April and Sieg have 1-1/2 year-old Morgan. Of course they are the cutest, smartest and brightest!

Shelley is our only single child. Her philosophy seems to be: "Why make one man miserable when I can make a multitude happy?" This summer she did a three-month internship at the University of Southern Connecticut, working with Bill Faraclas, who is married to our cousin, Nancy. She is currently attending BYU and teaching at the MTC. She will graduate this year in Health Education. Briggs will graduate from the University of Utah with an emphasis on physical therapy.

Heather and Ken moved from Spokane so Ken can finish his engineering degree at BYU. They will manage our rentals in Provo and will live in the basement of our girls' home. (Not an easy feat when they have had their own lovely, spacious home in Washington.)

Two quotes to share:

"Wise men still seek Him."

"Are you among the Inn group or one of the Stable few?"

1988--Having made my Korean contact relative to reprinting the cookbook last November, it seemed imperative to move on the possibility in view of our pending mission call and the fact that the cookbook is virtually "out of print." Hence, Phares and I boarded Delta Airlines and spent a most interesting week in Seoul, Korea, negotiating with Brother Han and Sister Jang relative to their printing 2,000 books. The price was most attractive since it was far less than we could print it for with Phares and I doing all the work and having the project consume our entire house! The difference, mainly, was that their bids did not include anything for labor, which, of course, accounts for half the cost in the U.S. (See Surprise Entrepreneur.) Our spending was a bit more fun than the first trip, since this time we just bought things for ourselves, knowing we would need certain clothes for our mission.

April and Sieg moved from Magrath to Salt Lake and Sieg is going to complete his studies in engineering. We are delighted to have the entire family in Utah, and of course, now we will be leaving.

Phares and I have received a call to serve a Leadership-Proselyting mission in the Halifax-Canada Mission!

* * * *

MISSION FAREWELL TALK
May 29, 1988

I am here today to make a public statement. I am the victim of child abuse. My children claim I forced them into the mission field, and now they are forcing me.

I have the advantage of the "gray hair" point of view, so from that very vulnerable station, let me make a few observations about life in general and mine in particular.

Life is real and life is earnest. It is a series of agonies and ecstasies, and so it was meant to be. Our first parents, Adam and Eve, were driven from that blissful garden with the stern admonition that henceforth they were to "earn thy bread by the sweat of thy face all the days of thy life". (Moses 4:25) Now I don't know of any change in that edict. In other words, the Lord has never said life would be easy, only that it would be worth it! Further, He is on record as saying, "To everything there is a season, and a time to every purpose under heaven. A time to be born, a time to die, a time to plant, and a time to harvest, a time to kill, a time to heal, a time to weep and a time to laugh, a time to mourn and a time to dance," etc. (Eccl. 3:1-10)

Wherever there is growth, it appears there must come some pain. What about your "green years"--that first real growing season? Did you find it easy to grow up? I think we all had a very common experience. It was a great deal of pain, as I recall, along with the few satisfactions, was it not? Most of us would not want to relive those teen-dating years again, would we?

Then we finally find "the right one" and think all of our troubles are over--when in reality, they are just beginning. Were the first few years of your marriage all sweetness and bliss? Mine were not. I quickly suspected that the Biblical quote of "they twain shall be one flesh" was the first blatant mistranslation of which I was aware. When you try to mesh the genetics of hundreds of generations just because of one simple ceremony, repercussions are bound to occur.

But oh, the maturing that takes place. The child-bearing years were difficult, but provided us glimpses into heaven and eternity. Surely that season of life was one of both agony and ecstasy.

Remember those wonderful years when Mommy and Daddy knew everything and no answer was challenged? Savor those times, you young parents, because it will only be a season before every answer is challenged and you go from the all-knowing parent to the square who knows nothing!

Raising our teenagers was challenging and frustrating. But oh, how I miss the crowds of young people at the table, or around the piano, or coming in or going out of our home. Even without major problems, seeing teenagers through the dating years involves a great deal of agony. It was a time to learn patience, requiring endurance, humor, cajoling, encouragement, tears--all of the virtues we thought we have already mastered. Perhaps it was a honing of those skills required for parenting--but indeed, it was a growing season.

We endeavored to "train up a child in the way he should go"--then finally came the harvest when they chose to fill missions, attend college, marry in the temple, and begin families of their own. It was always two or three in college, two or three on missions, two marriages in two months, or all of the above going on simultaneously. Believe me, those were tough years, and I don't know how we escaped with our sanity--and that is even up for debate. But the rewards--seeing testimonies grow--seeing them learn to give service and grow beyond themselves--what a joyful, bounteous harvest!

And then come the grandchildren--aren't they wonderful? I am so glad that it is now my children's season to bring these bright little stars into the arena of life. Had I known how much fun it was to be a grandmother, I believe I'd have started there.

The present season of my life I find the most challenging. Retirement ten years in advance of normal retirement age is for the birds! I told Phares I married him for better or for worse, but never for lunch. We'd have not survived this long had we not had a big house and we both hide a lot. In truth, it's trying to cope with half as much money and twice as much husband. Then of a sudden, or so it seems, we are called "empty nesters" and a new season is upon us.

The monetary needs of the family diminish somewhat, and it is natural that one begins to get caught up in acquiring more "things" to retain "fulfillment." Another car, a bigger house, a cabin in the mountains, a bigger boat, a little more real estate, more stocks and bonds, a condo in Palm Springs--now these have not been my temptations, but perhaps they are yours. (I merely wish they were mine!) But before these thoughts loom too high, we hear a prophet's voice and the voices of many in the mission fields recite the critical need for couples to add stability to struggling areas of new growth. Now that's a wet blanket of a different kind! And Brother Mabey comes to our ward and tells of the agonies, yes, but also of the ecstasy of bringing 1,200 souls into the Kingdom of our Father in Nigeria in one year!

Then the searching question--Am I doing all I can do to be a missionary, to actually teach the gospel to His children? The admonition to preach the Gospel to the world is meant for everyone, all of our lives. The field is white, ready to harvest, and the laborers are few.

Then Satan whispers, "You cannot leave your children and grandchildren! Your business is too complex for another to manage. And besides, I know of a couple who had been married 42 years who came home from a mission and promptly got divorced!" I can relate! Twenty-four hours with one companion and no place to hide, no hope of getting another companion in two or three months like the young missionaries. Now that is scary--am I ready for that?

Perhaps this is the season for introspection, a time to speak of service, to look beyond one's self. The Savior said, "He who would be the greatest of all would be the servant of all."

Last week I was talking to a stranger on the phone. She asked the question: "Do you think you will be earning money in 1988?" I laughed and said, "No, I don't think so. I am going on a mission and the wages are notoriously low."

"Oh, but think of the fringe benefits," she replied. "And I understand the retirement program is out of this world!" What a wise response! I knew we were "sisters" right away.

THE HILLS AHEAD

> The hills ahead look hard and steep and high
> And often we behold them with a sigh,
> But as we near them, level grows the road,
> We find on every slope, with every load
> The climb is not so steep, the top so far.
> The hills ahead look harder than they are.
>
> --Douglas Mallock

I am thankful for a church that continues to challenge me, and in so doing tries to meet the needs of all of its people. Essentially that is the difference between God's church and the churches of men. We are admonished to "endure to the end"--let us not rust away, but wear away in building His kingdom. It has been my observation that there is not a great distance between retirement and senility, so anything I can do to widen that gap, I would like to do. I am taking this new challenge to help stave off the rocking chair blues. At least when that time comes, we will have something interesting to talk about, assuming we retain our remembering faculty.

What better time to strengthen the kingdom than now? What better time to strengthen a relationship with a spouse than now? What better time to "let go" of the material things that so easily become our material gods than now? We know that "where our treasure is, there our heart is also." Further, we know that "the worth of souls is great to our Father in Heaven," and should we labor all the days of our lives, and bring, save it were one soul into the kingdom of our Father, how great would be our joy--and should that one soul be that of Phares or Hermine, does that make the quest any less important?

I don't expect the mission field to be all convenience and pleasure. If there is to be growth, there must be pain, some of the agony. But I am eager for this new season, with all of its challenges. And should we survive the MTC and survive a winter in Nova Scotia, we shall probably be asking for another similar assignment at a future date. Missionary work is important, and we are the only tools Heavenly Father has to accomplish His purposes in bringing His children back to Him. I am humbly proud "to be about His business," and pray that we might all catch this vision.

* * * *

The MTC experience was awe-inspiring. We met some of the most wonderful instructors, all young returned missionaries, who impressed us tremendously with their dedication and spirituality. We even had the privilege of having our daughter, Shelley, instruct us one day. We could see why so many people rave about her presentations and how lucky BYU is to have her. Approximately 4,000 missionaries were there while we were. It is surely a well-organized program and certainly one of the most inspired. What a mighty group of "Saturday's Warriors" they represent.

Elder and Sister Horman
"That's Where We Are!"

*O*ur District at the Mission Training Center, Provo

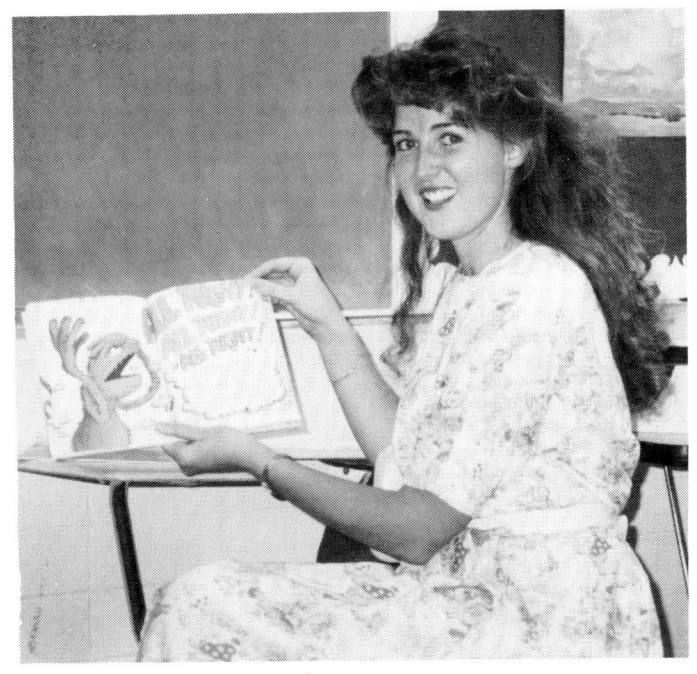

A Wonderful Instructor at the
M.T.C. – Our Shelley

290 HEART STRINGS

1988--Greetings from Atlantic-Canada. You wonder what we are doing up here? Sometimes we even ask ourselves this question! When we arrived in June, after having driven through the drought-stricken areas of the Midwest, this verdant greenland looked like the Garden of Eden. Being at sea level and just off the Bay of Fundy, the humidity is high as are the variables in temperature, winter and summer. Without a doubt, this is one of the most beautiful places in the world. Lots of woods, lakes and wild flowers.

Laboring in Moncton, New Brunswick, our work has been interesting and challenging, to say the least. We were called to "strengthen the ward and its members." We came with no "how to" books, so striving to accomplish our objectives has been a humbling, learning and growing experience.

We started out by conducting a series of weekly lectures dealing with Church videos, then our pet topics of archeology of the Book of Mormon, genealogy, family histories and journal keeping, family preparedness, filling one another's cup, etc. We gave 11 such lectures, one a week. The "getting to know you" was enhanced by entertaining two or three times a week in our tiny apartment. I sent for my quilting frames and taught tying swatch quilts and baby quilts from nylon tricot. Last week it was an ornamental Christmas tree with tiny multi-colored lights inserted. The finished product truly looked like crystal. This week we're teaching how to make and hand dip chocolates. Phares has enjoyed performing his magic on several occasions, and we've instigated the first-ever newspaper under the masthead <u>Chapel Chatter</u>. Our role as seen by the local members vacillates between villain and hero.

As is true in most branches and wards in the mission fields, Moncton Ward is suffering from the lack of trained leadership. They are good people, but have not had opportunity to see how a well-staffed ward operates. We are here to teach them, but how to do so is a challenge.

Our first payday came in October when 72-year-old Polly Ferdinand went into the waters of baptism after we had given her the discussions. She was as radiant as a new bride, and you should have seen the smiles on our faces!

New Brunswick is bilingual, English and French. Phares gets to use his Parisian French daily. He thinks he's died and gone to heaven. I think I've just died!

We joined a square dance group and in addition to getting some much-needed exercise, we enjoy the fine people with whom we dance. They are from all different faiths. We have entertained each couple in our home, and they have returned the favor. Of course we have ample opportunity to explain our mission and they are very interested in a passive sort of way. No doubt we are the "unique" ones of the group.

Recently we volunteered to assist the Red Cross with the Bloodmobile. We have met many wonderful people through this contact as well as through teaching English to non-English speaking residents. We took training through the literacy program and really are enthused about its possibilities, both as a helping agency and as a proselyting tool.

We're surrounded by industries typical of the Maritimes. There are fisheries (lobster, sardines, mussels, oysters and crab), boat and ship building, lumbering, paper pulp mills, and sea-faring vessels involved in international commerce.

Moist breezes from the Bay of Fundy, the Gulf Stream, and the Atlantic Ocean combine to create a damp, healthful atmosphere for growing myriad plants and people.

Springtime brings waving fields of multicolored wild lupines and other flowers. The verdant woods are dotted with apple blossoms attesting to Johnny Appleseed's earlier travels through these parts. Fall brings autumn leaves so daringly spectacular as to stop traffic on the well-built highways. The presence of sugar in many trees indigenous to the area, and the right blend of humidity and frost, produces autumn foliage that surpasses the imagination. Capturing it on film is at best, a poor substitute for experiencing it.

The storied Tidal Bore is a phenomenon wherein the tide from the Bay of Fundy ebbs and flows under and on top of the waters of the Petticodiac River. The two bodies of water run wild, carving deep banks in snake-like formations. At high tide the banks frequently overflow; at low tide the red mud banks are covered with seagulls and other birds scavenging marine life left by the tide.

On the Bay of Fundy strange rock formations create miniature islands, called flower pots, far from shore. Pine and other hardy trees seem to grow out of the rocks. The tides and winds are ferocious, resulting in the claim of the highest tides in the world measuring over 40 feet. Lush fern forests and wild flowers thrive on the misty spray felt several miles inland.

The sunsets and cloud formations in the area almost defy description. They change rapidly due to the many weather patterns playing upon land and sea. What an education in such a lovely place!

We know we'll return different people than we left. We should be more tolerant, more grateful, and more dedicated to the

Gospel message. We have a greater capacity to love those who are different than we are. Perhaps this has been our greatest learning experience.

As you might imagine, the mailman is about the No. 1 man in our lives. We are fortunate to have large families and many great friends. At 43 cents per letter, we have cause to more carefully evaluate our relationships; therefore, if you are a recipient of this epistle, you are likely a friend indeed!

* * * *

RECLAIMED FROM THE SEA
Baptismal Talk given in Moncton, N.B.
August 6, 1988

Do you know what this is? It appears to be just a round, almost clear glass ball. In reality it is a floater used on a fishing net. Many of them of various sizes keep the nets buoyant. Prior to World War II the Japanese fishermen used them extensively so that their full nets would not sink into the deep and lose their catch. The floaters kept the nets near the surface where the nets were more easily emptied.

Apparently the floaters were not very securely tied to the nets, as thousands of them came loose, were caught in the Japanese current, and eventually, many years later, made their way to the beaches of the South Pacific. They became the delight of beachcombers and novelty collectors. Several people with whom I am acquainted took their families to the beach for family home evening, searching for these "worthless" treasures.

One needs an educated eye to identify them. They appear round and black and are many times the size of this one. Attached to them during their long journey are seaweed, barnacles, and small marine life. They are not attractive and have a foul odor, but if you are fortunate to find one you might see it riding on the crest of the wave and eventually washing ashore. By rubbing it in the sand, which acts as an abrasive, it cleans up quickly and beautifully, and becomes again a clear, crystal ball, worthy of the search.

After the war, better products were found to keep the nets buoyant, things like plastic or styrofoam, which cost less and were more easily secured to the nets. Consequently there is a total absence of these glass balls on the Hawaiian beaches today.

Canadian Flag

Acadian Flag

294 HEART STRINGS

Tidal Trail · Le Sentier Des Marees
WORLD'S HIGHEST TIDES
SCENIC ROUTE TO MONCTON
ROUTE PANORAMIQUE VERS MONCTON
EXIT 430 ROUTE 114

DALHOUSIE
CARAQUET
NEW
BRUNSWICK
The Picture Province
SHEDIAC
CAPE TORMENTINE
FORT
BEAUSEJOUR
N.H.P.
FUNDY NATIONAL PARK
SAINT
JOHN

*Couple Missionaries in Halifax Mission Home
A Very Special Group of People
Pres. & Sister Wood (front right)
The Dietrichs, Tidballs, and Hormans (back center)*

*M*oncton Ward Chapel

*St*ake President Blaine Hatt

*The Hormans Aboard the Ferry
Enroute to Prince Edward Island*

*A Beautiful Inn at St. Andrews By the Sea
F.D.R. Had a Summer Home Here
Nova Scotia*

*P*hares in a Fern Forest

A "Gingerbread House" in St. Stephens, Maine

First Ward Dinner Ever Held in Moncton, N. B.
Sister Horman, Bishop Airey, Diane Smith, et al.

Moncton Ward Relief Society Participants in Program

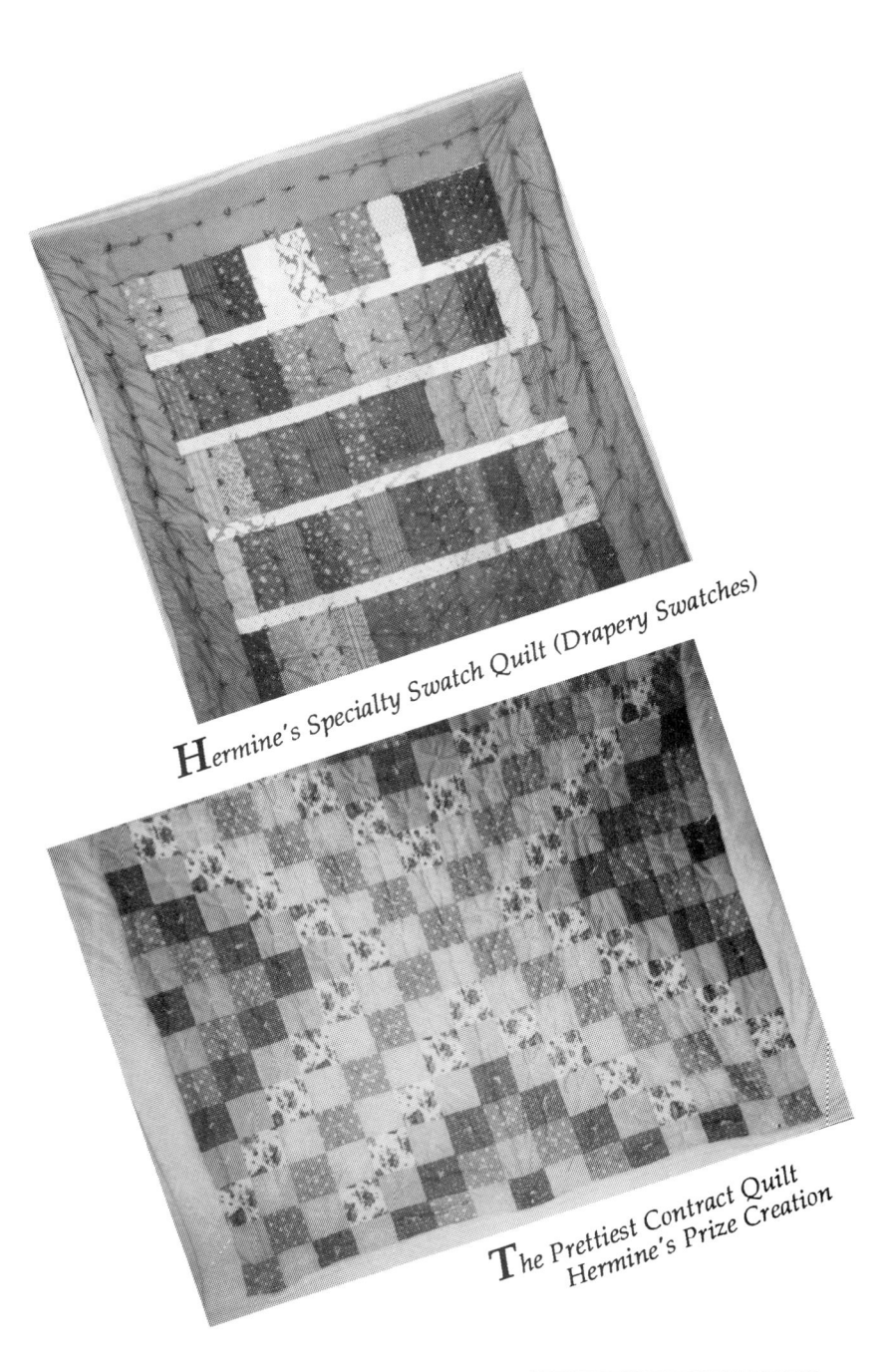

Hermine's Specialty Swatch Quilt (Drapery Swatches)

The Prettiest Contract Quilt Hermine's Prize Creation

*H*ermine's Lap Robe Made for Sister Wood

*S*ister Wood and Sister Horman Holding a "Contract Quilt" Made to Order

*S*ister Horman, Nicolle and Stacey Leaman
Learning to Make Chocolates

*T*he Missionary Magician – More P.R.

*S*elling Chocolates at the Mall in Moncton on Valentine's Day

*H*and Dipping Chocolates with Sister Cheryl Hebert

*A Crystal Christmas Tree
Made from Baby Food Jars
(Another Fund Raiser)*

A Missionary's Pay Day—Baptism of Polly Ferdinand, and the Vautours and the Hormans

*A*nother Baptism – Elder Wilson, Joey Arsenalt
and Elder Brooks – A "Magic" Convert

A Lobster Feed with the Elders, Vautours, Hormans
and
Polly Ferdinand

*P*resident and Sister Wood and Elder Burton Howard,

*C*ompanions to the End

HEART STRINGS 309

*O*n a Ferry to
 Visit the Dietrichs and
 Give a Magic Show and
 Interview the Canadian Broadcasting Corporation

The Biggest Egg We Laid – A Fund Raising Easter Project

The Dietrichs at Sommerset, P. E. I.

*O*ur Favorite P-Day Activity
Square Dancing at our Ward House

A "Wee Bit" of a Snowstorm in Moncton

*S*quare Dancing at a School in Moncton

*A*n Evening's Snowfall, Moncton

Recently a friend of mine was in Hawaii after a 30-year absence. She and her husband went to the same beaches looking for their glass treasures. They returned several times and found none. However, one evening, as they were about to return home empty-handed, they saw a floater coming into a small bay. They raced to claim it. As they approached, however, a stranger appeared as if from nowhere ahead of them and it became evident that he had the same thought in mind. From a short distance they watched him pick it up, examine it with a grimace, and throw it far back into the ocean. They awaited his retreat before running to the spot where they knew it would return with the incoming tide. Theirs was the treasure, the priceless collector's item.

Why did the man throw it away? Obviously he did not know its value. He could not see the crystal-like iridescence, the beauty of the glass beneath the seaweed, the barnacles, the sea urchins which had attached themselves to it. He witnessed only the malodorous exterior. How like the world he was.

Each of us is a child of God. Only our Father knows our true worth and our potential. He sent us to earth for testing, for experience, but with the charge to return to Him. Life buffets us all in countless ways. Being mortal, we are subject to temptation and become entangled in the seaweed of sin. Each transgression darkens our crystal image and purity. Some of us even have large sea barnacles firmly attached, or have our vision clouded by sea urchins. After a few years in the sea of life, we forget our great potential and celestial home from whence we came. Even our friends and associates help us forget this truth, as they too, esteem us as dross. Eventually the error appears a truth to even us.

But a merciful Father in Heaven can see beyond our exterior. He sees our hearts. He doesn't want us to drift aimlessly. He provided us with His Gospel, the Gospel of Jesus Christ, to help us in our journey back to Him. When one allows the Gospel to be effective in his life, a beautiful miracle happens. The abrasive gift of repentance removes the tarnish, the seaweed, the barnacles and sea urchins, if you will, and we begin to relearn the glorious truth that we are sons and daughters of our Heavenly Father, and are of inestimable value to ourselves, to the world and to Him. We catch the vision of who we really are, and have always been, why we are here, and where we are going. Our lives take on new meaning, purpose and beauty.

Brothers and sisters--this is the heart and core of the Gospel of Jesus Christ. Countless lives and souls are reclaimed from the sea, as it were, when the great gift of repentance takes us to the waters of baptism. By so doing we are saying to our Savior, "I accept your great atonement which makes me clean, and hereafter I will pattern my life in your way." God grant that each of us might re-commit ourselves to this sacred promise, I humbly pray.

* * * *

Our small apartment on the third floor of a building on Ann Street was hot both summer and winter. However in the summer, ill-fitting and holey screens allowed mosquitoes to enter in droves and they stayed the season. I dreaded nightfall, as I was defenseless against them. It was a source of much irritation that they did not bother Phares, only me! I deduced that I must be the most delicious morsel in all of New Brunswick, so popular was I. One night, as I heard several come in for landing (on me, of course), I was inspired to write the following:

ODE TO A MOSQUITO

He dined upon my carcass
As a king dines at a feast,
He filled his crimson wine-glass
From this domesticated beast.

> He paused for just a moment
> To more appreciate the view,
> Then asked his tortured victim:
> "Would you like one lump, or two?"

* * * *

An Old Fashioned Sleigh Ride in the Woods
Almost Like Home

*P*rize Percherons

The Quintessential Snow Blower, Moncton, N.B.

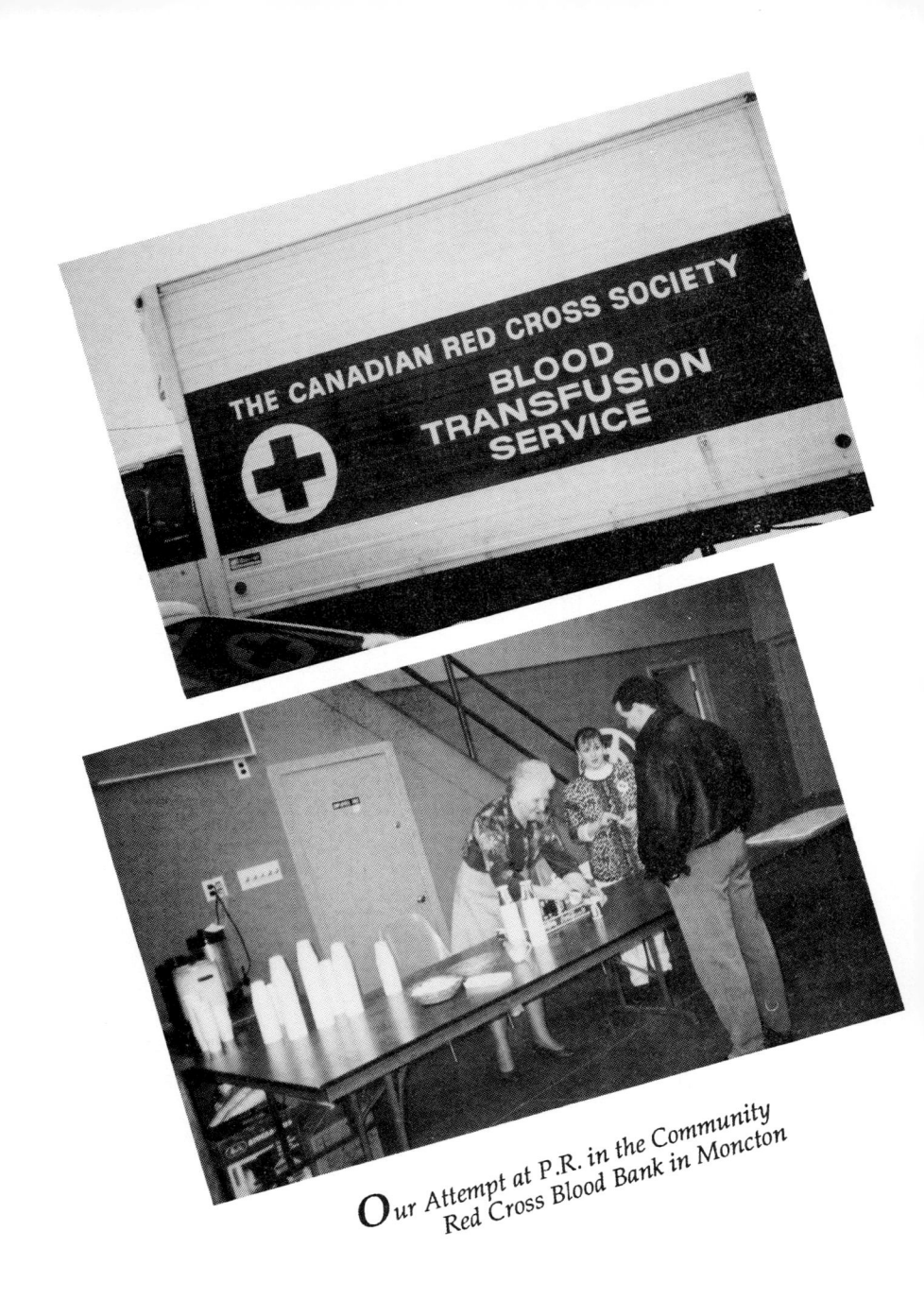

Our Attempt at P.R. in the Community Red Cross Blood Bank in Moncton

Missionaries in our Apartrment
Elder Larsen from Raymond, Alberta is at far right.

Lobster Boat and Traps

Farewell Party for the Hormans in Moncton

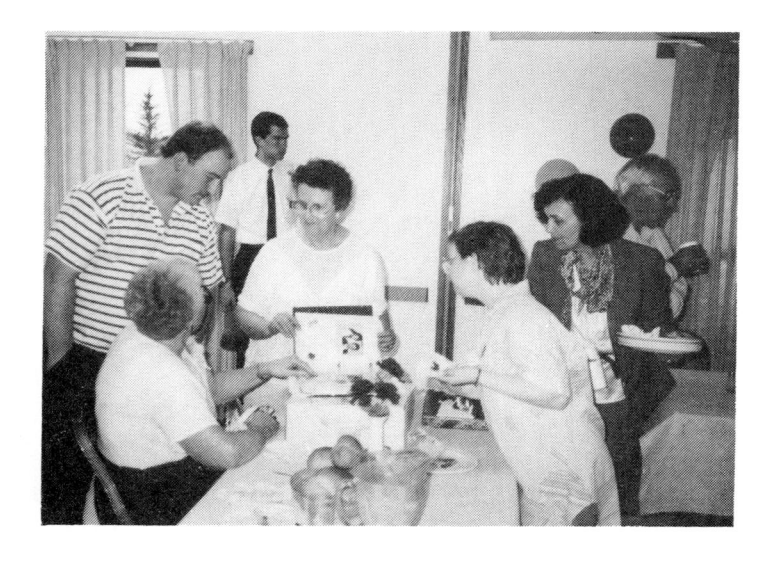

Ready to Leave – Goodbye to the Haydens

*The Hormans with David and June Dietrich
in our Anne Street Apartment*

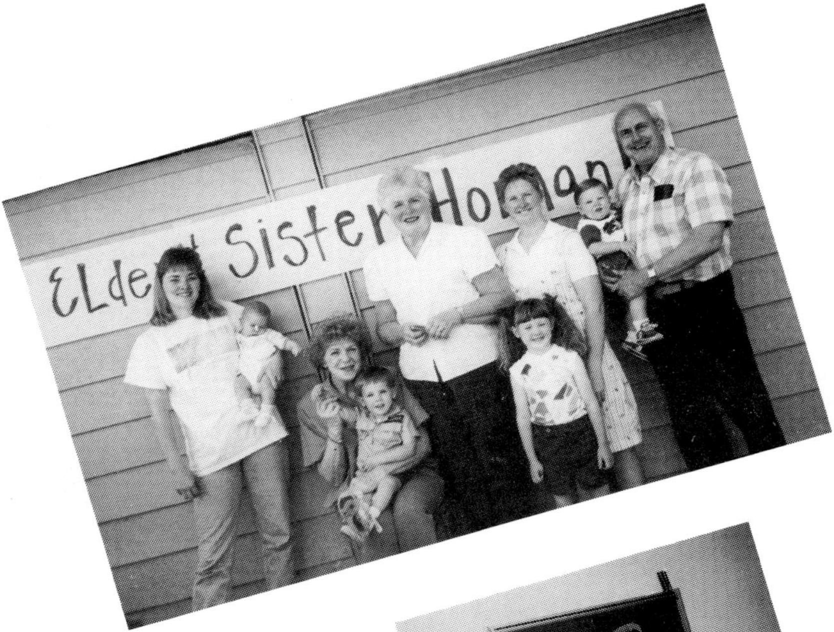
Sister

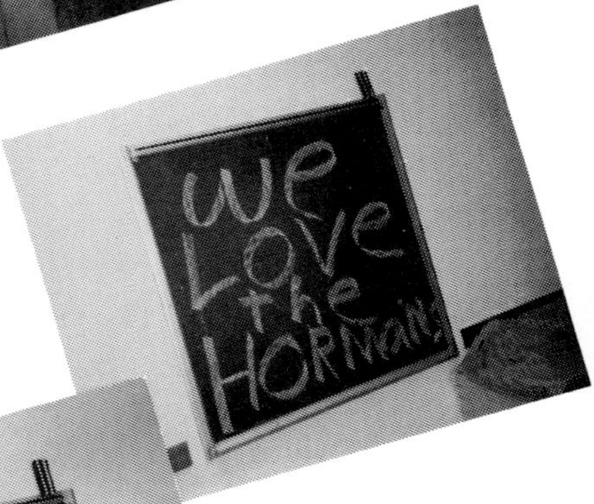
We Love the

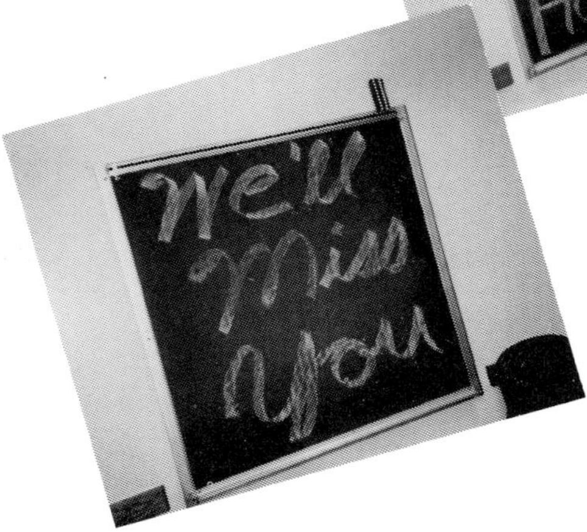
We'll Miss You

Welcome Home!

Grandchildren Grew and Multiplied in our Absence

*Our Japanese English-Learning
Students – Special Young Men*

*E*xtra Special Saints
J.M. and Claudette Belleveau
at their Salt Lake Temple Sealing

*T*he Belleveaus

Friends from the Missionfield
Belleaveaus, Frauzels and Hormans
Also Shelley and Elder Tomat

Mr. and Mrs. P.T. Horman

Missionaries arrive from Salt Lake City

Mr. and Mrs. Phares T. Horman have arrived in Moncton from their home in Salt Lake City, Utah to become missionaries of the Church of Jesus Christ of Latter-Day Saints.

Mr. Horman has had a long and colorful career as a civil engineer, working extensively on highways, bridges, buildings and utilities. Mrs. Horman has been a secretary, teacher, editor and author. They are the parents of seven children, five of whom have served as overseas missionaries for the church.

The Hormans have travelled extensively in Europe, The Orient, The Middle East, Africa, Canada, Mexico and the United States. Retirement posed new challenges for the couple, who called upon their time as youth missionaries to venture to Moncton as a missionary couple.

The Hormans will be giving a series of free lectures with film and video presentations at the Latter Day Saints Chapel at 2070 Mountain Rd. at 7 p.m. beginning Aug. 4.

Included in the series will be *Improving Your Relationship with Christ, The Lord's Plan, Ancient America Speaks, Families are Forever,* and *Man's Search for Happiness.* The general public is invited to attend.

Moncton Times Transcript, July 23, 1988

To all married couples that can serve: now is the time. Thrust in your sickle and serve the Lord with all your might, mind, and strength. You will know more love and fulfillment than you ever believed possible. A mission is a sacrifice, yet your sacrifice will bring forth the blessings of heaven. In reality the sacrifice of leaving home, family, and comforts truly turns out to be a sacrifice of something good for something better."
—Elder M. Russell Ballard,

BLESSINGS OF FILLING A MISSION
Given at Stake Conference in
Salt Lake City, Utah 1989

In the dark days of WW II, King George V of England gave an impassioned plea to his people on New Year's eve. He endeavored to give them courage through increasing faith in the Almighty. Said he:

> And I said to the man who stood at the gate of the year,
> "Give me a light, that I may travel safely into the unknown."
> And he said: "Go, and put thy hand into the hand of God and it shall be better than a light and safer than a known way."

Answering a call to fill a mission is an act of faith--launching into the unknown--but at any age, as one puts his hand into the hand of God, it most assuredly is better than a light and safer than a known way.

While in the MTC our zone included seven couples going to all parts of the world. We all came from different backgrounds, different experiences in the Church, and our preparation was as diversified as our personalities. Two couples were similar in that both of the men were converts to the Church, and were rather late bloomers in their commitment to faithfulness. But the one thing we all had in common was our desire to serve. We kept touch with these couples, and learned much from each of them. Without exception, the two who were a bit rough-hewn, less articulate, led us all in lessons taught, members reactivated, and baptisms performed. As the Spirit of the Lord moves upon his instruments, however humble, they are all magnified in their callings as we were.

When we arrived in Moncton, New Brunswick, we were as green as the grass surrounding us. Since no one, not even the members, was especially anxious to get to know us, we decided to devise ways and means of getting to know them. We invited them to lunch or dinner with us and did so three times a week. We were suspect immediately--missionaries inviting members to dinner? No doubt this was setting a new precedent, but we found that real concerns were aired as we broke bread together. We always invited them to tell us of their conversion. In doing so they experienced once again the warm feelings of the Spirit which might have been dormant for some time. They became stronger as they shared this time of joy in their lives.

Finding people to teach was our great challenge. I happen to be co-author of a cookbook, A Century of Mormon Cookery. While I was not out there to sell books, I thought that any way to get the word "Mormon" in the public eye in a positive way was worthwhile. I submitted to an interview and a feature article in the local newspaper and made the book available at the local bookstore. I also offered my services for food demonstrations, hand-dipping chocolates, and tying quilts. Now at home I never considered myself anything but a novice at these skills, but in the mission field, one is immediately "an expert." Before I got finished honing these skills, I did become quite expert. These were merely a means of bringing non-members into the chapel in a non-threatening environment so that they more readily agreed to take the lessons and befriend the Church. Our aim was to heighten the LDS presence in the community.

My good husband, Phares, is a magician. Evidently New Brunswick or the Maritimes in general is not on the "magic circuit," so his talents were an immediate hit. And believe me, New Brunswick needed lots of magic! As we presented his credentials to the local newspapers on Prince Edward Island, the magician-missionary combination piqued the interest of a reporter from the Canadian Broadcasting Corporation (CBS equivalent). She called us long distance for an interview and was extremely intrigued with the many things we were doing to carry out our mission. After an hour and a half interview which was video taped, we were presented on prime time twice on the date of the magic show, which was a sellout. The Catholics up the street were showing THE GODMAKERS to an empty house. Oh, how He magnifies his missionaries as they seek to serve Him. Countless doors were opened, and we saw a special young man of 18 come into the Church as a direct result of being introduced to the missionaries and Mormonism through a magic show.

When we had been out about three months and were feeling that our impact was quite insignificant, the Lord heard our prayers and blessed us with Polly. She was a 72-year-old lady who had seen the world and been a part of it. Upon meeting us, she said she "was born Anglican and would die Anglican." However because the second discussion asks for the baptismal commitment, Phares said: "Polly, we are having a baptismal Wednesday. Do you think that will give you sufficient time to prepare?"

Without hesitation she replied: "Oh, I think so." Neither of us could believe our ears!

"Are you sure?" said Phares.

"Do you understand the question?" I asked. Each time we gave her a lesson, her countenance seemed to lighten.

Brothers and sisters, as the Spirit moves upon the missionaries and upon the investigator, beautiful things take place. Before we had finished the six lessons, she fairly glowed! She entered the waters of baptism prepared and eager for membership in the Church. As inexperienced and as inarticulate as we were in presenting the discussions, the Lord accepted our offering of service and blessed us with this beautiful experience. He knew how badly we needed encouragement to help us move ahead.

We left our rentals in Provo and Salt Lake in charge of our children. What a blessing it was to see them grow with the experience. They learned how to work together, taught one another new skills, skills they didn't even want to learn, but which will be put to good use in their own homes. They were blessed to realize their own strengths, which might not have come for many years had we not gone.

Perhaps the greatest blessing realized through serving a mission is the renewed dedication one has to his or her companion. It has been upwards of thirty years since "it was just the two of us," and it is about as scary now as it was in those first heady days of marriage. It is also a most gratifying experience. Our main problem is that of not having a junior companion, both of us having served before. Once I gave him an understanding as to who was "junior," things moved along nicely--but he kept forgetting!

As we enjoyed companion study together, we both grew in our understanding of the marvelous work in which we were engaged, as well as in a knowledge and love of our Savior. We learned to laugh at ourselves again. Frequently we decided which concept each would teach, and just as frequently one would overlap the other, or change the order entirely. But we found it did not matter at all. If we taught with the Spirit, the message came through, and our efforts were understood.

What a blessing to mingle with the vibrant, young missionaries and partake of their "Helaman spirit" and maturing testimonies. And the other couples--their friendships will go with us through the eternities. They added so much to the areas in which they served. Every ward and every branch in every mission could use a missionary couple. <u>They represent the fulfillment of the promise made to the early converts.</u> Their example verifies the value of continuity in living Gospel principles. And how the members bless them! So many faltering testimonies are brought into the marvelous warmth of activity as concerns are resolved in ways only they are inspired to do. Perhaps it requires doing some gardening, picking blueberries, putting up pickles, baby tending, taxiing, making quilts and drapes, typing a resume--but it is all part of the service we are there to render.

We served in "Ann of Green Gables" country. What an education and blessing it was to have the privilege of seeing this part of the world where lobster fishing is the main livelihood, as well as logging and paper products. The ethnic differences of a bilingual province were also colorful and challenging. It takes one out of the comfort zone and gives an opportunity to grow.

Brothers and sisters, the bottom line is that every one who has a desire to serve can be a useful tool in the hands of our Father in Heaven. Wherever one is called he will be made equal to the task. I submit that when we "oldsters" are sittin' and rockin' we will have something more exciting and rewarding to talk about than watching the grass grow! I shall ever be grateful for the blessings of my two missions. The following poem expresses this view:

LIFE'S MIRROR

There are loyal hearts, there are spirits brave,
There are souls that are pure and true.
So give to the world the best that you have
And the best will come back to you.

Give love, and love to your life will flow,
A strength in your utmost need.
Have faith and a score of hearts will show
Their faith in your word and deed.

Give truth, and your gift will be paid in kind
And honor will honor meet,
And a smile that is sweet will surely find
A smile that is just as sweet.

For life is the mirror of king and slave,
'Tis just what we are and do;
So give to the world the best that you have
And the best will come back to you!
                    --Madeline Bridges

You are the best the Church has to offer, for you have been schooled in a Stake of Zion--a "School of the Prophets" if you will. You have the truth, the restored Gospel of Jesus Christ. You have the love and faith to share with your brothers and sisters, His children. There are countless loyal hearts out there awaiting you brave spirits who will give the world the best that you have--your willing heart, and I testify of God's promise that the best will come back to you in eternal blessings.

This is the greatest work on earth. Christ is at its head, and short is the time before He will come to claim His own. There has never been a more exciting time to be engaged in missionary work than now. The Gospel is true. Jesus is the Christ, and the Book of Mormon contains a fullness of this truth, of which I testify in His sacred name, Amen.

* * * *

1989--We returned from our mission in June, just in time to bid farewell to Briggs and Wendy as they took off for Chicago. Briggs will be attending Northwestern University, studying physical therapy. It was our first encounter with their tiny son, Steven, and Brittney, who was so young when we left. They had appropriate "Welcome Home" signs at the end of the lane, along the fence coming up the lane, and on the house as we entered.

How wonderful to "touch the green, green grass of home" and all the children and grandchildren! Heather and Ken had their fourth little boy just before Christmas. They named him Zachary James. He is from the same mold as the rest--big dimples, ready smile, and reddish hair.

My cookbook continues to amaze me, having sold over 35,000 copies to date. We're currently in our seventh printing in four years and have broadened our sales base from coast to coast in the U.S. as well as Canada. Emma Lou (my sister) did a terrific job of "holding" and even "lengthening" the line in my absence.

High on our worry and prayer list this year is my eldest sister, Beth. A retired school teacher, having earned a good rest, she is now plagued with multiple myeloma. She has had chemotherapy and radiation. She also tried a Mexican regimen. We hope remission is on its way!

What a momentous year this has been! Hurricane Hugo devastated the southern states; powerful earthquakes leveled parts of California and Armenia; tornadoes, floods and drought wreaked havoc in other parts of the world. Truly, we are seeing prophecy fulfilled.

On the brighter side, we have witnessed other history-making events: people in many lands have broken the chains of tyranny and cried out for freedom. As <u>glasnost</u> has taken effect, the walls of communism have crumbled, even to seeing the Berlin Wall, intact and destroyed, mirror the paradox of twice being the vehicle through which the East Germans were "kept in."

What a fast-moving, complex problem faces the heads of nations who must now decide which form of government will satisfy the needs of millions! Let's hope that they enlist the help of the Almighty as did our founding fathers when drafting the Constitution of this great land. It has stood the test of time in ensuring democracy in a free country. How blessed we are to live in America!

1990--This was a year filled with myriad activities, sufficient to keep these two "retirees" tired but not retired. At the conclusion of Legislature we spent a few days in Mesa, Arizona, on the occasion of meeting the Proctors there for their daughter's wedding. We were all guests at the Ernie and Betty Briggs' home.

In early spring April, Sieg and Morgan moved in with us. What a lively summer we had with Morgan enjoying her many cousins, picnicking on Grandma's big quilt, sharing her playhouse, and jumping on our giant trampoline.

July 4th was supposed to be a family outing at Bear Lake, but the stork pre-empted that plan and the day was spent awaiting Susan's delivery of Skyler Briggs Ray, our 13th grandchild.

Shelley and Vern Fuller became engaged. Upon seeing Shelley approach the house, April declared: "Here comes Shelley with her wheelbarrow to carry in her big rock!" And a beautiful diamond it is!

Mid-July saw the Briggs clan (104 of us) gathered at Badger Ranch near Waterton Park, Alberta, for a family reunion. It was a wonderful time of renewal of self and relationships.

Shelley and Vern's August wedding was one of the prettiest garden weddings I have seen. Our good neighbors, Naoma and Russ Hansen loaned us their back yard, complete with gazebo, swimming pool, and bowers of flowers. The following week we followed the newlyweds to Glendora, California, where his folks hosted them at another open house.

Sieg, April's hubby, graduated from ITT with an associate degree in electrical engineering. He secured employment in Logan, Utah, so their little family moved, leaving quite a hole in our home and hearts.

In October we flew to Chicago to attend Briggs' graduation from Northwestern as a physical therapist. We would have attended anyway, but it was especially joyful to hear him give the graduation address which was a "rap" detailing the many facets of preparing to be a therapist. He is now employed at the Back Institute affiliated with Cottonwood Hospital in Salt Lake City. We are happy to have their little family back home.

Since my cookbook, A Century of Mormon Cookery, proved successful, I optimistically put another one on the drawing board. Heart Strings From the Book of Horman will be out in 1991. It is a compilation of vignettes from my childhood, adulthood, marriage and retirement. Some of it is humorous, some inspirational, and at the very least, I hope it is interesting. It will be ready for the Christmas market.

President Monson provided my quote for the year:
"We make a living by WHAT WE GET.
We make a life by WHAT WE GIVE."

* * * *

SELF-FULFILLING PROPHECY

I sewed 36 yards of tricot for an elegant backdrop for Karen's wedding line. I stepped back to survey my accomplishment with a smile of satisfaction. It would look exquisite--the bride and groom in traditional white, the mothers in pink, and the bridesmaids in lovely, springy flowered voile. Tonight was the night and the setting in the ballroom of the Sons of the Pioneers building would be a bowery of flowers, with lots of guests and excitement.

I stepped off the deep-carpeted platform, which was placed in front of a long wall of windows covered with venetian blinds. The euphoria of the moment left me as I thought: Just the right size for someone to fall off. I tried to quickly erase such a misgiving because I had a day's work ahead of me. I hurried off to things more pressing.

By six o'clock all was in readiness for bridal and family pictures. Newman Studio had been hired for the job, and we expected something great in addition to his bill! To my consternation, the 18-inch platform was not flush against the wall. It stood away from the wall, with a row of folding chairs both behind and in front of the drapery. I had no time for major changes now. Besides, the chairs wouldn't show in the pictures, at least not the ones behind the drapery. Guests began to arrive immediately. Happy, chatty conversation replaced my concern.

After standing in the wedding line for 45 minutes without a break, I sought respite by sitting for a moment. Unbeknown to me, the two back legs of my chair were over the edge of the platform. I fell backwards, completely disappearing behind the drapery. When my chair fell against the chair behind me, I was pinned between them with my legs in the air, unable to extricate myself. I fell on my right shoulder, resulting in great pain.

My abrupt exit created a terrible noise as the two metal chairs clanged together and started a chain reaction. The wedding cake, which had a darling little fountain on top, was plugged in underneath the vertical venetian blinds. As the chairs hit one another, they pulled on the fountain cord, and clattered the blinds the full length of the hall. It was a miracle the cake was not upset in midfloor.

Phares became aware of my absence, lifted the drapery to my full exposure, and asked, "What are you doing down there?" I shrieked, "Drop that drape!" One look and he complied without an argument.

Unfortunately, many guests had gathered, heard the noise, and in my absence, assumed I might have been part of it. It seemed like an eternity before the groom's brother-in-law appeared and said, "Let me help you." He was a husky fellow and took charge of the situation. He took my hands and literally pulled me to my feet. I surveyed the damage which, thank heaven, was not readily apparent. I decided the best thing I could do to save face was to skirt around the far end of the line and quickly take my place. I gathered all the dignity I had left, passed the waiting guests and took my place in line. I curtsied and with a self-conscious smile said, "Now for my next act. . . ."

And the show went on.

* * * *

A Century of Mormon Cookery

Hermine B. Horman & Connie Fairbanks

*O*ur Korean Printer Brother Han and Sister Jang

*N*amdaemun Market, Seoul, Korea
Hermine and Sister Missionaries

*A*utograph Party at Deseret Book in Salt Lake City
Elder Richard Scott and Elder and Sister Ted E. Brewerton

*A*utographing in Mesa, Arizona

340 HEART STRINGS

SURPRISE ENTREPRENEUR

The idea of a cookbook was cooked up by Joan Ririe and me. It was past the talking stage and in the first phase of collecting when Joan's terminal illness took her life. I was personally distraught with her loss and was sure the cookbook concept died with her.

However with the heavy demands of a large family now all in their teens, with college, missions and marriages, I sought ways and means for supplemental income. Once again the cookbook idea came to the fore. Because Phares had retired, time was somewhat heavy on his hands in the first years of adjustment. If I could find someone to co-author, perhaps I could start again with my dream; and Phares could do the printing. I contacted Connie Fairbanks, my good friend in our ward. She eagerly accepted the challenge.

Had I known how the project would literally consume me and my home, I might not have had the courage to do it; but we were both optimists. We were cautioned that a project of this magnitude always requires $20,000 "up front." I acknowledge the fact that without Phares' tremendous help for that initial printing of 500, such a project would never have seen fruition. We paid the costs of production as the bills came in, but Phares worked for nothing until the sales were made. Of course, so did Connie and I, but we expected that! Before the book was off the press, nearly every copy had been "spoken for." We were encouraged to go on, so launched into additional printings of 1,000; 2,000; 3,000 and 5,000. Meanwhile we accrued additional equipment necessary for the project: two collators (gathering sheets), a laminator, an electric punch and binder, a light table for layout of negatives, and a copy machine, in addition to the metal plate burner and Multilith 1250 we already had in our basement print shop. One bedroom was converted to a collating room; another to an assembly room; and production control (checking) took place in the family room. Large boxes of printed papers were stacked in all three rooms and down the long hall, representing each stage of the book's completion.

A bank loan was secured for each printing. It then took us 3-6 months to pay off the loan and begin operating in the black. We printed the book on a shoestring because we paid ourselves last. We had good friends and family, however, who worked for minimum wage with the entire process issuing forth from our home.

In the fall of 1987 I was at my rope's end. I was pressured with the thought that every waking moment had to be devoted to the cookbook. It mushroomed not only into every nook and cranny of my house, but also in the recesses of my brain. It was an obsession. And being completely surrounded by it made the psychosis much deeper because I could never "leave it."

The supply of books was running low and three years of labor produced little more than "blood, sweat and tears." I approached Connie with the suggestion of dissolving the partnership, especially in view of the fact that we were anticipating a second mission in the spring. She agreed, so I repaid her investment.

Sales proved to be a one-man job. I took occasion to carry the book with me wherever our travels took us. If we went to visit family in Arizona or California, I sold going and coming. If I went to Canada, I repeatedly went via Jackson and Yellowstone, where sales were brisk. It proved to be the easiest selling I'd ever done. It merely had to be shown, and it sold itself. Its yellow, shiny cover and red spine were attractive. Its name, A Century of Mormon Cookery, whetted one's appetite to look through its pages (500 pages and 1,000 recipes) and the price was modest ($12.95 and $15.95) for a book of its size. Locally I credit Deseret Book for giving us our first big break, followed by the other book outlets at ZCMI, Waldenbooks, Dalton Books, and countless other LDS and non-LDS establishments too numerous to mention. An invitation to demonstrate foods during Women's Week at Ricks College in Rexburg, Idaho helped promote the book early-on, while current autograph parties at Deseret Book and Waldenbooks, and Relief Societies throughout the Intermountain West keep sales fluid. When autographing, I usually serve Tex-Mex dip with corn chips, and pumpkin coconut or lemon bread--all of which are crowd pleasers. Least-likely sales outlets have also proven productive, such as "Grandma Grunts" in Hatch, Utah and drug stores, curio shops and service stations. It sells equally well in LDS or non-LDS communities.

In 2-1/2 years I had not spent any book-generated revenue for myself. Since I did not anticipate the continuation of the book, I thought this a good time to "pay Hermine." I almost wore out my little blue Suburu in the sales process, so was excited to pay cash for a 1988 Toyota Corolla. It was the first such cash payment for a car in the Horman family history! It was worth the effort! We now had a reliable, new car to drive to our mission in the Canadian Maritimes.

Having run low on books and patience, I decided to put the project away. But fate interceded. I had opportunity to go to Korea with long-time friends and traveling companions, Cherie Pardoe and Beverly Mercer. It was purely a pleasure junket to do a little shopping for Christmas in early November, 1987. I took six cookbooks along to drop off in Hawaii on the return trip just so I could say we also had sales in the "Orient." Immediately some unusual events occurred: (1) Our tour guide in Korea was a former book publisher. I gave him a book and asked for a bid. (2) We went to the Seoul LDS temple and made contact with the temple president. He worked with an LDS printer and gave him his copy of the book. I not only had the bid from the tour guide but a comparable bid from the LDS printer. I felt more comfortable working with the LDS printer for the simple reason that he came recommended by someone whose opinion I trusted. I did not know the other man.

Either the book would be out of print in two months or I must go to Korea and arrange plans for reprinting. Printing costs were considerably less there than I could reprint in my home, so I opted for a trip to Korea. In March '88, Phares and I hopped a plane and spent a week working out details with Brother Hahn and Sister Jang of Shinsung Total Printing Company in Seoul, Korea.

What made their bid so attractive? First, it included no monetary figure for labor (which constitutes half the cost in our economy) and second, it removed the production project from our home, without either Phares or I having to do any of the work! I was ecstatic! My sister, Emma Lou Smith, reluctantly took over sales and quality control in our mission-absence, and did a first class job of not only "holding the line" but expanding our sales base. The first printing from Korea was for 2,000 books; the second and third for 3,000. But for the last printing I was able to pay cash without the customary bank loan! My "century" of mormon cookery had reached a milestone in profitability, at last!

While on our mission in Moncton, New Brunswick, I kept a high antenna for ways of "spreading the good word" by as many innovative means as possible. Since the title, A Century of Mormon Cookery, is a bit provocative, yet not as threatening as a book on theology, I approached the local major bookstore chain, "Coles," and asked if they would be interested in handling it. They eagerly accepted and suggested that the local newspaper would likely want to do a feature story on a local author. The author-missionary angle was intriguing, so I was given free publicity, which was also productive in friendship towards the Church. It also brought our presence to the attention of the reading public. I did not plan to make a profit on book-selling while serving our mission so wholesaled the book at little more than cost; however, it paid dividends in other ways. The book was in every Coles store in three provinces. Every mall has a Coles, as we have Dalton and Waldenbooks in the U.S. Upon our arrival home from our mission, I received notification of my vendor number from the head office in Rexdale, Ontario, which gives me license to sell to any of their stores in Canada. What a delightful surprise! I can hardly wait for my annual pilgrimage to Canada on the 24th of July and to journey to Calgary and Lethbridge to open new accounts. Perhaps this year I will venture into the capitol city of Edmonton, Alberta!

Since the first printing in December 1984 until the present (1991) over 40,000 books have been sold! The amazing phenomenon is that each year it gains more strength rather than reaching the saturation point some anticipated. I wonder if there will be a need for a good cookbook in the Millennium?

Vern and Shelley's Announcement

Horman Family at Shelley's Garden Reception

HEART STRINGS 345

*O*ur Shelley Bride

*B*riggs' Graduation from Northwestern
as a Physical Therapist – 1990

*O*ur Summer with April and Morgan
Three Generations – 1990

CHAPTER VII
NOSTALGIA

NOSTALGIA is a collection of essays and poems prepared, mainly, in the latest decade of my life. Some were talks given in a Church setting; others are writings by assignment or purely for enjoyment. Hopefully one will recognize a maturing-in-process.

TWENTIETH CENTURY PIONEER

What are the hallmarks of greatness that set one woman apart from others? Is it wisdom? Courage? Or dedication to a cause? Is she always a pioneer of sorts? A reformer? A rebel? Most likely our answers to these questions must be affirmative. Though the challenges of each generation vary, true greatness finds expression in the eternal principles of righteousness and human dignity.

I speak of a "modern pioneer" who left the security of home and family to conquer a wilderness in Canada. It was a wilderness made bearable only because of the love she had for her new husband and a belief that they might grow and prosper while helping build the Kingdom of God in that part of His vineyard.

My mother's first home was modest--two rooms and a path with a rain barrel that provided water for drinking and washing. Two large washtubs and a scrubbing board graced one side of the house. A kerosene lamp shed evening light. A coal stove baked crisp brown bread and warmed the thin, uninsulated walls. There was not a shade tree for miles around to break the prairie winds that whipped up dust storms in the spring and blizzards in the winter.

It was a hard life. The monotony was broken by driving a horse and buggy to visit neighbors some miles distant, to shop at the country store or to attend church on Sunday.

Her family grew fast. Nine children were born during the difficult years of the Depression. For eleven years she was deprived of a visit to her "mountain home so dear" and her loved ones in Utah. Possibly it was at this time one of her little ones inquired:

"Daddy, is Lehi heaven?"

"No," he replied, "but your mother thinks it is."

Hard work soon absorbed the adventurer into farm life. She never heard of a 40-hour week. Every morning of the spring and summer months started shortly after 5 a.m. and ended long after dark when the last tired, hired man came in for supper. She taught her children the blessing of work by canning fruits and vegetables in season, doing chores in the home as well as in the barnyard and fields. Making bread, butter, popcorn, hotcakes and biscuits, was a culinary art mastered by both boys and girls in the home.

Housecleaning was also a family project. The boys washed or painted the ceilings; the girls did the walls and woodwork. On these occasions the rafters rang with songs of home. The dishpan provided a daily setting for "duet" music where the washer and dryer sang harmony to a wide variety of songs. Work, music and fun were a happy combination in the home.

In those years she put her footprints in the sands of time. She was a teacher; she wanted good educational facilities for her children. She had filled a mission for her church; she loved things spiritual. She knew good music and the refinement of the arts.

She pioneered religious training in the little one-room country school her children attended. She looked beyond her time and saw fruition of her dream that allowed seminary in the high school years. She worked closely with the teachers in the rural school and tutored them in music, elocution and drama, until a reputation of "excellence" was recognized in local competition.

Her stamina never failed in championing the cause of women's suffrage or going on tours to lecture against birth control. She made her prairie home beautiful inside and out though her means were modest. Each trip to Utah saw her bring back new shrubs, flowers and bushes for her yard. They usually winter-killed with the heavy frost, but it did not dampen her spirit to try again the next year with plants of a more hardy variety. She wanted her wilderness to "blossom as a rose." Responsive to her tenacity and hard work, she soon had her yard bordered with shade trees, mostly poplars and willows because they are so hardy. Lawn, shrubs and flowers graced the home front.

With words of wisdom and love, and tears of sadness and joy, she and her strong, kind husband guided the destiny of their children. As they matured, she expected each child to fill a mission for their church, or go to college, or both. However, World War II intervened, upsetting their well-laid plans. She then encouraged her husband to fill his second mission, while her sons served in the armed forces. Precious were the newsy letters she wrote and still writes to her now scattered loved ones throughout the world. Her 45 grandchildren have each felt her firm, gentle hand, her fine generosity, and her great concern that they walk in the paths of righteousness.

She gave of herself to everyone in need, a selflessness which reached beyond the bounds of race or creed. She helped the Indians from the Blood Reservation as well as the immigrants from throughout the world who settled in her beloved prairie. If there was a void, she filled it. It was as natural as breathing. Truly, her hand of mercy blessed and fed the poor.

She was a dreamer, and dared to work her dreams. Hers was a profile in courage. Her life exemplified dedication to a noble cause. Her faith, her courage, her vision and wisdom, together with her proud, rebellious spirit, would not be conquered by the wilderness. She subdued it. She is my mother, Emilie S. Osterloh Briggs.

* * * *

CAN ONE PERSON MAKE A DIFFERENCE?
Salt Lake City, Utah 1979

Magrath is a small Mormon community. For many years it struggled to maintain a population of a thousand. After World Wars I and II there was a slight influx of people, primarily immigrants from Europe. The Japanese from the British Columbia coast came during World War II. These minority groups were tolerated but not integrated. None of their children progressed much beyond the elementary grades, even though they scored favorably on the provincial tests for high school entrance. Most of them were kept out of school to work on the farm late in the Fall and early in the Spring. Few, if any of them, participated in the social affairs of the school or community. It was almost an unwritten law that the original pioneer stock filled all the prestigious posts. Newcomers were referred to in such negative terms as "Japs, Nippons, bohunks, hunkies, or foreigners." They were relegated to the "other side of the tracks" though there was but a block or two difference between Main Street and the outskirts of town.

Magrath maintained its status quo for approximately 65 years. It was "Sleepy Hollow" with a capital "S." Its main street boasted one department store, a grocery store, a theater, a couple of Chinese restaurants, a pool hall, some farm implement shops, a drug store, and a shoemaker shop. We all knew each other and cared less for a broader environment. Most marriages were between local boys and girls, or perhaps from the nearby Mormon communities of Cardston and Raymond. Few graduated from high school, and those who did usually went to normal school in Calgary for teaching credentials. Very few went away for advanced studies. Wartime temporarily united the many factions in Magrath as native sons served shoulder-to-shoulder with their immigrant brothers. Both suffered great losses during World War II.

Then a beautiful thing happened in our town. A young man, fired with ambition, talent, enthusiasm and vision, came to teach band in the school. He had a dream of a nationally ranked marching band, and he rallied the support of every church and civic group in town. Within a few short years (not more than three), he had a marching band with national acclaim. Students who could not have afforded music lessons were taught by this fine teacher. Anyone who wanted to be in the band was offered the opportunity to do so. Practice and performance were the only criteria. Then a curious thing happened. The more they practiced the more they won--and the more they excelled academically. There were no drop-outs. They wouldn't dream of flunking; they wanted to be a part of the band. They traveled throughout Canada and the United States to compete. No one wanted to miss those trips.

All parents were excited and supportive in a common cause. The three denominational factions worked closely together in fund-raising projects, which were constant, to support the band. Parents from all sectors of town were chaperons for the many trips. Friendships flourished that heretofore were not impossible, but unlikely. It was apparent that the "foreign element" was just as talented musically and academically as the posterity of the "founding fathers." Each had leadership ability that could not go unnoticed. They began to have clout in the high school, on the city council, the school board, and in the civic clubs. With all the attention it received, the little town of Magrath began to grow.

People began moving into the farm community because they heard of the fine schools, especially the excellent band program. They wanted their children to have that experience. The natural consequence of one man's dreams surpassed the expectations of all. Hundreds of new homes cropped up. A new high school with an Olympic-size gym was built. The old elementary school was replaced with a larger, modern facility. Real estate values increased. The town started to hum with new industry. A new stake was formed. Where two wards had sufficed for 80 years, four were now necessary. New church facilities and buildings were provided. The town started to hum with new industry. "Sleepy Hollow" awakened with new life and vitality.

It would be less than fair if I failed to mention that the fine band teacher was Boyd Hunter from American Fork, Utah. I doubt that he even realized the impact of his personal ambition. He not only built a band, but built men and women of character, education, and achievement in every field of endeavor.

Magrath now has a first class hospital, staffed by local graduate nurses and doctors. Lawyers, engineers, teachers, all of the professions are represented by graduates of Magrath High School. They contribute in many positive ways to the communities in which they live.

I picked up the local newspaper last week and found an account of the high school graduation program. The Japanese studentbody president gave an address. The valedictorians were all emigres by name, names that never made the news in my day, much less excelled academically. The field and track stars were honored, as were the basketball stars and those receiving national music recognition. Musical numbers were rendered by the familiar names as well as those unfamiliar, but to a man, they were all band members. The local newspaper holds only human interest for me now, as the names I read are not the ones I remember. The town is a milieu of nationalities which gives depth and color to its growing population.

In the same newspaper was an account of students returning home for the summer who had been away attending college. The list was impressive--65 in number, studying throughout Canada, Utah, Idaho and Montana and in institutions of higher learning across the nation. And I thought--how times do change!

Can one person, just one individual, alter the course of an entire community? You'd better believe it, if that one person is fired with ambition toward a worthy cause and has sufficient leadership ability to rally others around him.

Throughout my life I have returned to my home town almost every summer. My children have grown up with my addiction and refer to Magrath as "Big M"--then we all laugh. But I am glad that I understand a part of its growth pattern. My only regret is that the band was a little late coming or I, too, might have been famous.

The Magrath Marching Band was invited to Lake Tahoe to compete with the 300 top marching bands in the nation. The awards were all given and much to everyone's surprise, they did not receive one. This band, the top band in Canada, had placed for the past ten years! Then the MC came forward and announced that it was the judges' unanimous decision that this year, for the first time, there was need for a new award--THE SWEEPSTAKES--to be given the band that excelled in every phase of the judging. It was awarded to THE MAGRATH HIGH SCHOOL MARCHING BAND! There was great jubilation in Lake Tahoe and Magrath that night!

Magrath celebrates its birthday annually on July 24th. I had the privilege of hearing and seeing this great band. It certainly has that "extra special something" that makes a winner, and my heart swelled with pride.

Boyd Hunter may not even know how he made a great little town even greater, but the fact remains that he did.

* * * *

WITHOUT PREJUDICE

Black Man

My earliest recollection of childhood involves a train ride when I was five years of age. I was standing on the plush maroon velvet seat when a black porter came through our car. He stopped and spoke to me. I was so frightened at the sight of someone different than I had ever seen, I wet my pants. Mother was embarrassed and tried to repair the damage to the velour. I just cried. I didn't see another black person until I was an adult. Magrath was 99 per cent LDS and ever had been so far as my experience was concerned. Other than the Chinese families who ran the two or three store-restaurants in town, all the people I knew were Caucasian. But with the war came many changes.

Japanese

First came the Japanese who moved in from coastal communities in British Columbia. Most of these families left established businesses. Some were second or third generation Canadians. No matter--the national political machine vowed they were strategically located and would conspire with the enemy--"The Nipponese." However, there had never been a documented case of any of their race being disloyal to the allied cause. Nevertheless, they were uprooted and sent inland. There they were left to their own devices to relocate and make a living in a very rough and foreign environment and one to which they were not accustomed. In Magrath's case they proved a blessing because farm help was sorely needed. This option was available to all who would work. They were usually afforded housing of some sort on the farm where they worked. They immediately made a reputation for themselves as honest, hardworking, and good citizens, loyal to the cause in which we were all engaged.

During the summer months the young people gathered at the softball diamond at Lehi School across from our farm home for games that lasted until dark. Many of the hired men from neighboring farms joined in, as did some of the farmers. The Japanese were the first chosen for a team because they were formidable at batting and ran like greased lightning around the bases. They were our friends, our good friends, and happily many remained and strengthened our community after the war.

German and Italian

German and Italian prisoners of war also came to Magrath. We had a bird's eye view as 150 POWs were encamped at Lehi School grounds during the summer months. The major encampment was in Lethbridge, but they were given the option of remaining in the prison confines or working on the local farms. Most of them preferred the relative freedom of farm work compared to the prison environment. However when not in the fields, they were in a fenced area and guarded by soldiers from the National Guard. Living in such close proximity (divided only by a ditch down our lane), our parents made many strict rules regarding our behavior, especially for Emma Lou and me. However, six-year-old Jim could "roam at will" and was a favorite with the POWs. It presented a paradox to my young mind. For sure, they were the "enemy," yet they looked like us and our neighbors, though few of them spoke English. Only on Sunday did they become strangers from a foreign land. That was the day they had dress parade and put on their full uniform and did the goose-step march and drills. We loved watching them and admired their highly polished boots and bloused breeches. But Monday through Saturday they were young men like our brothers and fathers.

Mother spoke a little German, having been raised by a loving German grandmother, and she was quick to engage them in conversation. Mother was also an avid missionary, so took every opportunity to talk to them about the Church. She distributed hundreds of German pamphlets she secured from Salt Lake City.

Years later we heard that at least two of them joined the Church in their native land.

Daddy was a kind and gentle boss who saw them as victims much as his own sons might be while serving in a foreign land. Two of the POWs were scarcely 17 years of age. However, most were in their teens and twenties. A few were slightly older. It was not hard to love them. It was impossible to hate them--any of them. We were told to "always be kind to them. We want the Germans to be good to our boys." It was expected that the farmers would provide morning and afternoon coffee for the workers. Daddy saw to it that at least a couple of times a week they were provided with apples, oranges, or a treat of some kind. They reciprocated warmly, and were very good workers.

While all Canadians were under stringent rationing of foodstuffs such as coffee, tea, sugar, butter and meat, POWs were provided the best of everything in compliance with the requirements of the Geneva Convention. They often gave us sugar, especially at canning time, as well as coffee and tea to take to the fields since we didn't get coupons for such items.

Every evening during the week the POWs lined the fence facing us, and sang their native songs to accompaniment of guitars, accordions, concertinas, mouth organs and jews-harps. They formed a grand chorus of four-part harmony whose rollicking melodies filled the twilight on the prairies. After one of their renditions, our Briggs clan sang one of our favorites. We had quite a repertoire because we sang together often all our lives. We took turns singing until Mother summoned us to bed. Reluctantly we left our friends, not our enemies. We slept well, and were not threatened in the least that they would harm us.

At the war's end, many a tear was shed saying goodbye. Several wanted Daddy to sponsor their return to Canada. All invited us to visit them in Germany. Jim has since done so on two different occasions.

With the cessation of hostilities in Europe, a steady stream of immigrants to Canada began. Many of the first to come were already "displaced persons" who had lost everything in their homeland and had miraculously survived in DP camps for extended periods of time. They looked to a future with greater opportunity than a devastated Europe could provide. Magrath received more than its share of immigrants. But good, bad, or indifferent, Mother (by now a widow) reached out like few others and tried to make their lot a bit easier. It was rare she didn't have a "little family of immigrants" living in the two front rooms of her home "just until they get settled." She could not separate herself from the Germanic blood which coursed through her veins. (See Mother and the Hutterites.)

Black Majority

Within three years of these events, I was called to serve a mission in the Southern States where Mother served 45 years earlier. Since Apostle Charles A. Callis interviewed me for my mission, it was almost a foregone conclusion that he would send me there. He presided over that mission for 24 years. He claimed Mother was, even then, "most unusual" as lady missionaries were few and far between. She was one of his favorites, and "certainly one of the prettiest."

I had scarcely seen a black person prior to arrival in the mission field. They terrified me! It seemed that at every door a black person answered. I found myself tongue-tied and unable to say a word. Quickly I knew that I must change my thinking or my mission would be a mammoth frustration, because I was surrounded by blacks! In Savannah, Georgia, for instance, the population was overwhelmingly black. Even the "poor" white people had nannies or servants, so virtually every door was answered by a black. Once I conquered my fear, I found them extremely polite, always addressing me "M'am." Their language was distinctly colorful. I knew I had the capacity to love all people, and I discovered blacks were no exception.

German

In 1953 I was a member of a group of language students (33 women and 4 men) who took the first BYU trip to Europe after WW II. Our visits in the German homes were most meaningful. The rubble had been removed from the streets, but the bombed out buildings stood everywhere as stark reminders of the ravages of war. Whenever we met with people on a one-on-one basis, they said, while pressing our hands, "We love you." Wherever we met with the Saints they said: "Tell them (Saints at home) that we love them."

Jewish: "Aunt Bertha"

While on a student tour to Hawaii, I became close friends with a woman three times my age by the name of Bertha Rappoport. She was Jewish. I found her a delightful traveling companion and a woman of great depth. Our lives were happily entwined for twenty years. My children grew up knowing how special "Aunt Bertha" was. We all mourned her death.

I married into a family who frequently expressed disdain or non-trust of any minority group. This was spawned not only from a background more narrow than mine, but because they had rentals and no doubt had some unfortunate experiences with minorities. However, I determined that my children would grow up without prejudice. My life has been so enriched by those of different cultures, I wanted the same for them. Now that they are adults, I am not sure how well I succeeded. However, I made an honest, conscious effort, and feel that perhaps their adjustment on their foreign missions was easier because of the attitudes fostered in the home.

Japanese Students

One of our family's first encounters with foreigners was being a "host family" for visiting Japanese. We found this to be a great deal of fun. Initially we had to rely exclusively on sign language, but it didn't seem to hamper our fun. Later we enrolled as a host family to students attending the Western Language Institute. Young Japanese executives attend the Institute to learn English and are boarded in local homes. Three or four times a year they were our guests. They loved the interaction with our teenagers and spent long hours in conversation with them. Often they were taken sightseeing, or invited to socials in our home. As a family, we thoroughly enjoyed this interchange, and still do.

German Student Exchange

Next, April had the opportunity to go to Germany as an exchange student, living in the home of the Grassmans (both teachers). She was in Ahrensburg, a suburb of Hamburg, for a year. She learned to be very fluent in High German, as well as having a good comprehension of her high school subject material. When she returned, she brought 15-year-old Annette Grassman with her to attend Skyline High School and to live with us. We loved her like our own. She made a great contribution to our lives.

In subsequent years, Heather filled a mission to New Zealand. Karen and Susan served in different missions in Australia (Sidney and Brisbane); Briggs went to South Africa and Shelley to the Philippines. As a result of these far-flung contacts, we have entertained people in our home from each of these countries. When the children went to college, we encouraged them to have travel experiences. Three of the girls participated in a six month BYU Study

Abroad program in Israel. They visited most of the Biblical lands and gained a rudimentary understanding of the Jewish-Arab conflict which is almost as old as the Cain-Abel scenario. Karen and I also the had opportunity to visit Israel for two weeks. We enjoyed the company of my sisters, Emma and Beth.

<u>Horman Hostel--League of Nations</u>
During April's senior year at Skyline, we collected girls like honey collects flies. Sarah Scott of California was a carry-over from the previous year and was a special friend of April's. Annette from Germany was an exchange student; Dana Smith from Calgary, Alberta, was a cousin, as was Camille Briggs from California. Blonde-haired, blue-eyed Maggie was from Mexico, and was with us at the behest of the Scotts in our ward; Carol Clark of Salt Lake City was the daughter of my cousin, and had been having trouble at home. It was an interesting, taxing, but remarkably enjoyable experiment in a merging of cultures. I almost put my shingle out, "Horman Foundling Home," but felt we had tremendous magnetic power without advertising!

Phares was the one who "suffered" through most of the above. Without a male ally (Briggs was on his mission), he felt quite dominated and definitely a minority. I might add that never before had our piano, washing machine, dishwasher and bathrooms been so fully utilized. Every inch of the house was truly lived in. One of my greatest challenges was to prepare meals that were acceptable to the individual tastes and diets of eight temperamental teenagers. I was used to a houseful of teenagers, all of them being mine. But I found that it was a horse of a different color to fill one's home with someone else's teenagers! Still, it was a good experience. As for Phares and me, we were grateful for our big house, and the ability to find our old hiding places!

* * * *

MOTHER AND THE HUTTERITES

Each year as I returned to Magrath, it was customary to visit the local Hutterite colony. Mother knew most of them on a first-name basis, and we always got the VIP treatment as long as she was with us. The "VIP" treatment usually consisted of an invitation to dinner or lunch in a large mess hall type setting, where the women sat on one side and the men on the other. The children were served in a separate dining room, and the food was served family style. They conducted a personal tour for us to any of the facilities we desired to visit, such as the dairy, egg farm, bakery, pig farm, sheep farm, etc. We chose our tour by the interest of the children. They were intrigued by the many shy, yet beautiful, children hiding behind their mothers' voluminous skirts.

All men dress basically the same in black pants, jackets and plaid shirts. Blouses and aprons for the women are colorful gingham over full black skirts. Their local cobbler fashions the same black shoes for the men as for the women.

After our tour was complete we made it a point to visit the flour mill where we purchased unbleached white flour, cracked wheat, wheat germ, germade cereal, and Coyote Pancake flour. We felt their product was superior both nutritionally and price-wise. We returned to Utah every year with a supply of wheat products to last until our next annual visit.

Having established this practice over a 10-15 year period, the miller would frequently ask (if Mother was not present), "Now let's see, who is your mother?" As soon as I told him who I belonged to, we were well on our way to an order efficiently expedited with 15 pounds of wheat germ thrown in for good measure because he liked my mother.

Then came the car accident of 1974 which claimed Mother's life. I didn't go to the colony that year because of my injuries. I flew directly back to Salt Lake City. But I well remember the entire back rows of the chapel filled with Hutterites at Mother's funeral.

The following year I made my annual pilgrimage to the colony and the friendly miller. He met me with the customary, "Now let's see, who do you belong to?"

"Mrs. Briggs," I replied.

"Oh yes, Mrs. Briggs. She was a very, very good woman."

I agreed, but argued that "Magrath is full of good people."

"But none like your mother," he replied seriously.

"Oh, I am sure that if you knew the others as well as you know my mother, you'd find many good women among them," I replied.

"No, I don't believe there is another woman like your mother anywhere," he said firmly.

My curiosity was piqued at his insistence, so I asked, "What makes you say that?"

"Let me tell you about your mother," he said, and the following story unfolded.

One fall Mother was in the local hospital as an out-patient undergoing some tests which required her to remain in the hospital overnight. She was not feeling sick, so mingled with the other patients waiting in the foyer. One of them was a young married Hutterite whose wife was having her first baby. The hours waned on until it became dark, and all of his people returned to the colony. The darker it became, the more severe became the blizzard that engulfed the community. Still, the baby did not come, and it became apparent that complications had set in necessitating a caesarean section for the mother. The expectant father voiced his concerns, and Mother, always a good listener, tried to allay his fears since her daughter (Hermine) had had five caesarean sections. This made her quite an authority on the subject. A healthy baby boy was finally delivered at about 10 p.m., and the parents were jubilant.

Mother saw beyond the emotion of the hour, and inquired of him: "How are you going to get back to the colony?"

"I don't know," he replied. "I am sure they won't want to come and get me in this storm. I suppose I will just stay here all night."

Mother had thought well ahead by this time. Reaching in her purse she took the house key from her key ring, and handed it to him, saying: "You know where I live--just across the street from the Health Center?" He nodded affirmatively.

"You take this key and go into my house, and go into the little north bedroom and stay the night. When you want to get up, help yourself in the refrigerator; there's milk and cold cereal and bread for toast if you want it. Then when you feel you'd like to return to see your wife and baby, bring the key back to me in the room assigned me."

The young man was nonplused. He could not imagine that anyone would trust him or any other stranger to admittance to her home in the absence of a family member. She was totally trusting, even to inviting him to fix breakfast! He was moved to tears. He carried out her instructions precisely, and the following morning returned her key to her with great expressions of gratitude.

But the story didn't end there. As soon as he was able to return to the colony he told his incredible story to everyone and the "powers that be" agreed that Mrs. Briggs was indeed "one among women." They unanimously agreed that hereafter they would not charge her for any of their services, be it labor in her yard or produce from their garden. They were very thoughtful of her and her needs and she appreciated anything they did for her. A unique bond of trust and friendship was formed. They both knew the meaning of "filling one another's cup."

As he told the story to me, we both became a little emotional. But he ended the saga by saying: "No, there are no women like your mother. She was such a good, good Christian. She loved everyone and thought only the best of them."

Now I understood his firmness. I was humbled to say I was her daughter, and the story was enhanced even more by the fact that this event took place several years ago, but mother divulged it to no one. We had to come to the source to hear it at all. It pleased me to know that her score of admirers was increased by the addition of 200-300 Hutterites!

* * * *

FOR NAME'S SAKE

Brother Bartley Heiner, formerly of Ogden, Utah, was transferred to Edmonton, Alberta to head the Institute program. He wrote a short satire making fun of the names of Canadian cities. I could not let it pass, so took opportunity to remind him of some of the peculiarities of his home environment.

Dear Brother Heiner:

Well MALAD, I received your epistle and am sure you could FILLMORE pages were you so inclined--but being somewhat EAGAR myself, let me be your little HELPER and tell you of things familiar in ZION or the TROPICS to you.

If LEHI had a vision in the MERIDIAN of time, I am sure it wouldn't include anything on the GLOBE like MOSCOW or PARIS--both far too worldly for him; and I am sure MORONI would have broken out with PANGUITCH had he envisioned any of EPHRAIM with a BLACKFOOT. He'd have really put them in JACKSON'S HOLE just for fun to see the SPARKS fly, which, of course, could have been extinguished with a few SNOWFLAKES or a HURRICANE--both at quite a PRICE, and for which he'd have to PAYSON, but then he probably had a RICHFIELD as the NEPHITES had BEAVER.

Yes, I agree that Canadians are different, and if this letter has made you tired, just sleep on some SODA SPRINGS.

Just one more word of caution. Be a bit careful in your criticism of the Canadians and their towns or they might KANAB and

SIOUX you and you'll find you have no car in which to CIRCLEVILLE or anywhere else!

With all good wishes.

/s/ Hermine

* * * *

I HAVE A STORY TO "TELL"
Farewell Address for Susan and Karen prior to their
Australian missions, November 2, 1980

Those who have been to Israel know what a "tell" is--but for those of you who haven't had that opportunity, let me explain. A tell is a Hebrew word meaning hill or the highest point in a geographic location from which fortifications were made to protect the people of the community. Sometimes it was surrounded by a wall, and always it had a water supply that was accessible only within the walls; thus, a complex network of chariot-rutted roads, towers, granaries, cisterns, dwellings, business houses, community baths, and synagogues developed atop the tell.

Beautiful marble pillars often were part of its construction. One wonders how such massive weights were put upright, and why in modern days all of them are lying prone among the ruins. It was explained that they were supported by beams of wood. When the invaders came to conquer the land, they merely set fire to the beams and the beautiful foundations crashed earthward. When the fire had completely demolished the tell and its occupants taken captive, the invaders covered it over with their earth-movers and built another civilization in its place. Hence today there are countless tells in the Holy Land, and in excavating them they find as many as 125 civilizations occupied the same hill at different time periods. Of course the hills got higher and higher as one city was built upon another.

Those who make a vocation of studying these digs, relating them to a time period and identifying them with a particular civilization, are known as archaeologists, and they in truth, have a story to "tell." From the artifacts uncovered they are able to discern the age of the dig, the degree of refinement of the culture and the types of civilizations they represent. Much of this information is gained from the clay pots, from the color of the clay, its composition and structure, and of course, from weapons and other metal artifacts.

I, too, find this study fascinating. As I drive up our beautiful canyons and over the highways of this spacious land, I wonder what stories we are leaving behind. Pretend that Mt. St. Helens covered our civilization as Mt. Vesuvius covered Pompeii in 79 A.D., what would the people in the year 3000 A.D. be able to learn about us? Surely one of the great puzzlements would be to give meaning to the thousand of zip-top can keys that line our parks and roadways. It would be interesting to hear the name they give our aerosol cans, ski equipment, and robots. Will they find shrines built to our manmade gods?

Thinking on these lines, Carol Clark Ottesen has written a poem I dearly love.

PROGRESS

Paper napkins
Paper dolls,
Plastic flowers
Plastic balls.
Disposable spoons,
Throw-away knives,
Disposable husbands,
Throw-away wives.
Cardboard chairs
And building facades,
Plastic people,
Dispensable gods.

This is a glorious time in which to live, but so were the wonders of Athens acclaimed worldwide. It seems that history repeats itself over and over again. Once a civilization reaches its apex, great is the fall thereof.

Need this happen to us? The Lord once preserved an entire city by plucking it up, so righteous were its inhabitants. It can happen again, but only when we are "all of one heart" as were those in the City of Enoch.

But in conjecture, I pray to God that should an archaeologist in the year 3000 A.D. dig inside America, he would find much that was good:

1. That we were a Christian nation, family oriented.
2. That we were temple builders--not of temples to an unknown god, but of temples dedicated to the true and living God, which temples blessed all the earth's inhabitants.
3. That we were a literate people, a record-keeping people, who recorded dealings with all peoples of the earth, regardless of race, color or creed, and that those same people found freedom within our shores.
4. That we had a highly developed civilization, spending as much money on "weapons" of peace as weapons of war.

5. That we developed technology that not only put a man on the moon, but eradicated from our lives the diseases which take such a toll of mankind today.

We have an obligation to leave a greater heritage than that given us, because our opportunities have been greater. I sincerely believe that those who write histories or keep family records, or serve missions at home or abroad, are enlarging that heritage. Anyone who earnestly lives the Gospel of Jesus Christ is contributing to our proud heritage.

I have always been proud to be a mother, especially proud to be the mother of seven children, five of whom were willing to leave their lives for a year and a half so that others might hear the Gospel message. I pray that we might all do our part in serving as well, that we might all grow where we are planted, and that the heritage we leave posterity might be pleasing to our Father in Heaven.

* * * *

April, our youngest daughter, writes beautiful original music. On occasion she asks me to help with the lyrics. Her most recent request (April 1991) was for words with an Easter theme. The following poem resulted:

THE STONE WAS ROLLED AWAY

When Mary went to Jesus' tomb,
To her wonder and dismay,
Her eyes beheld the empty crypt
And the stone was rolled away!

In fright she approached a stranger,
And asked with sorrowing breath,
"Oh, where have they lain Him?
Is there no peace in death?"

Then came the wondrous knowledge!
Within her heart she knew
Before her stood the Risen Lord
Whose promises were true!

The Savior by a stone entombed?
"Nay! Nay!" the heavens shout.
It was to permit us entrance,
And not to let Him out!

It seems so very strange to me
That the One who calmed the waves,
The One who moved the mountains,
And freed believing slaves--

The One who caused the blind to see,
Who raised souls from the dead
Was deemed incapable that day
To cure man's greatest dread.

The cold despair of the dreary tomb
Was dispelled that glorious day,
When light o'er came the darkness
And the stone was rolled away!

Roll back the stones of doubt and gloom
And behold the glory of the tomb!

* * * *

A HOLY WAR

Perhaps you are familiar with the infamous Three Day War fought between the Israelis and the Egyptians in 1967. The Egyptians were armed with the very latest in tanks, planes, and thousands of soldiers. By contrast, the Israelis had a dozen tanks, a few fighter planes, and a few hundred soldiers. Still--they won the three-day war! It appears that the Russian-made tanks were manufactured for fighting in any part of the world except the region to which they were deployed. The battle front was a virtual desert, the Sahara. Immediately the engines became corroded with sand which blew into the motor systems, demobilizing them after only a few hours of use.

As the Israelis came in for an attack, they found the Egyptians fleeing afoot before their scanty troops. They were amazed, to say the least, because they had little mechanized warfare to match their opponents. They were curious as to why they were abandoning their armored tanks as they fled. An examination of the tank motors verified that they were indeed immobile because of sand in the oil. The ingenious Israelis quickly deduced that the simple addition of an oil filter would solve the problem. Within a few hours of finding the immobilized tanks they had them running, repainted the red star and sickle with the white Star of David, and were using the enemies' own tanks against them. That accounted for the speed of victory in favor of the Israelis.

Our Father in Heaven has sent us all out to battle. We face foes of many kinds--temptations become our greatest enemy as we succumb to habits that rob us of our freedom. The subtle seeds of complacency immobilize us for battle readiness. Tiny grains of compromise make us vulnerable to the enemy. But we were not left without hope to fight our battles alone, any more than were the Israelis. The Gospel of Jesus Christ was given us as a guide to bring us safely home, victorious.

Perhaps we can liken the Gospel to the all-important oil filter, which is in place to save us from immobility or destruction. If we let it refine our lives, filter out the negative influences which face each and every one of us, we will not be giving in to the enemies of righteousness, but will hold on to the Iron Rod with banners high. This is the crux of missionary work. This is the call to serve given each of us. We must recognize the divine tools at our disposal and put on "the whole armor of God."

We are engaged in a Holy War--one between the angels of darkness and the angels of light, even our Savior, Jesus Christ. Only by a full understanding of His Gospel can we become familiar with and effective in the use of our tools. More than a physical battle, Satan is doing hand-to-hand combat for the minds of men. Are we prepared? Our minds must be filled with as much good as his angels are filled with evil. It requires a constant vigil to keep the channels of communication open with the Great Commander, who shouts or whispers orders to us frequently through his living prophet. Live close to the Church, learn the beauty of the scriptures, "for they are they which testify of Him" and great strength and power will be ours to fight for the right in life's battlefield.

* * * *

A REASONABLE, PATRIOTIC AMERICAN
Thanksgiving, 1982, Spurlocks' home, Spokane, Washington

I pride myself in being a reasonable, patriotic American. When the President said: "Set your thermostat at 65 degrees to conserve energy," I complied, even though my body thermostat was stuck at 72. I donned another sweater and sweltered.

When the nation went from a speed limit of 70 to 55, I suspected the world would come to an end, but with time and a ticket or two, I adjusted.

I burst with pride when the hostages returned from Iran, and cried with all America. And even though I have only one son and he is 18, I encouraged him to register for the draft.

What I want you to know is that I am all-American, as American as moms and apple pie. I am even guilty of being a mom who makes apple pie, and I do try to be reasonable.

When I was a teenager and wrote to my sister in Canada, it required a three-cent stamp and a wait of from 3-5 days on an unreliable bus or train for delivery. The postal service was then operating in the black. Now I pay thirty cents for the same letter, delivered by air, with the added advantage of automation, modern technology and zip code, and it arrives at its destination in three weeks or not at all. Still, I remain philosophical and hope the next administration can solve the problem, given time.

As my Utah car traverses from California to Arizona, I set my watch up or back an hour, willingly telling myself it is no more serious than resuming or ending daylight saving time. After all, I am a reasonable, patriotic American!

But there comes a time in the life of even reasonable, patriotic Americans when mind and body cannot cope. Recently I find a spirit of cynicism creeping into an otherwise optimistic mind. It all happened when I took a trip to Israel. After spending 24 hours in darkness, the flight attendant announced that our date of arrival was the same day we left New York! This announcement boggled my mind. No matter how I rationalized and explained to my body it remained in open rebellion with my mind. An intellectual fuse blew and my equilibrium came unglued.

Was this a plot by the PLO to undermine the American dream? I did not see them coming forth to claim credit for this misdeed. Or was this another of Menachim Begin's dirty tricks for which he'd have to answer to the U.N.? Even credibility on the home front came in for question. Was Ivory soap really 99-44/100 percent pure? Did they actually remove 97 percent of the caffeine from Sanka? Is 7-Up the only drink that is not detrimental to my health? I was not at all surprised when, despite "most doctors recommending Extra-Strength Tylenol," it spelled the demise of seven patriotic, reasonable Americans.

Unless someone comes to my rescue quickly, my fears might make terminal the malady others refer to as jet lag. I can find a logical, reasonable or patriotic reason for most things I encounter in my everyday life. But to arrive the day before I leave? Now I ask you!

* * * *

"MY SHEEP KNOW MY VOICE. . . ."

It was 4:30 a.m. in the teaming city of Jerusalem. The clamor of the city beneath my hotel window was stilled, and hardly a sound broke the early morning silence. The pristine sunlight was just beginning to lighten the horizon.

I walked to my window to reinforce the reality of "my actually being here." Very faintly, in the distance I heard a sound, almost like crying. I strained to identify it, but it was entirely foreign to my ears. The sound began to take shape into melodic calls, coming from diverse quarters, some nearer, some further away, until a muted, almost choral chant was heard. I tingled with a new insight and a spiritual confirmation that I was, indeed, witnessing a phenomenon used frequently in the teachings of the Savior.

Some five miles distant lay the hills of Bethlehem where countless shepherds tended their flocks. However the sheep frequently mingled as one flock at night, while their shepherds sought each other's company. In my mind's eye, I saw re-enacted a scene almost as old as time. Each shepherd has his own unique call, and as each sounded, the sheep arose and obediently followed their master's voice. After the choral chant, a chorus of bleating and bells was heard as the separate flocks dispersed, each going its own way.

It was an electrifying moment for me to realize that I was witnessing the fulfillment of the Savior's words when He said, "My sheep know my voice."

Are we as wise as sheep? Let us learn well the sound of our Master's voice through His anointed servants and our scriptures, and follow obediently.

* * * *

World, O world of muddled men,
Seek the Peace of God again;
In the humble faith that kneels,
In the hallowed Word that heals;
In the courage of a tree,
In the rock's integrity;
In the hill that holds the sky,
The star you pull your heart up by;
In the laughter of a child,
Altogether undefiled;
In the hope that answers doubt,
Love that drives the darkness out.
Frantic, frightened, foolish men,
Take God by the hand again.

--Joseph Auslander

* * * *

My heartstrings have been tugged and loosened through this exercise in moving memories. The interweaving of relationships is both sad and glad, but all add color to the rainbow. I have always believed that life is a worthwhile journey--each phase lived and in retrospect bringing joy. My conviction is now more sure than ever that the happiest journey is made with Him and His children as constant companions.

"May you each live it up in your day, time and period of life. Kiss while you can kiss, swim while you can swim, see while you can see, and sing the song of sixpence while your pockets are full of rye. If you do, then life will be adventuresome and your lantern will be swinging even if the light is dim as you make an exit."

--Dr. Harold Glen Clark

* * * *

APPENDIX A--LEHI SCHOOL

School's fate undecided

By Andrew Stuckey

The fate of the old Lehi school building, which currently sits behind the Magrath School, is in the hands of the people of Magrath.

At a regular meeting of the Magrath town council, councillors decided to let the people of Magrath determine whether the old school should be saved.

"If someone can come up with the funds or will do some fundraising for the school then they can save it," said councillor Greg Strong. "Otherwise I don't see how we can save it."

Councillor John Brunner, who attended the Lehi school when he was younger, said he had examined the building. "As far as I can see it's not worth saving," he said. "Push it over."

He added he doubted the building could be moved. "You're going to lift it up and the walls are going to collapse."

"If that happens," said Strong, "then the decision is made."

Council had earlier requested bids for removal of the building to another site. The lowest bid tendered was $4,000. An additional $10 to $15,000 would be necessary for renovations and upkeep.

Council decided it could not afford those costs.

Grant Stevenson, chairman of the Magrath Museum and Historical Society, said his group is interested in saving the building. "It's going to cost a lot of money to move it," he said. "But we're approaching government agencies for help."

The school was built around 1911 and served as a country school house for numerous years until it was moved into town. It now is being used for storage but will either be moved or torn down by May. It currently sits on the site of the proposed school gymansium.

Most involved with the school feel its value as a historical resource lies in it possibly being the last remaining single-room school in the province. Largely though, the town is interested in saving the building because of its sentimental value.

"There is really nothing of structural significance in the building," said town administrator Rod Bly. "Mostly it's just of sentimental value. A lot of citizens went to school in that building."

The fate of the old Lehi school is in the hands of the citizens of Magrath.

374 HEART STRINGS

Magrath, Alberta Nov 1934.

Dear Alice :—

We went to Sunday-School to-day. The wind was very cold. We, Daddy, Mama, Fred, Ernest, Maxine, and I, all rode in the cab, comeing home. Ant Francis made,

Hello Alice (Joseph)

Emma-Lou and I.
A new coat. Now I will tell you my marks that I have taken so far.
Arithetic, 100.

Spelling, 100.

In writing, My Shadow I got, 98,

With love Hermine Briggs.   (1st grade writing)

FIRST PRIZE

Writing

A B C D E F G
H I J K L M N
O P Q R S T U
V W X Y Z

Silver
Walter de la Mare

Slowly, silently, now the moon
Walks the night in her silver shoon;
This way and that she peers, and sees
Silver fruit upon silver trees;
One by one the casements catch
Her beams beneath the silvery thatch;
Couched in his kennel like a log,
With paws of silver sleeps the dog

From the shadowy cote the white breasts peep
Of doves in a silver-feathered sleep;
A harvest mouse goes scampering by,
With silver claws, and silver eye;
And moveless fish in the water gleam
By silver reeds in a silver stream.

LEHI SCHOOL - 1933-36
- by EMERSON BLUMELL, teacher

I recall, most vividly, Lehi School. It was my first school and as I look back now, I knew so little about human nature and human learning, and indeed, about human beings. But I have learned since that these understandings come slowly and gradually and that they are cumulative. It would have been great to bring all those things to bear at the beginning.

Lehi is an odd name--certainly not a common one on the Canadian prairies. The surrounding lands were taken up in the main, by people who emigrated from Lehi, Utah, e.g., the Bradshaws, Briggs, Sabeys, Karrens, etc. As was customary in Western America, when people settled, they marked off an area and formed a school district. They built a one-room school, hired a teacher, and the great business began. The "great business" I refer to was the three Rs-- basically. People had to learn to read English, to write, to spell, to count and to calculate, to learn the multiplication tables, the Imperial measure, e.g., acres of land, gallons of milk, and so on. But perhaps some other things might come almost incidentally. I refer to literature and a bit of history. I recall so well Tennyson's "The Brook." Such a beautiful and nostalgic piece of literature! In it was a "thumbnail" history of the growth of the British Empire and a nostalgic sketch of a beautiful philosophy about love of home and love of country. Perhaps other values were seen in the intermingling of pupils and teacher, i.e., the ideas of work, of honesty, the development of helpfulness and goodwill. Some of these things probably happened at Lehi.

As I said earlier, this school was typical of the schools in early rural America (Canada and the United States). The United States developed earlier than Canada, and as they filled up, there was a "spill-over" in Canada. The job in America was to teach (in America) the English language and a bit of the early culture. A magnificent job was done in the U.S. and perhaps in Canada, too. It is reported that the State of Kansas had 4,000 of these school districts. Alberta had hundreds of them. They all had basic objectives that I have mentioned and all achieved a measure of success.

Lehi School was not unique. As I recall, there were eight grades and about 30 students. What a tremendous responsibility rested on the shoulders of young, uneducated teachers! The reading lessons began with Grade One and moved on up the line. Older pupils always gave a certain amount of time to help younger ones. It had to be that way. Arithmetic, spelling, penmanship and geography, as well as other subjects, followed in the same way. In 5- or 10-minute lessons, some points were "fixed" in mind. Books always went home and reading in the long winter evenings was "the-order-of-the-day." Books were exchanged among students since the library always had too few.

But everything was not confined to the school's four walls. Sports, in season, were important, too. Teachers and children played softball together. I recall serving as "catcher" for one of these teams. Merlin Sorenson, the batter, struck out. I dropped the ball, so had to throw to first base ahead of the runner. I aimed carefully, threw the ball and hit Merlin on the back of the head. He dropped and we all waited while five minutes ticked away and he finally opened his eyes. What a relief! We had track and field activities and occasionally contests with neighboring schools. Such events were highlights!

Preparations for Christmas were important. Small drama, songs and recitations were in order. All the parents came and everyone seemed to enjoy these events. These experiences all made their contribution to the total learning package.

The rural school has been gone for years, but one may still ask if it really achieved its goals. I have thought about this many times. I recall meeting Hermine Briggs in Lethbridge a few years ago and asking her: "Hermine, you attended a rural school. You learned to read and write and converse there. Did you really lose anything by spending the early years of your education in a rural school?" Her answer was quick and precise and affirmative. "I learned," she said, "so many vital and important lessons there. I wouldn't have had it otherwise."

As Hermine left I recalled a very verbal, well-spoken, outgoing, well-educated girl. The beginnings at Lehi School couldn't have been so bad!

The rural schools of Canada, and especially Western Canada, sought to Canadianize students, i.e., make them aware of this large country and perhaps develop some loyalty to it and its institutions. And additionally, to develop in the three "Rs." And in an incidental way, something of our literature, history, and geography as well. This was a big order when one considers the restrictions of time, space, materials and teachers. Lehi School, like many other rural schools in Western Canada, did achieve some of these objectives at a time in history when they were difficult to achieve.

* * * *

LEHI SCHOOL - 1936-37
- by BETH BRIGGS, teacher

Teaching at Lehi School was a milestone in my career, perhaps because it was my first school teaching and also because it was at this school that I received my first eight years of formal education.

In 1935-36 I attended Normal School in Calgary, Alberta. I knew that the teacher at Lehi School, Emerson Blumell, was leaving to further his education at BYU. Hopefully I thought I could take his place and teach at my beloved alma mater. I don't remember having any difficulty getting employment there and signing a contract as I talked to Azer R. Briggs (my father) and Estella Karren, our neighbor. It seemed they represented the school board at that time. My salary was $840 for the year.

The fact that I would be teaching Fred, Hermine and Emma Lou, my much-adored siblings, did cause me a little concern. But they had always been such wonderful and obedient youngsters. I found myself looking forward to it. The truth of the matter was that my parents and family were very proud to have me teach at Lehi School.

On my first day of school I was prepared to be "Miss Briggs" to Fred, Hermine and Emma Lou, as well as all the neighbor children. Very prim and proper, I began to call the roll but was interrupted by the clear soprano voice of five-year-old Jimmy. He was on Tom Karren's horse, Topsy, and was circling the school, chanting, "Miss Briggs has some pigs!" Any dignity Miss Briggs had went right out the window. If he couldn't be with the rest of the family, he at least was going to be heard. Bless him!

Long and enjoyable were the hours spent getting my first school room decorated as a place of learning. I had always known I would be a teacher; now it was coming to pass. I made dimity curtains, orange and white plaid, gathered on a string, covering the bottom half of those tall drafty windows.

There was no tac-board, so every picture was put up with a tack and a hammer. Every inch along the four walls was decorated with this long line of pictures. There were pictures of animals, children, and landscapes, all from my huge collection of colored magazine pictures. Well, so much for the outward trappings.

As I recall, Hermine took great delight in helping me after school. She swept the floor and dusted the desks, and wrote assignments on the blackboards for the following day. The blackboard writing probably helped her develop beautiful writing. I took great pride in the writing of my students. My! They were beautiful writers, but Hermine was the best! I can't think of anything my students didn't do well, from elocution and singing to drama and the Christmas program.

My athletic ability left much to be desired. When I went out to play ball with the students, one of them would run around the bases for me (provided I hit the ball).

Emma Lou was a source of pride to me, being a good student and such a darling. Fred was arriving at the age of independence, but was always good to me--and what a whiz! He was always very S-M-A-R-T!

Mother and Daddy were so helpful with any of our projects. I wish now I had stayed longer than a year. But I moved on the next year and taught at Beazer Elementary up in the foothills of Cardston.

* * * *

LEHI SCHOOL - 1937-38
- by JAMES E. BLUMELL, teacher

I remember:

1. My salary was $68 per month (no deductions) for 10 months; $6.00 per month for janitorial services. (I always said this was the profit side of my earnings!)

2. The teacherage was really the entrance to the school. When the north winds blew, the curtains raised to about a 45-degree angle from the wall.

3. The day that "Muck" Sorenson decided to test the authority of the teacher. It was after school when I saw him carrying a large axe, coming along the south windows toward the door. I was waiting inside the door and when Merlin was poised to chop down the door with one mighty swing, I swung the door open, gave him the meanest gaze I could summon, and demanded (also in my loudest authoritative voice): "What do you want?" He retreated hurriedly to the barn and my authority remained unquestioned!

4. The kind meal invitations and other generous handouts of the Briggs and Sabey families. They tolerated me with their generosity and kindness and support at all times. Surely I would have perished physically if it were not for this timely, delicious and frequent aid. I always will treasure the memory and the kindnesses of the Briggs and Sabey families.

5. The ball games, races, etc., held at recess (sometimes extended) at noon and after school. We all participated and enjoyed the exhilaration of the physical activities. Since I was somewhat athletically inclined, I enjoyed a "star" role as we played.

6. The continuous learning activities which were carried on in the classroom. If my memory serves me right, grades one through eight were taught. It was teach, then seatwork as the teacher proceeded from one grade to the next. Actually, the work was well-organized because I had received some careful instruction from my brother, Emerson, a very careful and learned scholar. I worked hard at my task of teaching, and the learning activities seemed at least somewhat adequate.

7. The Inspector's visit. This was probably the teacher's most dreaded experience. However, he was an elderly man and wise in many ways. He seemed pleased with most activities, but warned me to have the students keep careful notebooks.

8. The winning of First Place in the musical festival for rural school choruses. (I still have the certificate to prove it). This was clearly a case of students with pleasant voices carrying the whole thing through in spite of their inept teacher.

9. The many rides to town in a horse-drawn gig with Lloyd Sabey as we participated in Senior Basketball. You had to really love the game to put that much effort into it. Again, many pleasant experiences and lunches as we came home late.

I have many fond memories of events at Lehi School which started a teaching career of 46 years. My last ten years were served as instructor for the Lethbridge Community College.

* * * *

LEHI SCHOOL - 1938-40
- by SARAH GIBB LOW, teacher

You ask me to try to remember but memories are too short. However, it has been real fun trying to recall way back when. . . . Finishing Normal School in Calgary, Alberta, the next step was to try to persuade a school board to desire my expertise, and let me demonstrate it in some school. Upon hearing that the Lehi teacher had moved on, I called upon Brother Briggs, chairman of the local school board. From him I learned about divisional boards--higher authority than local boards. Brother Briggs helped them to decide that

Lehi School wished the services of Sarah Gibb. Thanks to Brother Briggs and the local board for persuading them.

It was an interesting experience. I had never been in a one-room school or even in a multi-grade one-room school. What to do with first grade while trying to see to the work of Grades 2, 4, 5, 6 and 7? I filled the blackboard and wrote exercises on slips of paper to give to them. Thank goodness many of the students had been in this school for some time and they were patient, most of the time! It was soon obvious that the upper grade students could do their work without supervision and their spare time was recruited to help the younger children.

One time while teaching a Grade 1-2 class, I thought how nice and quiet they were. I looked up to find the Inspector had entered unannounced and was sitting in one of the desks at the back. An Inspector was a person who could drop in any time unannounced and terrorize even well-seasoned teachers. What had I said while he was there? How many times had I "yelled" at the kids? etc., etc. He gave me a good report--thank goodness.

Recess was an experience too. In the spring the ball games filled the recesses. I would go out to get them going, and referee some. Gordon Sabey said he had forgotten more about ball games than I ever knew, and what do you know? He was right! But someone had to do the job, and all the students were needed to make the teams.

Rural schools were centers for neighbors to hold dances and parties. The teacherage (living quarters for the teacher) was a small room. The entrance of the school was modified to fill this purpose. In the bottom of the cupboard was a box of coffee cups. It was nearing time for a party, so one noon hour while the students were eating lunch, I decided to get the cups out of the cupboard and get them ready for the party. I pulled out one cup by the handle, and little pink and white--you guessed it--baby mice slithered across my floor. In terror I rushed into the classroom. The boys really laughed, but went in and cleaned them out. Mice are another story. I ran a trap line and every weekend, on return from town, I'd have to empty them!

I usually returned from town with the Briggs' upon their return home from Sunday night church. We enjoyed singing our favorite songs in four-part harmony all the way back. It helped me forget the trap line awaiting me!

It was very rewarding to go to a school where music was well grounded and enjoyed, because that was one of my loves too. The annual music festival was the highlight of the year. I was told we had to win this year because they would be able to keep the silver cup for winning three years in a row. We worked and drilled and then because we needed an accompanist, we took the whole group to Magrath. Grace Bingham was accompanist and graciously agreed to come to Mother and Dad's home. It was Saturday, the first of April. The practice went well. The "rote" training had been quite accurate, and rough edges were quickly smoothed over. For a treat the teacher had homemade chocolates, some of which had been doctored with soap. Soon it was forgiven and they enjoyed the good ones!

The night before the festival I was riding my trusty steed home to get ready for Lethbridge. As we started off, the horse decided to run. I couldn't stop him. I tried to think what to do. Should I fall off and let him go, or what? I couldn't decide because the festival was the following day. So I hung on for dear life! The horse stopped at Dad's farm (long since abandoned). I got safely into town and made it to the festival. Our chorus won first place and the silver cup, but it somehow we didn't get to keep it.

Life in the teacherage was not always roses. It was quite lonesome and even scary. Often I would stand by the open window on the south of the school and sing. Guess it got a bit loud, because the Briggs' could hear it and someone would often come and visit a while. Jimmy was especially good to come. He even pretended he liked the soup we had for supper if he was over when I was eating. He could report he had two vegetables for supper, if the health lesson next day said you should have two vegetables for the day.

It was interesting to see the students come to school on their horses with their lunch pails hanging on the side. In the winter the kids huddled round the furnace to "thaw out" and dry their wet clothing.

One requirement for getting a teacher's certificate was "practice teaching." Lehi was the spot for Reece Gibb to do some of his practicing. While he was there some of the young men of the school decided to smoke out in the trees. Their telltale perfume was detected and all were questioned in the teacherage. All but one confessed, and he said, "No way." All the others implicated him. He still denied it, so out came the dreaded strap, not for smoking but for telling a lie. Years after he accused Reece of doing the strapping. So in his eyes I was cleared. I never got a chance to clear Reece's name with said student.

When the war broke out and the call for volunteers came, my neighbor, Lorin Low, was first to enlist with the Calgary Highlanders.

He was the first volunteer from Magrath. He went to Calgary for training. No phone at school, so he called person-to-person to Briggs' for me. We wondered why the connection was so poor, until we learned about "rubbering" in on rural phones. Everybody in the district seemed to know our business--even when he could come home to marry me. I finished the year. He went overseas and I went on a mission to Eastern Canada.

I met Arden Olmstead in Edmonton recently. We were excited to see each other and remember Lehi days.

* * * *

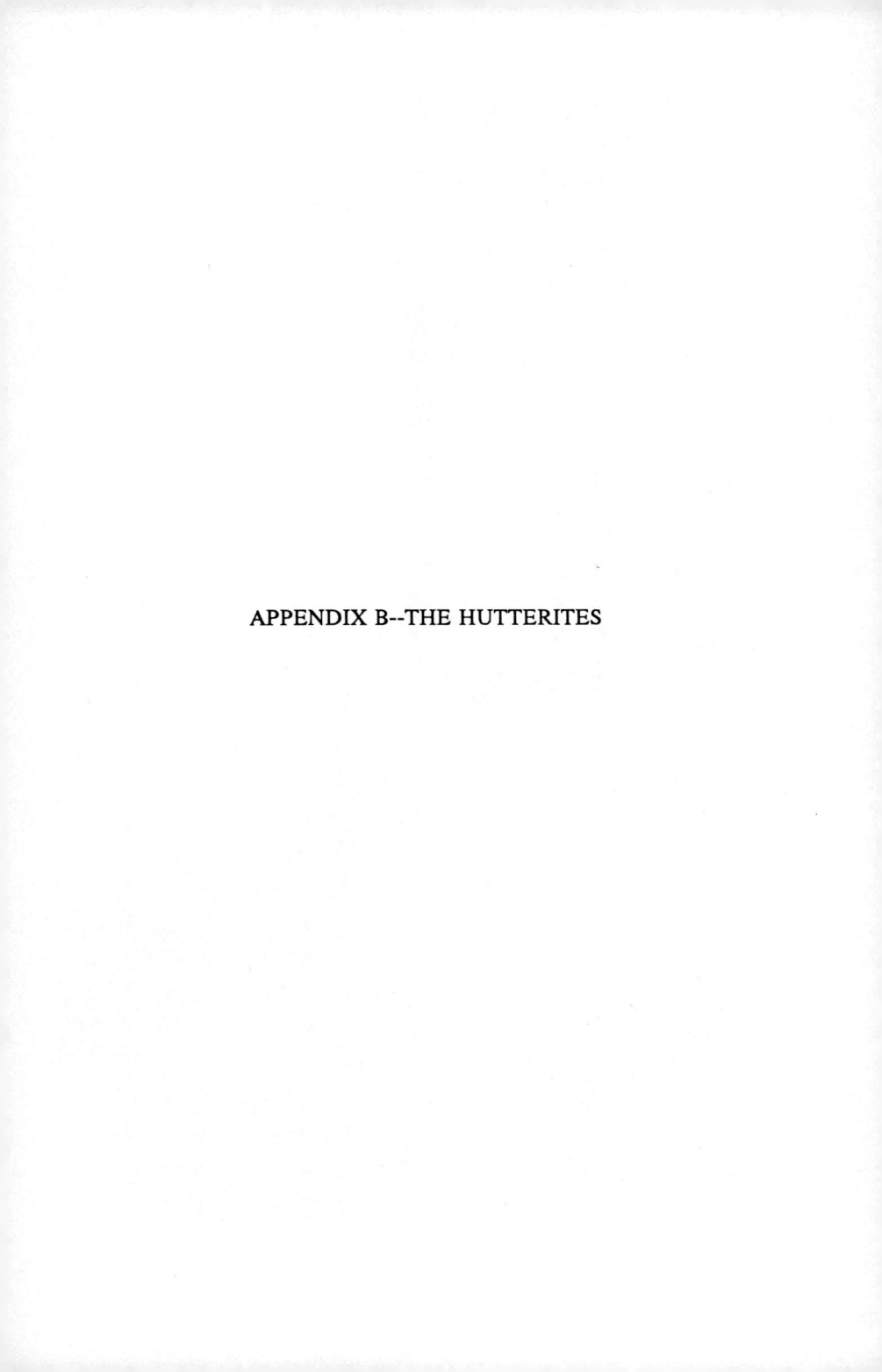

APPENDIX B--THE HUTTERITES

388 HEART STRINGS

THE HUTTERITES

The Hutterites are a group of people living in Southern Alberta, Canada, who are of Prussian extraction. They are discernable in any community by their black clothing, bearded men, bespectacled faces, and German language. They date back to the Huguenots of Europe who eventually made their way to America. In an effort to keep their ideals intact and live according to those ideals, they opted for communal life. Today they are found in the Dakotas, Montana, and Southern Alberta. "Living their religion according to the dictates of their own consciences" has resulted in some unusual circumstances (1) physically, (2) socially, (3) politically, and (4) religiously.

1. <u>Physically</u>. The idea of communal living appealed to them because they desired to be self-sufficient, meaning they provided for all their needs within the confines of the colony. Of necessity, the woman all share the same fashion, as do all the men. The single men are clean-shaven with their married counterparts full-bearded. Women of all ages have their heads covered with colorful bandanas, with only the edges of twisted or plaited hair showing around the face. All men and boys, likewise, wear stiff-top hats with visors. Further, it is apparent that the men and women have the same cobbler, as he has one pattern for all. The fact that most of them wear glasses is due to extensive intermarriage. Since new families are not coming into their order, they divide every ten years with other colonies in an effort to add new blood lines.

2. <u>Socially</u>. It is difficult to live in 20th century America yet cling to many of the mores of the Puritans. They have no radios, no musical instruments, no television, no movies, no dancing, no socializing apart from the colony. Still, they utilize the most modern equipment available in vans, suburbans, and equipment available for their farms, herds, dairies, butcher shops, flour mills, bee houses, and fruit farms. Their young people often become disenchanted with the strict confines of their lives and leave the colonies. It is extremely rare to hear of the addition of new blood by way of an "outsider" joining the colony. They live frugally, and can do so because they pay no community taxes, nor do they pay wages for any cause. They have no need for money because their needs are taken care of by the "system." Their education ends with the eighth grade and they are then apprenticed to a trade "boss" who will prepare them for their life's work. Because they are able to accrue great wealth, they are unfair competition to the average or small farmer. They can buy the

best parcels of land available and make it more productive by their advantage of manpower as well as modern equipment. They spend little money in neighboring communities to aid local economy. The one exception to this rule is their need for health care which is paid for and provided in local communities. It is understandable that their presence in any non-communal environment is cause for resentment.

3. <u>Politically</u>. The Hutterite is viewed by his non-Hutterite peer as a parasite. He does not vote, does not pay individual taxes, does not serve his country in times of war, but stays home safe and sound while his brothers "outside the colony" give their life's blood so that this land might remain free for the practice of his religious freedom. In the framework of a land founded on the free enterprise system, maintained by the taxes of its people, and idealized by the stories of Horatio Alger--there is some resentment for a people who seemingly contribute nothing to this great philosophy of life.

4. <u>Religiously</u>. Religiously he is free, free to exercise his religion as he sees fit. Services are conducted in German by a layman. German is the language of their homes, but law dictates that English must be taught in their schools.

Hutterites are good Christian people. They live temperate lives and help their neighbors. But as long as they want and get the best of both worlds (past and present), living peaceably with them will remain a challenge.

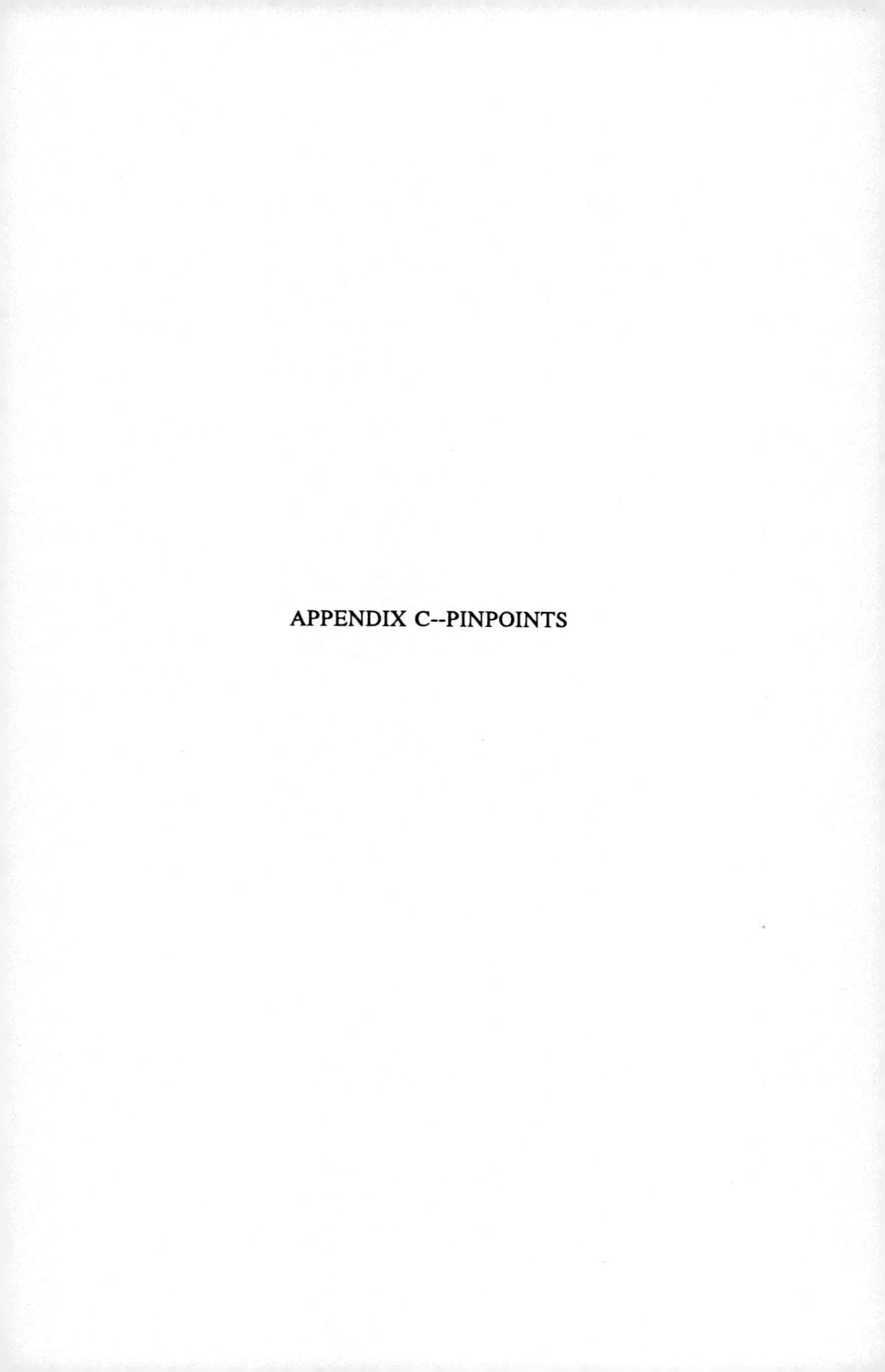

APPENDIX C--PINPOINTS

PINPOINTS

While working in the capacity of editor of the Church Department of Education, we initiated a publication called PINPOINTS. It was a digest of current writings devoted to teaching techniques, classroom and counseling skills, human relations, etc., printed in magazines, journals and periodicals. The seminary teachers reviewed the articles and sent them to the office for editing before being republished. It was a fascinating segment of my job description. Writing an editorial each month was challenging, as I tried to incorporate the LDS philosophy of religious education. During this assignment the <u>Improvement Era</u> published my contribution, "Unto Every Man. . . ." also included in this appendix.

While these articles deal with teaching per se, one might ask, are we not all teachers, either by precept, word, or profession?

* * * *

DESTINATIONS

It was a stormy night in the English Channel, 1950. A shrill wind dashed high waves against the sides of a small craft which bobbed cork-like on the choppy waters. Now and then one could discern a swimmer re-enacting the great epoch drama of the many who aspire to conquer the Channel. Florence Chadwick had trained rigorously and long for this feat. She had been successful in even more difficult endurance tests--but on this murky night she tossed in her victor's cap when only a few hundred feet remained between her and the shore!

The next day the United Press interviewed her on the air and asked the question: "In view of your past accomplishments, what single factor contributed to your failure to swim the Channel?" Her response was quick and terse. Said Miss Chadwick: "It was foggy and dark. I lost sight of my objective."

Life's byways are crowded with wanderers who have lost sight of an objective. Perhaps they will never know how close they came to success. The real champion gives all he has and then gives just that little extra bit more which makes the difference. A strength beyond one's self does not come, however, until one's whole soul is immersed in purpose, in desire, in faith.

How about your objectives for teaching? Are you able to tie your daily lessons into some phase of your over-all objective? When you counsel students does your objective have any influence upon your approach? Does your out-of-class conduct reflect your well-defined objectives?

Certainly in every teacher's day there come clouds of doubt and discouragement which obscure the goal. On other occasions it appears as if the fog literally rolls in to thwart a noble purpose. Even a master teacher cannot see immediate results from his efforts, but must chart the true course and not be deterred therefrom. Occasionally, the sun breaks through just long enough to discern a heart warmed through his labors, a soul walking with renewed faith because he cared, and the hills ahead seem not quite so steep, not so dark-shrouded as he contemplates these things.

Life is made up of many objectives--some of little importance, others of eternal consequence. We must first learn the difference, and then utilize our full energies in their accomplishment.

THE HILLS AHEAD

> The hills ahead look hard and steep and high,
> And often we behold them with a sigh;
> But as we near them, level grows the road.
> We find on every slope, with every load,
> The climb is not so steep, the top so far,
> The hills ahead look harder than they are.
>
> And so it is with troubles, though they seem great
> And men complain and fear and hesitate,
> Less difficult the journey than we dreamed,
> It never proves as hard as once it seemed;
> There never comes a hill, a task, a day,
> But as we near it, easier the way.
>
> --Douglas Malloch

* * * *

IDEALS

A school teacher was trying to impress upon her young students the contributions of great men in history. At the close of the discussion, she asked each student to write down the name of the person who, in his opinion, was the greatest living American. The answers ranged from presidents to sports heroes, but all were men of national renown. However, one name submitted caused the teacher to question the student further, as she was not familiar with the accomplishments of the individual. The name scrawled in childish script was that of the young boy's older brother.

Whether you realize it or not, you are someone's ideal. It is not a responsibility all would choose, but is one none can shun. Man has always felt the need for an ideal, a goal to follow, and whether the ideal takes the form of one whose virtues are worthy of emulation is not always paramount in the thinking of a child. To discern true greatness, then, becomes the task of the parent or teacher, and to be worthy of a child's ideal becomes the challenge to all.

Carl Schurtz has said:

"Ideals are like stars; you will not succeed in touching them with your hands, but like the seafaring man on the desert waters, you choose them as your guides, and following them, you reach your destiny."

* * * *

LET PEACE PREVAIL

With the Yuletide season we once again join in singing the songs of "Peace on Earth," "Joy to the World," and our voices echo a "Merry Christmas" in the crisp December air. Such phrases and songs are generations old, but the little thought we give to their meaning makes them as sounding brass and tinkling cymbals.

All America prays for peace, but too frequently we think in terms of peace only as an international problem. We view it as a utopian objective cloaked in austerity as its use comes into the forefront at the conference tables at Geneva. Its personal significance escapes us.

Yet, peace is a very personal thing. Its small flame must be kindled within every human heart before it can become a reality. When you and I are so living the commandments of the Prince of Peace that we can enjoy peace of conscience, it will then be a universal move into our home, our community, and our nation. When such becomes the goal of each and every American, we can then stand as an ensign to all other nations in charting the course to that coveted peace.

LET PEACE PREVAIL

O God, this Christmas Eve let peace prevail.
Let love abound for all beneath Thy sky;
Let hearts lift up hosannas to Thy name,
And weary souls have strength to live, not die.

O, give us hope and faith to seek Thee out.
Teach us how to find Thee. Bring us near.
Let us know the wonder of Thy love,
And may our hearts know naught of hate and fear.

O God, this night we pause to seek afresh
The path Thy Son trod. Guide us then aright,
And may our faith, like lanterns in the dark,
Lead us on to everlasting light.

* * * *

"LEAVE US NOT TO SOW ALONE. . . ."

Is there one among us who does not note with pleasure the changing season? Pert pussy willows bring spring's first promise; colorful crocuses and daffodils nod reassurance of the end of winter chills; and the farmer turns his thoughts and hands to the soil.

How careful and painstaking are his methods of soil preparation for the planting of grain. Experience with the seed and season has taught him the most advantageous time to sow.

As the good farmer knows the soil and the seed, so must a good teacher know his students, know when to grasp the opportunity to say the right thing at the right time to reach the wayward child; know how to nurture and encourage the shy student who feels as if others are crowding him from the light, the right to grow.

Great is the responsibility of all who teach, for we learn from the Master Teacher "good seed bringeth forth good fruit"; thus we, too, must prepare well the seeds we sow. Unless the inspiration of the Lord is invoked for this preparation, we can expect the seeds of a full and useful life to fall on barren soil, to be lost among the rocks and crags of misunderstanding, or, having fallen on shallow ground, take root briefly but become dwarfed because of the lack of life-giving light.

Though we must prepare the seeds, others have gone before us to make ready the soil. Each eager, youthful face holds great promise for our planting. Each has come to our class enhungered and needing to be filled. See that they leave refreshed, having tasted of the bread of life, and having drunk deeply from the fountains of living water, because we, the sowers, are equipped, and know our students as the farmer knows the soil.

> Thou who knowest all our weakness
> Leave us not to sow alone,
> Bid thine angels guard the furrows
> Where the precious grain is sown.
>
> Till the fields are crowned with glory,
> Filled with mellow-ripened ears.
> Filled with fruits of life eternal
> From the seed we sowed in tears.
> --From the hymn, "We Are Sowing"

* * * *

"LIVES OF GREAT MEN. . . ."

Life is spent in the pursuit of success. What means success to one may be regarded as failure by another; the basic difference lies in the true value of the objective. For our purposes, let us consider the man a success who has attained greatness of character.

One who is great never resigns to defeat, but rises every time he falls. In the annals of history, the names of Lincoln and Washington are usually associated with this term. An analysis of their lives seems to point up that their greatness is attributed to the fact that they were firm in their belief that their cause was right, and they expended all of their energies to prove it.

Many of us merely "window-shop" our way through life. We are ever seeking an "easy bargain" but never buying because the price of greatness is always high. Consequently, many of us are lured to purchase a substitute, a counterfeit reality, and thus miss the joy and satisfaction of true accomplishment. Perhaps proper motivation is lacking because our goals are not well defined, and thus we do not expend our full potential in their attainment.

As Washington's weary troops faced a bitter winter with inadequate clothing and rations at Valley Forge, he knew the course he must then pursue. After exhausting all human effort, he sought the guidance of Him who rules in all the affairs of men.

When the dark clouds of the Civil War hung low, President Lincoln was asked: "Do you never fear that the Lord may not be on our side?"

"Sir," he said, "I am not worried as to whether the Lord is on my side, so long as I am sure that I am on the Lord's side."

> Lives of great men all remind us
> We can make our lives sublime,
> And departing, leave behind us
> Footprints in the sands of time.
> --Longfellow

* * * *

IN SEARCH OF TRUTH

We fear that which we do not understand, but with the proper application of knowledge, fear is dispelled by truth.

The powerful forces of nature which our pagan predecessors feared, an enlightened generation has come to know as electricity. Columbus did not believe that the world was flat. Against the prevailing belief of his time, he set sail for the "New World." Galileo developed an instrument through which he could view planets not visible to the naked eye, and he was branded insane. The great French physician, Laennac, invented the stethoscope, and for so doing was committed to a mental institution where he died a miserable death. After the First Vision the Prophet Joseph Smith advanced concepts so revolutionary to Christendom that his life's blood was shed by his enemies in defiance of these truths.

Because the world has not been ready to accept these truths, many have suffered persecution, but this has not changed the eternal verities.

Was Christ just speaking idle words when he said, "Know the truth and the truth shall make you free"? Free from what? Free from fear, from ignorance and superstition. Truth paves the way for free exercise of thought and action in every sphere of life.

We have the Gospel truths to teach, the truths for which others have died, forsaken family, friends, and country, and pioneered the long, dusty road, that they might be established on a firm foundation. But ours is not an easy task. Each day these same truths are on trial anew, and through our guiding influence must triumph over skeptical or agnostic views of men. Inspire your students with a thirst for knowledge and a love of truth, that they might know that truth is its own reward and the price paid is never too high.

* * * *

VISION IS MORE THAN SIGHT

Have you ever been on a sight-seeing trip with a blind person? Recently a tour group to Hawaii included such a lady and, surprisingly, many were unaware of her handicap until the tour neared completion. Her traveling companions observed the tender consideration shown by her husband, and thought it an unusual manifestation of companionship.

Those who knew commented, "With so much beauty on every hand, what a pity to be unable to see." Others lamented, "A sheer waste of money." But their pity was soon replaced with admiration, and at length they became aware that she saw at least as much as they saw, and understood, discerned, and enjoyed much more.

It has been said that "one who will not dream has no advantage over one who cannot; and one who will not see is often blinder than one who cannot."

How is your vision? Fortunately, science has done much to improve defective eye sight, but many with unimpaired vision walk in total darkness oblivious of the panoramic view around them. How long has it been since you climbed a mountain, or stopped to stand in awe before the beauty and majesty of a sunset?

Have you had your spiritual eyes checked lately? How do you view the world from your soul-windows? Do you look upon your fellowmen as fool mortals? Or as gods in embryo? Frequently those who are near-sighted become so involved in their work-a-day world that they do not raise their vision to behold the glorious view of the eternities. Conversely, there are those whose malady is far-sightedness, who overlook the joys and blessings provided in their earthly home, and constantly yearn for a haven unlike their own. Herein they err, for the Gospel teaches that heaven hereafter is merely a projection of heaven earned in mortality.

Others have only a mild astigmatism which merely requires a slight adjustment of their spiritual lens. Though easily corrected, its effects can become serious if not given immediate attention.

Wise is he who, having sight, possesses the full vision of life.

* * * *

"ALL HOODS MAKE NOT MONKS"--Shakespeare

The sun hung like a speck on the golden horizon as a farm boy returned home after a long day in the fields. The hours and days and weeks seemed all merged together as each dawn brought the same tasks as the previous day. The monotony of his life was broken, however, as he dreamed upon the distant house with the "golden windows." He was confident the owner was very wealthy, that every night the sounds of music and laughter of happy people filled its spacious halls. Almost unconsciously he prayed that some day he might be rich, and experience a new, exciting life. At the moment, however, his greatest desire was to see the house with the gleaming windows.

He arose one morning, just as the sun began shooting slim rays of amber on the eastern horizon. This would be the day, he thought. He would go to the house with the golden windows!

The hike was much longer and more difficult than he had supposed, but the curiosity and anticipation of youth spurred him onward. It was evening before he reached the house, and eagerness gave way to disappointment as he realized that the windows were not gold, but plain glass. Shattered were his dreams of the festive halls!

Heartsick, he turned homeward, and his footsteps were heavy and slow. As the sun raced to its setting, he saw, silhouetted in the western sky, his own home with windows illumined with golden light.

Countless lives are spent in search of golden windows. We might call them by another name--glamour, social prestige, or a job that will put us on "easy street." Individual concepts may differ, but all agree that our modern world presents countless "golden windows" to blind one's vision of the diamonds in his own back yard.

Won't you take time to count your many blessings? As you become truly grateful, pastures cease to be greener and taller across the fence and your own becomes as velvet to your touch.

MY FRIEND'S HOME

"My friend has a beautiful home," I said,
Then I stopped, why that's not true--
For the porch is sagging and the paint is gone,
And the roof lets the rain seep through.
To others it must appear ugly--

Just another house, old and gray,
But I'd seen the glow of love within
I was blind to its outer decay.
I'd seen the windows, wide to the sun,
The old fashioned garden of flowers.
The open hearth, the winding stairs,
The beauty of evening hours.
I'd seen the very soul of the place,
Fresh and sweet as the ocean foam
And the house may be shabby, ugly and old,
But they've still got a beautiful home!

Lay not up for yourselves treasures upon earth, where moth and rust doth corrupt, and where thieves break through and steal; But lay up for yourselves treasures in heaven, where neither moth nor rust doth corrupt, and where thieves do not break through nor steal; For where your treasure is, there will your heart be also.--Matt. 6:19-21

* * * *

A TEACHER'S GIFT

Just for a moment, suppose that this were your last year of teaching, that you were to be separated from your students for the rest of your life. There would be no exchange of letters, no newspapers or radio, carrying account of graduation, marriage, or other activities. Not a very pleasant thought, is it? Were you given such a decree, what parting gift would you desire to leave that would be of value to them throughout their lives?

Such a difficult choice actually came to one Great Teacher. What weighty, deliberate thoughts must have been His as He worked with saw and plane in those thirty preparatory years! He knew that His days were numbered, and that His ministry among men would be cruelly shortened by the cry, "Crucify him!"

He took his classroom with him, to the shores of Galilee, to the Temple, to the Upper Room, and to the mountain top. His students were the learned Scribes, Pharisees, Rabbis, and the humble fishermen, shepherds, or people from the streets. With a full realization of the nearness of Gethsemane, His every word contained the bread of life; even His writing in the sand had purpose.

He, too, desired to leave a gift with his students, his disciples, a gift that would be an anchor to them when the tempests of life were almost tearing their soul moorings from their foundations. His only gift was the gift of truth, which encompassed a testimony of His divine manhood, His mission, His relationship to the Father, and His promise of eternal life.

This Christmas season, won't you share this priceless gift with your students? No matter what your life span, the season of teaching and learning is short, indeed. Teach and live as did the Master Teacher, and both you and your students will be fortified for life and will possess the greatest gift of all--a testimony of the truth.

> I gave a beggar from my store of wealth
> Some gold. He spent the shining ore,
> And came again, and yet again
> Still cold and hungry as before.
>
> I gave a thought, and through that thought of mine
> He found himself, the man, supreme, divine.
> Fed, clothed, and crowned with blessings
> Manifold. And now he begs no more.

* * * *

LOOK UP TO THE LIGHT!

The elevator was crowded with last minute shoppers, and the operator's request "Move to the back" seemed to be the trigger that set off a downpour of tears from a little boy who held tightly to his mother's skirt. The elevator's quick movement accelerated the child's screams, but above them the mother's calm, clear voice was heard saying, "Don't be afraid. Look up to the light!" The crying ceased as quickly as it had begun. Adults and child raised their eyes heavenward, and a deluge of thoughts accentuated the mute, close atmosphere.

How frequently we play the role of the child and clutter our minds with fears, doubts, and uncertainties of the day, which real or unreal might take on correct proportions if we would but "look up to the light." When one becomes head and shoulders above his fellows spiritually, is it not because he faces the sun rather than turns his back on the source of light? Such a spiritual giant was the brother of Jared as he prepared for his journey into the wild and pathless wilderness. Ridiculing scoffers did not deter him from his mission. The Savior's words, "I am the light of the world," must have echoed and re-echoed in his ears, and when he had done all humanly possible for complete preparation, it was a natural thing he did in requesting more light in order to carry forth the will of the Lord.

His prayer was heard, the stones were illuminated by the touch of the finger of God, and the vessels he had prepared were filled with light.

Every soul must traverse unknown paths, and each has need of guidance. With head erect and full purpose in view, all may receive the reassurance of a kind and benevolent Father who pleads, "Look up, look up to the light!"

And I said to the man who stood at the gate of the year,
"Give me a light that I may travel safely into the unknown."
And he said, "Go, and put thy hand into the hand of God.
It shall be better than a light, and safer than a known way."
--New Year's Message from King George V, 1930

* * * *

THE PRICE OF GENIUS

The auditorium was hushed and dark. The visitors at Forest Lawn had been prepared for the spectacle they were about to see. The rich curtains parted, and bit by bit the stained glass representation of DeVinci's "Last Supper" came into full view. Sharp, quick flashes of sunlight played upon the face of one apostle, then another, until weary of its play, the light rested on the central figure of Christ. The minute detail of His kindly face and eyes appeared framed, as it were, by the vivid color and texture of his flowing hair and beard. The heavy silence which fell like a shroud upon the spectators was broken by one who exclaimed, "How wonderful is genius!" Others joined in the assertion.

Yes, such rare talent is enviable, but too few of us ponder the hours, and years, and lives spent in preparation for one such masterpiece. Brunelleschi devoted 35 years to carving the golden doors in Florence, Italy; Michelangelo worked ceaselessly, lying on his back for five years to give life and form to the mosaic tiles in the dome of St. Peter's basilica. And people exclaim, "How wonderful is genius!"

Every one of our Father's children is endowed with a spark of deity, genius in embryo. It may seek expression in music, in science, in sculpture, in poetry, in teaching, or, as is often the case, it never finds expression. Many there are who go through life content to follow the path lit by another's lantern, never daring to strike out with only their own resources and the inspiration of Him who gave them life. Thus the surface of their potential productivity is not even scratched by a personal awareness of their own capacity. They are the masses, who sit smug and satisfied to boast a noble heritage, failing to realize that such a gift is to be earned by each individual.

Would you like to create a work of art to live through the eternities? If so, you must be willing to devote the time and effort necessary for thorough preparation of mind and body. Such is the price of genius, of real art, of all masterpieces.

As you stand before the Great Judge to give account of the talents loaned, fortunately He will not require a work of art which has received the acclaim of men, but more acceptable will be a life well lived, a soul matured through varied experience in earnest effort, and tempered by love, a faith in God, in self, and in others. Such a life is a masterpiece, a work of art, and surely will earn the plaudit, "Well done, thy good and faithful servant."

* * * *

ALL THE WORLD'S A STAGE . . . .

> All the world's a stage, and all
> The men and women merely players.
> They have their exits and their entrances
> And one man in his time plays many parts. . .
> --Shakespeare

So you're an actor. Does that startle you? Perhaps you shun the title, remembering the "rogue" in the current movie; but you acquiesce to your title as you envision the "hero" who is more to your liking. One doesn't often play both parts, for though all are cast in multiple roles in this great human drama, one cannot be truly effective if any of them are in serious conflict.

Your particular role is unique, because as a teacher greater versatility and quality performance is demanded of you. It is hoped that you fit rather naturally and well the part of parent, Church worker, community builder--such characterizations are taken for granted by the "critics" who meet in your classroom.

But what of the "other" roles in which you are called to portray the wisdom of Solomon, the strength of Samson, the faith of David? You must know all the cues, for these lines must be flawless and performed without prompting. You cannot ad lib, for to do so might "take you out of character." You must be able to discern the real tragedy or comedy in the drama of life.

"The show must go on!" is the cry echoed by your eager, responsive, but critical audience. You may become weary of the long acts, but the rules call for no intermission in the part you play. They expect a twenty-four hour daily performance--all inspiring. They will not be deceived by your portrayal, and can readily detect whether you fit best the role of "The Disciple" or a "Shylock" who demands his pound of flesh. In your classroom production, you may teach the sanctity of the home and the importance of spiritualized family life, but the critics still may know that "on the stage he was a natural, simple, affecting. 'Twas only when he was off, he was acting." (Goldsmith)

Ponder the scope of your influence. Have you ever been faced with a greater challenge? You may never see your name in colored lights on a marquee, but perhaps you will find that the real "Oscars" are ofttimes awarded in more subtle ways and in the confidence of a child's heart.

> To wake the soul by tender strokes of art,
> To raise the genius, and to mend the heart;
> To make mankind, in conscious virtue bold
> Live o'er each scene, and be what they behold.
> --Pope

* * * *

BE YOUNG THIS SPRING

I approve of a youth that has something of the old man, so I am no less pleased with an old man that has something of the youth. He that follows this rule may be old in body, but can never be old in mind.--Cicero

Since the beginning of time the attributes of youth have apparently been most elusive and ever desired. The Spaniard, Ponce de Leon, traveled halfway around the world in search of the "Fountain of Youth." He claimed success in his quest and, had his discovery been authentic, the story of mankind from the year 1500 to the present would, no doubt, have been much different.

No matter how difficult those teenage years, we seem to constantly reflect upon them as the "happiest time of our lives" and recall that we were then full of hopes, dreams, aspirations, and life was a great new experience. Thus approaching middle-age and old age becomes something of a stigma to be postponed as long as possible, and we feel a sense of pity for those apparently "resigned" to acceptance of their declining youth. I followed this school of thought until the theory was proven wrong.

I was waiting for a bus to take me to work when I first met Brother Brown. He was resting heavily on a cane and his gnarled, strong hands bespoke a life of hard work in the out-of-doors, despite the crippling effects of arthritis. I observed him and mused, "How sad and unkind is old age." We met on that same corner each morning for over a year, and in that time I came to know a man whose body portrayed the three quarters of a century he had lived, but whose mind was ever an inspiration to me. His blue-gray eyes twinkled with enthusiasm as we discussed the current football race. He was an avid sports fan, and could always tell who "muffed" the play or missed the signal. He was anxious for the next election, and made me shamefully aware of the items I missed reading in the newspaper. He loved the youth of his ward, and apparently they reciprocated as he was frequently sought after to speak at their various meetings. He was eager to relate a visit with his numerous grandchildren, who were all "tops."

Brother Brown had a realistic philosophy of life. He said, "You die a little every day unless you learn something every day." His objective, then, was to "live a little every day" by expanding his scope of knowledge. Brother Brown will leave this life with many hopes and aspirations fulfilled and unfulfilled, but he will ever be young.

The "Fountain of Youth" is within your reach. Be young this spring!

* * * *

LEST WE FORGET....

The story is as old as time, and history continues to repeat itself from generation to generation.

The Children of Israel had miraculously been delivered from the chains of their captors. The Egyptian yoke which had burdened their lives for 400 years had been heavy, indeed. At last they were a free people, free agents unto themselves, free now to pursue their journey to their Promised Land. Yet how bitter proved the dregs of their first fruits of freedom!

Moses had gone up on Mount Sinai to inquire further of the Lord. Aaron and Joshua had been left in charge of the camp. The children of Israel wearied of the absence of their great leader, saying, "Make us gods, which shall go before us, for as for this Moses. . . we know not what is become of him." (Exodus 32:23) They prevailed upon Aaron to make a god whom they could see, touch, and worship. Thus they returned to all manner of idolatry and wickedness. They had forgotten the goodness of the God of Abraham, Isaac, and Jacob, at whose hand they had been delivered from the Red Sea, at whose hand they had been provided manna while in the pathless wilderness, whose power they had seen manifest in turning a reed into a serpent and back into a reed. They had forsaken the God of their fathers!

How could they so soon forget? This query and countless others are indignantly asked by succeeding generations who deride the weak faith of a driven people. Rare, if ever, is the finger of scorn pointed at self.

Have we not known the painful fetters of spiritual bondage? Have we not strained beneath the yoke of oppression or sin? Have we not also labored in vain for "the meat which perisheth?" Has not a kind and benevolent Father led us from darkness into light? Has He not lifted His cup of "living water" to quench our parched souls? Has not his protecting mantel comforted and sustained us in time of sickness and pestilence? Have we not witnessed the serpents of fear, doubt, and despair, devoured by His Word? Yet mankind today, "like the pyramids themselves, doting with age, have forgotten the names of their founders." (Fuller)

This is a month of remembrance, a time to reminisce on many events, many times, and many seasons. Let us recall Israel's later history as well as its prophetic destiny, and realize that we too, are Israel, chosen of the Lord. By exercising a living faith in the God of Abraham, Isaac, and Jacob, we, too, may ascend the heights from which we may ultimately see in vista vision, our promised land. We will not then be found guilty of the poet's claim:

> Our God and soldier we alike adore
> When at the brink of ruin, not before;
> After deliverance both, alike requited
> Our God forgotten, and our soldiers slighted.
> --Quarles

Let us, therefore, examine our own hearts, lest we forget!

Conducted by
the Unified
Church School System

"Unto every man..."

by Hermine Briggs Horman

LDS Department of Education

"Now the Lord had shown unto me, Abraham, the intelligences that were organized before the world was; and among all these there were many of the noble and great ones;

"And God saw these souls that they were good, and he stood in the midst of them, and he said: These I will make my rulers; for he stood among those that were spirits, and he saw that they were good; and he said unto me: Abraham, thou art one of them; thou wast chosen before thou wast born." (Abraham 3:22-23.)

What a dull world this would be if every man and woman were the same in feature, stature, ability, likes, and dislikes! It was never intended to be so. In his wisdom our Heavenly Father has given unto each of his children to develop in his own way, in his own time. Yet how often does the shortsightedness of men endeavor to distort this pattern by setting a universal pace for all, regardless of the innate abilities or personal desires of the individual! Whether one is a professional teacher, a community leader, or lays claim to the "teacher" title only at Church functions, there are certain fundamental factors of which he should be cognizant if he would "really teach." Henry Van Dyke has given us a little insight into the "ideal teaching" which will aid our basic understanding:

"And what of teaching? Ah, there you have the best rewarded of all vocations. Dare not to enter it unless you love it. For the vast majority of men and women it has no promise of wealth or fame, but they to whom it is dear for its own sake are among the nobility of mankind. I sing the praise of the Unknown Teacher. . . .

"Famous educators plan new systems of pedagogy, but it is the Unknown Teacher who delivers and guides the young. He lives in obscurity and contends with hardship. For him no trumpets blare, no chariots wait, no golden decorations are decreed. He keeps the watch along the borders of darkness and leads the attack on the trenches of ignorance and folly. Patient in his duty, he quickens the indolent, encourages the eager, and steadies the unstable. He communicates his own joy and learning and shares with boys and girls the best treasures of his mind. He lights many candles which in later years will shine back to cheer him. This is his reward.

"Knowledge may be gained from books; but the love of knowledge is transmitted only by personal contact. No one has deserved better of the Republic than the Unknown Teacher. No one is more worthy to be enrolled in a democratic aristocracy—king of himself and servant of mankind."

A prominent contemporary educator, G. H. Reavis, has penned a satire which cleverly points up problems which may exist in school situations.

The Animal School

"Once upon a time the animals had a school. The curriculum consisted of running, climbing, and swimming, and all the animals took all the subjects.

"The duck was good in swimming, better in fact than his instructor, and he made passing grades in flying, but he was practically hopeless in running. Because he was low in this subject he was made to stay in after school and drop his swimming class in order to practise running. He kept this up until he was only average in swimming. But average is acceptable, so nobody worried about that except the duck.

"The eagle was considered a problem pupil and was disciplined severely. He beat all the others to the top of the tree in the climbing class, but he had his own way of getting there.

"The rabbit started at the top of the class in running, but he had a nervous breakdown and had to drop out of school on account of so much makeup in swimming.

"The squirrel led the climbing class, but his flying teacher made him start his flying lessons from the ground instead of from the top of the tree down, and he developed charley horses from over-exertion at the take-off and began getting C's in climbing and D's in running.

"The practical prairie dogs apprenticed their offspring to a badger when the school authorities refused to add digging to the curriculum."

Is it not somewhat of a paradox that we readily accept the limitations and abilities of our animal friends, the "lesser of God's creations," but fail to acknowledge individual differences in our fellow beings? Because many of those who educate the mind have seemingly turned blind eyes to this truth, we find in our modern culture a frustrated society, clamoring to be that which they are not, or cannot become, or perhaps were never meant to be. The result is chaos and confusion, and an environment which lends itself to the ways of war rather than peace.

As we take the chalk in hand and face the eager, responsive group before us, we will, if we are to touch their lives, accept the fact that we are not all created equal; *we will accept every child where he is, as he is,* and make certain that each has equal opportunity to find his better self. We can then begin to formulate objectives which will be beneficial both to the teacher and to the learner. May I suggest the following plan of attack, which will work equally well with a group studying the scriptures or a 4-H project:

Objectives of Teaching

Our method of approach should be:
1. Conduct-centered and not activity-centered.
2. Built around personality needs.
3. Reveal the world as it is and not partially or superficially.
4. Meet individual differences and not just get by with them.
5. Evaluate pupil progress in terms of personality development as well as academic achievement.
6. Provide sensory experiences to relieve tensions and to crystallize attitudes into dynamic moral behavior.
7. Develop attitudes that are adjustive to an ever-changing world.
8. Teach followership as well as leadership.
9. Help students live a more abundant life, for "Men are, that they might have joy."

With realistic objectives, the teacher has a better concept of his own role in the learning process. Some argue that they would rather not "narrow" their scope of teaching by an established protocol, while the professional educators find the "defined" field one of unlimited challenge.

"I shall not make the dreams, the aspirations, the ambitions, the hopes of these strong, rested, restless, curious children all come true. But I shall wake in them new dreams, new visions of Canaans that each by effort may call his own, and arriving there find the joy of labor and success. (*Continued on page 547*)

"Unto Every Man"

(*Continued*)

"To better God's work!
What audacity, and yet
His will
And my privilege."
—Thomas H. Briggs

Understand our "Samenesses"

An acknowledgment of the fact that there are redheads, brunettes, and blondes in our group should not limit our building upon certain fundamental "samenesses" which are common to every class. There are techniques of teaching to which all personalities respond, i. e., the three basic drives must be satisfied:

1. *The need for belonging.* This implies the universal need to be loved, to be wanted, and to become a part of the group. Perhaps this is one of the most difficult needs to satisfy, since according to psychologists, it is frequently when a child least deserves love that he is most in need of it! But have it he must!

2. *The need for a sense of achievement.* Each student must experience a consistent number of successes. These may be major or minor in nature, but if he is to achieve, he must be made to feel that he is progressing. Methodology comes forcibly into play in this area. The use of a question can be most effective. The good teacher knows that there are few "wrong" answers. "Perhaps you are thinking of the John Jones of which we spoke yesterday—let me restate the question." The instructor can always re-word, giving sufficient clues to insure a correct answer, if the particular student needs this type of encouragement. "Who is buried in Grant's tomb?" may not always be a facetious question! Conversely, the questions or other requirements should be geared to fit the capabilities of the student. Unless the abilities of the individual are challenged there is little motivated learning.

3. *The need for recognition.* Everyone loves to hear his name spoken publicly. Even the shyest among us beams with pride when the smallest achievement is given recognition. Meeting this need helps establish a place, or "status" for the individual, and can be a part of every phase of our student-teacher relationships.

A well-told story, demonstration, or example has universal appeal to the young and old alike. After a concept is taught, repetition or "re-experiencing" cements that learning, *if the value of it has been clearly defined.*

If the influence of a teacher does not extend beyond the classroom, he has not taught, and his students have not learned. Unless that which we teach has meaning and importance in the everyday life of the student, we have wasted both our time and his. It is not important that the Church history student memorize dates and places, and how many Saints made up the first handcart company—but it is of vital importance that he understand that during a certain period of our country there was a cause deemed great enough that thousands left their families, friends, and worldly possessions, to endure hardship, conquer a wilderness, and even give their lives rather than deny the truths of the restored gospel. This type of knowledge has meaning. It fosters power sufficient to change the life of a student! Teach facts, yes, but make them live by teaching feelings, too!

We can vary the approach, but must always be enthusiastic about the thoughts we desire to convey. "A passive recipient is a two-gallon jug. Whenever the teacher does not first excite inquiry, first prepare the mind by waking it up to a desire to know, and if possible to find out by itself, but proceeds to think for the child, and to give him the results before they are desired, or before they have been sought for, he makes the mind of a child a two-gallon jug, into which he may pour just two gallons, but no more. And if day after day he should continue to pour in, day after day he may expect that what he pours in will run over."
—David P. Page

Coping with the "Differences"

Since literature is replete with helps for the average student, let us confine our discussion to those who do not fit the norm of the classroom—those students who are exceptionally slow or unusually bright. Before remedial steps are taken for these students, we would do well first to endeavor to understand the reasons behind their performance. In addition to the clinical tests made available through the schools for this purpose, possibly the greatest aid to the teacher is his power of observation. Much can be learned about a boy or girl if special note is made of their clothes, their friends, their speech, their nicknames, and their interests. And of course, a home visit is of inestimable value in understanding the "whole" child.

The Bright Student

This student can either be a troublemaker in the classroom or a valuable teacher-helper, depending on the climate set for him. If his abilities and interests are not constantly challenged, he becomes restless and bored, and thus seeks expression through disrupting others' studies. One alert to his needs might:

1. Give him leadership of small groups. (This might be a group of others like himself or slower students.)

2. Assign him special projects which are independent of the rest of the class.

3. Encourage him to go beyond the scope of that required by the class as a whole.

4. Counsel with his parents to assure that his out-of-school activities are also varied and meaningful.

5. Avoid "busy work" such as chapter outlining and excessive note-taking.

The Slow Learner

This child, like the bright student, is frequently the cause behind problems in classroom discipline. Too often the pace set for the group is beyond his capacity and speed. We must ever be aware that "every child is an individual and he travels by his own tailor-made time schedule." (Arnold Gesell.) Perhaps the following suggestions will be helpful:

1. Group the slow learner with those of similar capabilities.

2. Explain each principle to him in more than one way, then repeat it frequently.

3. Develop full sensory teaching techniques so that if he fails to respond to reading, he can understand the material visually presented.

4. Praise him frequently for the slightest progress noted. Perhaps the best he can do is write his name, but if so, find a way of sincerely acknowledging improvement in this feat. He must enjoy at least one "success experience" daily if he is to be motivated to learn.

As teachers in the vineyard of the Lord we must realize that there is more to a student than mind or intellect. We must explore every aspect of his personality in order to help him become a useful citizen. "Unto every man he gave, according to his several ability," and it must be within the reach of all God's children to live the abundant life. To assist students in the achievement of this goal poses the greatest challenge to those who teach!

APPENDIX D--ONE TIME CELEBRITIES

Twins For S.L. Family
2 More Children Makes 6 In 4 Years

By STEVE HALE
Deseret News Staff Writer

A Salt Lake mother who says she feels like "the little old lady who lived in a shoe" really isn't.

Mrs. Phares T. Horman isn't an old lady and she isn't living in a shoe.

The reason she feels that way is that she has six children—all born during the past four years.

The newest twins, Phares, a boy, and Shelley, a girl, were born just Jan. 17. That was just about the time the Hormans were readying to move into the house that Phares built—at 3481 S. 3530 East.

Mr. Horman is a civil engineer who works for the U.S. Bureau of Reclamation.

Mrs. Horman, a native of Magrath, Alta., Canada, was at one time a member of the Young Women's Mutual Improvement Assn. General Board, Church of Jesus Christ of Latter-day Saints.

The breakdown on their family goes this way: Heather, 4; twins Karen and Susan, 3; Becky, 2; and the newest twins.

Little Phares was the last one born—the family's first boy.

"My husband's still walking on clouds," said Mrs. Horman.

A television repairman visiting the Horman household recently inquired if Mrs. Horman were operating a day nursery.

"Yes," she sighed, "but we operate at night, too."

The older children are a help. So is Mr. Horman.

But Mrs. Horman is happy her mother, Mrs. Emelie S. Briggs is visiting from Canada just the same.

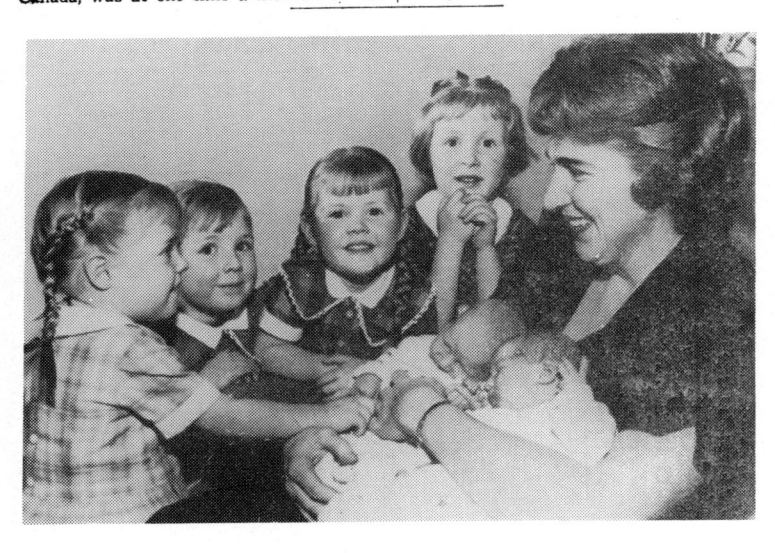

414 HEART STRINGS

DESERET NEWS
World of Women

Thursday, December 8, 1966   D 1

Deseret News photos by Ray G. Jones

Mrs. Phares Horman and her little daughter, Becky, put finishing touches on their Christmas cookie tree. Try making one yourself.

round cookies, then the largest star cookie, 2 more round cookies, another large star, and so on, using the stars in graduating sizes, with the smallest as the top.

When all branches are assembled, use a cake decorator and make white frosting snow on each branch and drifts of snow on the base. (You may wish to frost the cookies before assembling either way will do.)

On the point of each star (or just on some of the points) put a little rosette of frosting and place in it a small birthday candle. On the topmost star place a larger candle, and the cookie tree is complete.

To make the tree stand: Use a sturdy piece of wood about 6x6 inches and drill a hole in center. Firmly secure a 15-inch stick or dowel in the hole.

HEART STRINGS   415

A Cookie Tree—
Just For You

By WINNIFRED JARDINE
Deseret News Food Editor

This is the time for a cookie tree . . . this very season . . . this very week (if you're to get it done before the demands get too heavy.)

And our suggestion this year is something a little different, for rather than having cookies hanging from branches, the branches themselves are the cookies!

Yes, this cookie tree is a series of cookie stars made in graduating sizes and heaped over a wooden dowel onto a base, rising 15 inches high to a dainty candle on the tip top.

The recipe for the dough is our favorite cut-out cookie which has provided much delight through the years. A double batch, given below in its entirety, will make all the cookies needed and a little to spare for nibbles along the way.

You may make the star patterns yourself, 8 of them, graduating from 7 to 2½ inches (measuring from one point across to inner point on opposite side).

Or you may send in to the Deseret News (enclosing a self-addressed, stamped envelope) to Cookie Tree, Deseret News, P. O. Box 1257, Salt Lake City, Utah 84110, for a pattern and complete directions.

A cake decorator may be used for drifting snowy frosting onto the branches and base, or 7-minute icing may be piled on with a knife. If the latter is used, let the icing begin to firm up before setting in the candles, so they will hold.

Decorate it otherwise as you might wish, with silver dragees, bits of candied cherries, colored candies, or simply with candles.

Cut out cookie stars to form branches of your tree. Such a merry holiday idea!

Assembling your own cookie tree is really very easy to do, as demonstrated.

Here exactly is how to make this delightful tree:

CHRISTMAS COOKIE TREE

1 cup shortening
1½ cups sugar
2 eggs
1 teaspoon vanilla
1 teaspoon almond extract
4 cups sifted or stirred flour
½ teaspoon salt
1 teaspoon baking powder
⅓ cup milk

Thoroughly cream shortening and sugar. Add eggs and beat well. Add vanilla and almond extracts. Thoroughly stir in sifted dry ingredients alternately with milk. Chill for 1 hour, if desired.

Roll ⅛-inch thick on lightly floured surface. Cut out and bake one cookie the size of the base, then make star-shaped cookies in graduated sizes (measuring from 2½ to 7 inches) making two cookies of each star size (a total of 16 cookies).

Cut out 32 small round cookies (about 1¾ inches in diameter) to go between the star-shaped cookies. Make a hole in center of all cookies before baking (we use the lid of a small extract bottle to make the holes).

Place cookies on lightly greased baking sheets and bake at 375 degrees F. for 12 minutes or until cookies barely begin to go brown.

When cookies are cool, slip the cookie which fits the base over the rod first, then 2

DESERET NEWS Saturday, August 19, 1967   **B3**

A Red Letter Day For Karen Horman

Silken red hair that flowed to her knees was the pride of 7-year-old Karen and her parents, Mr. and Mrs. Phares T. Horman Jr., 3481-3530 East. But a day comes in every young girl's life when a short bob becomes more practical and more grown up. The cut hair has been saved, however, and made into a hairpiece which the mother, who has the same color of hair, will wear until Karen is old enough for it.

QUIET AND PRAY

THE NEW ERA
by April Horman

October 1979

It's a long drive from Magrath, Alberta, Canada, to Calgary, and the torrents of rain pelting the highway didn't make the trip seem any shorter. Most of us were tired, so we stretched out on the seats and mattress in the back of the family van while mom and Grandma Briggs sat up front and talked. I remember thinking we were in the middle of a real cloudburst and then drifting off to sleep.

When I regained consciousness, I ached all over. No wonder. The impact of a violent crash had stuffed me into a small space near the side door. My legs were scraped and bleeding; my breath came convulsively. I seemed to be alone except I could see grandma lying in the wreckage, and I heard moans. Soon strangers pulled me from my painful trap, and I approached grandma, who whispered, "Everything is going to be all right."

Briggs, my 13-year-old brother, had been thrown out the rear door of the van. He said that when he found me I was hysterical. He shook me by the arm to help me get control of myself and told me to quit screaming and pray. I calmed down. And I did pray. He stumbled back to the highway and flagged down a car, even though his arm and collar bone were broken and his head was cut.

Evidently my mother had lost control of the van when it hydroplaned through a large puddle.

---

418 HEART STRINGS

has ...sed the road, ...ed down an embankment, ...n continued forward until ...els hit a culvert and we ...airborne. We crashed ...t and rolled several ...came to rest upright ...ad that led to a ...ther was seriously ...crushed chest ...forehead; she ...the wreckage and ...ved without help. ...not to panic. We ...home on vacation, ...we had been on our ...aunt's new home, we didn't know anyone in the immediate area. (We were later to find out that we were close to Vulcan, a small town about 35 miles from Calgary.) And we weren't where we could be easily seen from the road. But my brother's words stuck in my mind, that I should be quiet and pray. Whenever I did start to get upset and worried, I prayed and felt calm again.

There were two girls in the car Briggs flagged down. They in turn stopped a car with a CB radio, and an ambulance was at the scene in two and a half minutes. We were lucky. There was a small emergency hospital in Vulcan, and we received care quickly.

There was only one phone for patients to use. My mother asked to be wheeled to it. She called my father back in Salt Lake City; then she called my uncle in Calgary, and he came immediately. When he arrived, the first thing mom asked him was if he could find the elders. Approaching the hospital desk to inquire, he was met by two men in their 50s or 60s.

"Has anyone here been asking for elders from the Mormon church?" they asked. "Yes!" he said, and led them to our rooms. They said they had been driving down the road, had seen the Utah license plates on the smashed van, and felt inspired to check at the hospital. They said they were both high priests. Before leaving, they gave a blessing to my brother, my cousin, my mother, and me. We never did find out their names or where they were from, but later we sent a letter to the editor of the local paper in an effort to thank them.

It was in the hospital that we also learned that Grandma Briggs had died at the scene of the accident. But her words of assurance had helped me to understand that she was ready to rejoin grandpa in the spirit world and that she had felt peace in her heart as she passed to the other side.

I learned another important lesson, too. And that is that the Lord does hear and answer prayers, and that he can direct worthy priesthood holders to be in places where they can help others. Though we all suffered serious injuries, we recovered. And the priesthood blessings at a time of need were a great comfort to us. I will always be grateful to those two men who took time to obey a prompting of the Spirit that led them to the hospital, and thankful for the peace that came to my heart when I prayed, telling me everything would be all right.

Illustrated by Paul Mann

horizon

VOL. XVIII NO. 10   SKYLINE HIGH SCHOOL — SALT LAKE CITY, UTAH   APRIL 24, 1980

Briggs To Lead Eagle Cheers

For Briggs Horman cheerleading is more than a social event, it is a position. "Next year we will have a strong squad," says Briggs and adds, "the competition is stiff."

Briggs enjoys all sports and is looking forward to the upcoming year; intending to focus on each individual sport he said, "We need to give more attention to such sports as girls basketball."

"Getting the studentbody involved is important and with a good attitude involved it will get better," said Briggs. He hopes that with this involvement the school will win more games. Briggs supports the statement that school support is a domino effect. Once you have the support of one you gain the aid of another and ultimately massive cooperation.

"The program is worthwhile," says Briggs, and adds, "I expect an exciting year."

Shelly Horman

Shelly Gains WA Victory

"I really want to represent Skyline women in 1980-81, and I hope to increase school spirit," stated victorious Shelly Horman.

Shelly has achieved her goal to become the Women's Representative by stepping in to Skyline's WA position. Shelly plans to increase student body interest in dances. "I want people to really enjoy the dances and the games." She feels that more unity between the grades would greatly improve the school spirit.

This enthusiastic junior is active in choir and band, and is an outstanding student. She enjoys her classes and especially likes poetry. Shelly plans to attend college in California or Hawaii. One of her long-term goals is to become an actress, which is why she is active in drama. "I really like to act and I think it's a great profession and hobby."

Two months ago Shelly decided to run for office, hoping to make her senior year fun and productive. Now she is determined to achieve that goal.

Briggs Horman

420 HEART STRINGS

APPENDIX E--TRIBUTE TO MY CHILDREN AND
MY BROTHERS AND SISTERS

TRIBUTE TO MY CHILDREN AND MY BROTHERS AND SISTERS

Being one of the younger of nine children in our family, my brothers and sisters played an important role in my upbringing. The threads of their lives are also the fabric from which I am made. Similarly, the anecdotal accounts contributed by my children are an integral part of me. Perhaps one lends understanding and credence to the past; the other points bravely to the future. Both have contributed substantially to my joy and growth in the journey. Here I pay tribute to them.

MEMORIES OF GRANDMA BRIGGS
by Karen Horman Phelps

When Grandma stayed at our place she often gave us pennies, sometimes for good behavior, sometimes just because. I asked for Canadian pennies which I deposited in a piggy bank and tried to remember to take to Canada when we went the following summer.

I have great memories of our trips to Canada every summer. Mother liked to visit her hometown and Grandma; of course, we loved to accompany her. We usually got involved in the July 24th parade (mainly because they paid us a quarter to enter, and it was fun). After the parade we went to the fairgrounds where there were children's races and horse races and a softball game. We all entered the footraces and sometimes some of us won. I believe Heather was the fastest runner in the family, and she once won a quarter or fifty cents. We were all jealous! Grandma loved to see us participate in the events of Magrath. She acted as if she were proud of us.

by Becky Horman Ririe

Occasionally when we arrived the front room was full of Hutterites whom Grandma invited in to watch TV while waiting for friends or relatives at the Health Center across the street. TV was forbidden at the colony, so the novelty of it was quite a luxury to them. Grandma usually shared some lemonade or cookies with them, whatever she had. They helped her in her garden. Thinking back, I realize what a large garden she had for just one person, but I believe she enjoyed sharing it with us and countless others. I can still see her bending down, straight-legged, to pull weeds, which she hated with a passion. Her back must have ached as she spent hours hoeing.

I remember the beans, peas, beets and my FAVORITE, spinach, that I helped her pick. Often she rewarded me by sending me to Lila's or Stevenson's store for one of my favorite bars or English Toffee or a Mr. Freeze. I thought it really neat that I could charge on her tab. She never accepted help without some form of payment.

When July 24th came around, our Smith cousins from Calgary joined us in marching in the parade, along with the Ernie Briggs kids who lived in Magrath. By some miracle, costumes were created for each of us. We loved being with our cousins, and Grandma was proud to watch us march by. In the early morning she lined the street in front of her house with chairs so that friends and relatives had a bird's eye view of the parade. I remember the many horses, Indians, and farm equipment in the parade. All were new to me. On Grandma's lawn several tents were pitched, indicating that she had more guests than she had room for in the house. We loved sleeping out but living in like we did at her place. In addition to the tents, telling the Magrath residents that the "Briggs clan was gathering" I liked to think they also knew by the many new cute girls who paraded Main Street. I know my opinion was not shared by the local girls, but it was by some of the guys!

* * * *

A CANADIAN BLIZZARD
by Don Briggs

When Azer Briggs (my father) went to Canada early in the 19th century, he worked for his brother-in-law, John Bradshaw. At the time of this experience he was a young man in his early twenties. He and John had taken a herd of cattle to Lethbridge where they were to be sold. It was a distance of about 26 miles from the ranch at Bradshaw Siding. The sun began to drop slowly in the western horizon and John knew that someone would have to return to the ranch to be with his wife, Emma, Azer's older sister, who was expecting a child.

At this time, it began to snow heavily and, along with the north wind, it soon became evident that a Canadian blizzard was in the making. The cattle were not yet sold, so my father knew that he was that "someone" who was to return to look after his sister.

He told John he would go if he would trade him horses and give him Little Jack, who was John's favorite horse. Little Jack must have been a noble animal for Azer trusted him to take him back safely in a snow storm that would not allow him to see six inches beyond the horse's nose.

As my father recounted the story he said: "I gave Little Jack his head and after what seemed like a long time he stopped at the only fence between Magrath and Lethbridge which was located on the Pot Hole Creek having traveled some 18 or 19 miles from our starting point. I got off the horse and walked for a few minutes up the fence line until I came to the gate. Little Jack had just missed it by about 100 yards in a blinding snow storm. I went through the gate and mounted my horse again. I gave him his head and after traveling another seven or eight miles, he stopped again, this time at the barn door of the ranch."

I include this story of heroism so that my children and my grandchildren, or any of the progeny of Azer Richard Briggs might know of the kind of ancestry from which they are descended--that in knowing about the man he was, they might better know themselves. He was and is a fine, noble and worthy patriarch of the Briggs family, dedicated to his loved ones and to his religion. He was a good friend to all who knew him.

* * * *

THE MAY STORM OF 1903
and Tom Purcell

The Mormon settlers who went to Canada at the turn of the century took cattle and horses with them that they might utilize the great abundance of feed that nature supplied in native grasses, most of which was as high as a horse's belly.

Some of the people in the area were not of the Mormon faith. One dubious character was Tom Purcell. Allegedly he was wanted in the United States. Had he gone back there, he would have been brought to trial and jailed. So he was in Southern Alberta as a fugitive from justice. In about 1899 or 1900, he was running cattle south of Lethbridge at old Fort Whoop-Up which was established by trappers and traders some time earlier. The point of embarkation on the Missouri River was Fort Benton in Montana. Much of the liquor was then sold to the Blood Indians who inhabited the rolling plains east of the Rocky Mountains in Southern Alberta. Later law and order came with the Royal Canadian Mounted Police, who soon made the traffic of liquor unprofitable and Fort Whoop-Up fell into disuse.

At this point in our story, the liquor trade was taken over by the "old outlaw," Tom Purcell, and also a man by the name of Dave

Akers, who ran cattle in the surrounding area and raised vegetables within the old fort. These men had a disagreement over their joint property and one day as Dave Akers was getting on his horse at the corral, Tom Purcell came out of the cabin with his rifle in hand and shot him. Dave Akers was killed on the spot. Tom was brought to trial and given three years for manslaughter. My father told me he was sent to prison on the same train with a young man who stole a calf who was sentenced to seven years. Dad noted the discrepancy of "British Justice."

Tom Purcell served his term and came back to Magrath and began some small scale ranching between Magrath and Bradshaw Siding, where my father was living and working. Dad said that Tom Purcell would point to a cow and tell him that she came home with triplets every spring. The truth of the matter was that she would have one calf and Tom would steal two. This is the background needed to fully appreciate the rest of the story.

The May storm of 1903 was a late spring storm that caught many of the settlers unaware. The livestock that was out on the open prairie drifted with the storm for miles and miles until they came to a river bank or cut bank, when they fell over the precipice and were killed. Some drifted south for many miles and were later found in the United States. Those that were in an enclosure drifted to the farthest southern corner and ultimately froze to death.

At the time of the storm, my father was in Magrath some three miles east of the ranch. He started for home but found the fury of the storm too much for him to travel by horseback. At mid-point in his journey, he was forced to stop at Tom Purcell's cabin and seek shelter. Tom greeted him cordially and invited him to stay the night, since further travel in the storm was out of the question.

My father relates that he spent an uneasy night sleeping next to the "old cut-throat," noting that there were look-holes in each corner of the cabin through which Tom might shoot a rifle to protect himself from his adversaries. He awakened the next morning to find the storm abated, and he completed his journey to the ranch.

* * * *

NOSTALGIA
by Fred A. Briggs

One of the saddest feelings that a person can have is to return to the place of his youth and find that all has changed.

I drove to the farm where I grew up as a boy, where the old farm house still stands, where the huge barn (by my standards) still stands but houses only grain now, not horses as in my day or cows in later years. I had never known this place to be really quiet. There was always the noise of animals even if the family was gone. On this occasion, the only form of life around were a few chickens soon to be picked up by the last tenant, and a scraggly tomcat pursuing his usual tomcat goals. The granaries all stand like guards at a castle, unpainted, like the rest of the buildings, and empty of their golden grain.

In past years, the yard at the farm house was full of machinery of all kinds: tractors, discs, cultivators, rodweeders, trucks, harrows, drills, combine harvesters, plows and other miscellaneous equipment necessary to operate a farm. This time, all that is left are a few rusted pieces of equipment, including a couple of power-take-off combines with their elevators standing like snorkels in the spring Canadian sky. The formerly well-kept corrals and sheds are falling down. Gates which used to be kept shut are now wide open, having no reason to hold in cattle, sheep or hogs that have long since gone to their reward.

I looked out across the acres of ground always so precious to me. There was, of course, activity by the new owner and a lot of planting, weeding and growing. But it wasn't the same at all because I knew that the farm had been sold and was no longer a part of our family or our lives.

On the north side of the half section and on the east side of the same half, in the days of my youth there were two separate pastures, to which, it seemed, I was always taking or bringing back cows or horses. I observed these two areas, not fenced, that will soon be broken to the plow. The part of the farm known as the "80" was sold earlier along with an adjacent 80 acres that my brother purchased thirty years ago. The pond on this property as well as the pond at the farm house property are now dry except after heavy rain or in early spring. The irrigation ditches, so necessary in past years and now no longer needed, are overrun with grass and weeds; and their banks are falling in.

At the time of my youth we had no electricity nor plumbing. The hauling of water, wood and coal was always something of a chore. Those trips to the "john" in the dead of winter at 30 degrees below zero didn't seem to bother me at the time, but I remember we were not interested in reading a magazine; anyway, it was probably out there for other purposes. The huge structure which used to harness the wind to pump water is now merely holding up a yard light, while an electric pump provides the pressured water for the house. The circular mill with its wind-catching vanes has been removed and the upper part seems denuded.

I stood in the large yard and looked to the west. The hill which seemed to dominate that part of the sky somehow looked smaller. I reminisced standing on that hill, where I could see as far as Lethbridge to the northeast, 20 miles distant; eastward to Raymond, 12 miles; to the south the McIntyre Ranch; and to the west to the Blood Indian Reservation and the Rockies' great peaks beyond. The familiar farm homes in the general view from our yard are still there, although some have changed hands. Lloyd Sabey's would never be the same. Stella Karren's, Dave Whitt's, Cliff Whitt's, the Shelton property, Esser's, Louie Felger's, the Horace Ririe property (farmed by Mike Schneyder), Charlie Felger's, Gibbs', Meldrum's, and Hockings' in the distance are the subjects of a bird's-eye view from the hill.

Now, even though my heart is full and I realize that things will never be the same, I also realize that change is not necessarily bad. Without change, there would be no progress.

In the years ahead, as I ply my trade to earn my keep and pay the bills that keep piling up with my family, I hope that I will be able to go back to this farm again and have my memory piqued, that I might relive to some extent the good memories I have of my youth in Southern Alberta.

* * * *

The following poem was written by Beth while undergoing her valiant fight with multiple myaloma in 1991.

MY CELEBRATION
by Elizabeth B. Hackney

And so tonight, I celebrate
The body bright,
Miracle of delight!

The wondrous skin,
The shape within,
Where I begin!

Eternity!
The child that's me,
Unique and free!

The awesome head,
Communion's bed,
In His own image
So He said!

My feet that run
'Til day is done!
My hands that move
And serve and love!

The wondrous eyes
That don't deny,
The laughs and cries
And hopeful sighs!

The mouth that seeks,
And nobly speaks
The soul's best thoughts!

The knees that bend
My thanks to tend,
My ways to mend!

Existence dear,
A gift so near,
I cannot hear

My heart that beats
Dependably.
That's true and kind,
And not resigned
That life's complete!

And so today I celebrate,
And thank my God
He did create
This soul and body that are mine!
Pray, let me use a longer time!

APPENDIX F--FRIENDS FOREVER AND MY "POMES"

ANOTHER SPRING. . . .

Josie Green Knowlton was the lovely mother of good friend, Beverly Knowlton Mercer.

Today they told me, "Josie's gone." It prompted many lovely memories flooding in of the years we had known together. You see, she was the mother of one of my dearest friends. She came into my life when I was adult, but she changed me, nonetheless. She made me feel responsible for her precious Beverly, and told me she didn't worry about her when she was with me. I grew taller in her trust.

Her well-kept yard bespoke her love of nature and beauty. She was the first in the neighborhood to plant the bulbs of fall, and lovely annuals brightened her outdoors. Inside her modest home were ample signs of her educated taste in art and handiwork. An Oriental rug, a piece of Dresden, a Hummel, a Royal Daulton, were but a few of her many "love gifts" she enjoyed sharing with others.

Her piano was stacked with music, old and new, and melodies echoed through the house either of her own making or Beverly's. She loved to sing and instilled in her children an appreciation of music and the arts. The best in literature lined her book shelves. She enjoyed teaching and was well versed in the classics and the Gospel she knew so well.

When she laughed her whole face lit up. She laughed easily and often. Little crinkles appeared around her blue-gray eyes as she recalled a funny story or shared one from her youthful days. Her philosophy was always upbeat and forward looking. Her countenance was happy.

Josie was a people person. When Beverly and Ted were at home, the rafters rang with the voices of many. Their home was always open to friends, and friends they had in abundance. Almost any Sunday their home was the scene of a fireside or informal gathering. Homemade ice cream and cake or cookies "from scratch" were the rule rather than the exception.

She became most animated when talking of the adventures of Ted or Beverly, or of their achievements in their married years. And when talking of grandchildren, she became the typical grandmother! How proud she was of all of you!

Ill health forced Josie to accept a less strenuous life than in her younger years. She loved independence and hung to it tenaciously. She went to the temple frequently when her health permitted, and I am sorry that I did not follow through on my promise to pick her up for that purpose.

I'll miss talking to Josie on the phone--miss her laughter--miss her strength, but as long as Beverly and Ted are here, Josie will always be with us. She is so much a part of them. Her goodness, her fun and laughter, ring through their voices and promise we will all be together again. . . another spring. . . .

With fondest love,
Hermine

* * * *

ODE TO JOAN

Joan Harker Ririe is the mother of Kevin, my son-in-law. She died of polymyositis, a disease which affects the extremities of the body and the respiratory system. We dreamed of sharing the same grandchildren, and it did come to pass, but not while she lived. We loved her dearly.

One of life's greatest blessings is to find a special friend with whom one can communicate spirit-to-spirit. Joan Harker Ririe was of that kind.

Confined largely to her home and wheelchair, she brought the world within her walls that we all might share in its wonder and majesty. From her hand went countless notes of love, praise and encouragement, which usually ended with "but most of all, I treasure your friendship."

The telephone might ring several times a day, just to share a thought, ask a question, or voice concern for someone else, usually terminated with "Have a happy day," or "Be happy like a bird."

Almost any occasion called for a party. She loved entertaining and gift-giving. Her desk was piled high with mail order catalogs from which she chose unique and meaningful gifts for her many recipients. Large or small, each was carefully wrapped in a colorful package of love.

As she daily sat by her card table, each visitor was greeted with a smile and warm handclasp. She was always busy there, writing letters to her missionary sons, her many Canadian sisters and friends, or reading the scriptures, a good book, or studying a recipe book, adding to her large repertoire of gourmet delights. If her facial expression was less than pleasant, it was likely she was "paying bills." She was as meticulous in balancing her books as she was her life.

"I have to be careful what I put into my mind," she said. "It stays there forever, so I must be selective."

If a special poem or story was needed for a particular talk or lesson, Joan usually knew just the one to fill the bill. She had her files, her cupboard and pantry shelves, her life, so well organized that retrieval was miraculous to those who joined in the "find."

Never was the chapel so quiet as when Joan took the microphone in her hand and bore beautiful testimony of the truths she held most dear. There was always expression of gratitude for her many blessings brought to her through others. Tears of love and understanding were mirrored by those of us who listened, for we knew that compassionate service supposedly rendered in her behalf became lessons in patience, long suffering, faith and hope to those who came to give.

Her eyes lit up and tiny wrinkles crinkled her face when friends, young and old, shared a humorous incident. She loved keeping up with the activities of young people. She rejoiced in their successes or wept with them in their disappointments. Involvement was her middle name.

Most of us only knew Joan three short years, but in that time she endeared herself and her family to each and everyone of us. She entered our lives suddenly, and left in much the same way. But none of us will ever be the same since knowing her. Each of us has a little more empathy for one another, love more freely, give thanks more readily, and stand a bit taller because of her. The world and we are better because of Joan.

* * * *

TRIBUTE TO JUNE MEINERS HORMAN

June Meiners Horman was first my friend, my roommate and then my mother-in-law. She died in 1974 after five short years of marriage.

Now may I, Hermine Horman, a former college roommate and long-time friend, and more recently a daughter-in-law, pay tribute to June.

JUNE--the name brings to mind a soft spring breeze filled with the delicate aroma of flowers and blossoming trees; that puts in the mind's eye a mischievous youth with a fishing pole over his shoulder, skipping rocks in a clear mountain stream. JUNE--the name that evokes happiness and laughter and good books read while the camper bumps down the highway, and gales of laughter as she joins the countless grandchildren in a Big Swim at Lake Powell. Always the center of their activity, she led the way to much excitement. For many, she gave them their first swimming lessons.

JUNE--June is a picnic at a roadside table or a turkey dinner in the family home. JUNE--Dad's beautiful, lithe and youthful dance partner, who delighted audiences across the state wherever they performed, be it on the ukulele, mouth organ, the piano or organ, or teaching the hula. JUNE made every performance an occasion.

JUNE--She's Love and Beauty and Spirituality, whether in a formal dress or in levis--she's Prose and Music and Poetry, wearing sneakers; she's a Child, a Woman, a Wife, a Sweetheart, a "Grandma June" and a Wonderful Friend--to all of us she's Inspiration--to follow where she led.

* * * *

JOHN HEIDENREICH

My association with John Heidenreich spanned a period of 18 years. I first met him when he was hired by the Church Department of Education as a Seminary teacher. I was aware that he was a former Congregational minister of 26 years, and a recent convert to Mormonism. I was immediately attracted to this middle-aged man, both from his background and stature. Our paths were to crisscross many times and with much pleasure over the intervening years.

After moving to Salt Lake City, my typing skills kept me in touch with Seminary men needing help with their theses. John Heidenreich was one of those calling for help, and he was conveniently located just across the Boulevard at Skyline Seminary. I really learned to know and love both him and his wife, Bernice, through this interchange. Later, however, I began substitute teaching and he called me frequently. I had him speak at a fireside at our home at which time he related his incredible conversion story. I knew he was "an elect person" in our Father's Kingdom--both by word and by spiritual manifestation.

John retired early from the Church School System because of several massive heart attacks. He moved to Mesa, Arizona, where the altitude is lower and dryer, hoping his health would improve. During this time he had an insatiable desire to complete his life story and solicited my aid. It was from this experience that I realized the depth of the man and understood why he was "elect." He had been "carried in the hollow of His hand" his entire life so that he might accept the Gospel and have opportunity to teach it. Together we put together a handsome maroon bound copy of <u>An Acorn Became an Oak</u>, of which we printed 150 copies. I had the privilege of helping with their distribution throughout the United States to the many who loved and respected this great man.

His health did improve, and he and Bernice were able to accept a call to serve a mission to the Los Angeles Temple. While so serving, he had more heart trouble, and called me the day before Christmas to tell me that he was due for a multiple heart-bypass operation right after the holiday. I was devastated, but he reassured me by saying, "It is all right. I have heard Him call me by name." In this frame of mind I wrote him a letter, one of the many we exchanged since his move from Salt Lake, and felt I was inspired to write "John the Beloved."

John did not survive the surgery. Bernice called me and asked that I speak at his funeral, using the tribute I wrote. I was humbled to be a part of the service shared with a General Authority and head of the Division of Religion at BYU. I lost a dear friend for this life, but was grateful that our relationship is eternal.

JOHN THE BELOVED

What's in a name? Does courage, strength, dedication and faith come with a name? Perhaps so. John, son of Zebedee, brother of James, was busy mending nets when came the call, "Follow me, and I will make you fishers of men."

No thought took he of the morrow, but eagerly he accompanied his brethren as they taught at the Master's feet. What matchless faith rose in John's bosom as in those early hours with Jesus he witnessed Him heal a woman of a fever, cast out devils, turn water into wine, cleanse a leper, and heal the blind. So great was his testimony of the Divine Christ that John was labeled "Son of Thunder" and with unbounded energy he proclaimed the Gospel message throughout early Christendom.

John's love of Christ was paralleled only by Christ's love of him. He was one of the chosen few present at the Transfiguration when the voice of the Father bore witness of the Son; again, John and only two others shared in His anguish as they accompanied Him into the Garden of Gethsemane. In the Upper Room he learned humility as Christ washed the feet of His disciples.

Of such great companionship, John wrote: "Of His fullness have I received. . . ." From this fullness came a desire perceived by Christ that "he might tarry until He came again."

Once more the question: Does courage, strength, dedication and faith come with a name? Perhaps so, for I know another John-- John Heidenreich, son of Ernest and Nellie, husband of Bernice, father of Joan, Paul and Fred. He too, heard the call "Come follow me." He forsook his nets, his father and mother, and went about the land proclaiming Christ. Countless souls bless his name for bringing them into the Gospel net. Tribulations dogged his footsteps, but with a profound love of Christ and testimony of His divinity, he developed a faith like unto that of his namesake, so that even angels minister unto him. He enjoys a speaking acquaintance with Him of whom he testifies! Little wonder, then, as John approaches his Gethsemane today, he pleads for one more miracle to "tarry a little longer" to continue the work he knows and loves so well. This prayer is echoed by all who know him, and by countless others whose lives he has not yet touched, but who wait in the wings to hear this great disciple "show them the way."

* * * *

Written from Whitehorse, Y.T. 1945
My first Christmas away from home.

TO ALL OF YOU

We don't have to see the snow fall,
Or hear the sleigh bells ring,
We can do without old Santa
And the pack that he will bring.
We can do without the turkey
And the Christmas fixins' too,
But it won't seem much like Christmas
If it can't be shared with you.

LOVE LETTERS

After evening chores were done
The youngsters tucked in bed
Mother got her writing pad
And Daddy sat and read.

I'd often watch them for a while
Discuss the book at hand
And gravely ponder prospects
Of the newly seeded land.

"Shall we get some baby chicks?"
"Is this an early spring?"
"What price do you suppose
The barley crop will bring?"

Small problems, large problems
They'd carefully peruse
And mention in the letter
With the home and family news.

The room grew very quiet
And nothing more was said
'Til Dad awakened with a start
When he bumped his nodding head.

And down the neatly written page
A dot or two would tell
The place where Mom took twenty winks,
And there the ink dried well.

If I might have one wish today,
I would that I might see
Mother making inked-in dots
Of her own telegraphy.

And sitting close beside her chair,
Contentment at its best,
Daddy's sleeping overture
In harmony with rest.

MY PRAYER

My Father who art in heaven,
With all Thy love and care,
Wilt Thou lend a listening ear
To the petition of my prayer.

There's a sweet little Mother with hair silver gray,
With a pure love that mothers possess.
So Father, do bless her and keep her I pray,
May each day bring her new happiness.

And there is my wonderful Father at home
Who, through years both of good and the bad,
Proved worthy indeed of the title he bears,
The noble and proud name of Dad.

A home of kindness and goodness they built
For a family fast grown to nine.
They wanted not the things of the world
But to teach them the things that were fine.

Now Father of mine in the heavens above
Thou knowest the things we can't see,
But return unto them the joy and the love
That they have given to me.

TO MOTHER AND DADDY

Your love and kindness unto me
Were signs of true divinity.
Your patience of my childish pranks,
Put you both in the "expert" ranks.

The lives you live, so sweet and fine,
Inspire me to so fashion mine
That I might mold a better me,
Worthy of you for eternity.

SPRING SONG

I'll sing you a spring song,
A butterfly-bring song,
A joy-laden song from the heart.
Of pert pussy willows,
And bridal wreath billows,
Combined in harmonious part.

I'll sing you a gay song,
Fly troubles away song
Accompanying a meadow lark's tune.
Of daffodils dancing,
Spring breezes enhancing,
A long quiet walk 'neath the moon.
I'll sing you a sweet song,
A very discreet song,
Of mountain slopes greening with May.
Of nature united,
Of mortals delighted
To sing praise of this beautiful day.

FAR AWAY PLACES

There must be something I don't know
About my family tree,
For surely gypsy blood runs high
In the uncharted pedigree!

The stork dropped me in Canada,
And there I was content,
'Til I learned of greener pastures,
So to Alaska I went.

A greater call then came my way,
(You may think me arbitrary),
But my next stop was the Southern States
Where I served as a missionary.

They say "when sand gets in your shoes"
Nature makes you roam,
It must be true, for soon I knew
Utah would be my home.

But once again my wandering soul
Was eager to break its bands,
I set foot on new continents
And Scandinavian lands.

This life's ambition is now fulfilled
I've mingled with many races,
But know my heart will always hear
The call of "Far Away Places."

LIFE'S MOUNTAIN CLIMB

I climbed the mountain top today
The way was hard and steep,
The rocks and crags were threatening,
And there were chasms deep.

My feet, unsteady for the task
Would often slip, and then
They'd find a rock firm planted
And scramble back again.

At last I reached the summit,
Triumphantly I stood
And quenched my thirsty gaze
Of home. The land so good!

The pines so straight and beckoning,
The mirror lakes below,
Nestled in the mountains
Capped with crisp, new snow.

The town I thought "just happened"
Now showed a well marked plan.
The sun smiled down approval
On animal and man.

I contemplated, standing there,
Is this not true to life?
It takes a lot of climbing
And overcoming strife

To really learn to see the best
And good the world can give.
You might need to take a tumble
To learn to really live!

It's not the little fall we take
That really is the test,
It's how we rise to face it
And go on to do our best.

It's a constant job of keeping
Our eyes upon our goal.
It's a never-ending effort
That's ennobling to the soul.

We all should climb a mountain
If only once a year,
To get a true perspective
To make life's vision clear.

Perhaps you'll find your answered quest
When you mingle brawn with sod.
You'll find your soul uplifted
And nearer to your God.

FANTASY

I saw the strangest things last night
While I in slumber lay.
I saw four locusts prancing
As they pulled a load of hay.

I saw a tiny little mouse
Swallow whole a cat.
On streets of candy bars I tread.
What do you think of that?

I saw a multi-colored sky
So beautiful to see.
Then a cloudburst of balloons
Came showering down on me.

And when I almost did awake,
I was so shocked to find
A great big round brown elephant
A-swinging from my blind.

And then a silver fairy stole
Up to my door to say:
"Wake up, get up, you sleepy head.
It's such a lovely day!"

And so I jumped right out of bed
Swung wide the door to see
A world so bright and beautiful
Surpassing fantasy!

ON BEING A BIRD. . . .

I wish I were a little bird,
With feather dress so gay,
That I might perch on any twig
To rest, then fly away.

And should I go a-visiting,
I'd soar through azure space
To join the hosts of heaven
Of the feathered angel race.

But then on second thought, I muse:
Bird traits make me squirm.
For I am confident that I
Could never eat a worm!

RENAISSANCE WOMAN

I wish that I might claim the brush
For just a day or so
To paint the treasures of Europe
As did Michelangelo.

Or borrow talent from his hands
To rebuild, very fine,
The cities of the Fatherland,
And bridges o'er the Rhine.

Or if with Verdi I could sing,
I'd tell of Plato's home,
The famed Blue Grotto, Venice,
The Vatican and Rome.

In Byron's tongue I'd like to tell
Of a country richly blessed,
Of Switzerland, the land of dreams
Build on the alpine crest.

Or if I could be Rembrandt
I'd sketch the scenic view
Of Holland's dikes and tulip beds,
Radiant with morning dew.

If Kipling could but loan me verse,
Or if Mozart's score I'd claim,
I'd relate events in Gay Paree,
And highlight Austria's fame.

Just for an hour, pray, let me use
Shakespeare's quill to pen
England's dramatic history,
Endeared to the hearts of men.

But I can't borrow from the bards,
I must conform to rules;
For I can only offer my own
Tarnished, worn out tools.

And hope that in my humble way
My life will help you see,
The value of this experience
And what it means to me.

BEFORE THOU THIRST. . . .

I sipped briefly of the cup, brim-filled with love.
I heard mortals must partake, while those above
Knew life's full joy and happiness while here--
A taste on earth of a sweet celestial sphere.

I took the cup with trembling hands and prayed:
"Please let this be fulfillment of a dream, an ecstacy."
Scarce had my lips grown moist and the cup was gone!
Vanished from my sight! And then the dawn mocked back at me.

O youth, keep faith in self, and then
Wiser grow before thou thirst again.

TO APRIL

The storm was heavy in '64
When an April stork came to our door.
We welcomed him as we always did,
But disappointment could not be hid.

You see Mama had gained fifty pounds!
To be sure of more "double rounds"
We'd grown accustomed to the pace
Of two each year to win the race.

We really hoped for a boy or two,
One with red hair and eyes of blue.
But when the nurse brought you to me
You won our hearts just instantly.

And we have never known a day
We'd part with you, or give away
Our April girl with happy grins
We'd not replace her for any twins!

MOTHERS

She sobbed when she came home from school,
The world had done her wrong.
She played the same piano tune
But she didn't sing the song.

She showed the wounds sustained today,
The friends who broke her trust,
Who shunned her every suggestion,
Turning castles into dust.

We sobbed when she came home from school,
The world had done her wrong!
We played the same piano tune
But we didn't sing the song.

Another child, misunderstood,
Another mother cried.
While people mocked, and one betrayed
And Him they crucified.

* * * *

While with Susan enroute to Mother's Week at Dixie College in St. George, Utah, I was writing a talk to be given on Mother's Day the following Sunday in my home ward. As I wrote, I read it to Susan. Upon its completion, Susan requested that I read it on the program at Dixie. The impromptu performance was fun for us both.

TO ALL MOTHERS OF TEENS
(With Sincere Sympathy)

"I admit that my youth is well spent,
That my get-up-and-go has got up and went.
But I really don't mind, as I think with a grin
Of all of the places my getup has been!"

I didn't get these gray hairs easily--
I earned them--every one.
You see--I am the mother of seven teenagers!

About the time you think you're through
With diapers, bottles, pins,
There's a new crisis coming up
That's not confined to twins!

I speak with some authority
And suggest you listen too--
Cause if you have one child,
The same applies to you.

The malady is the teen years,
And if you should survive,
There's little consolation
In coming through alive!

The symptoms are varied,
But most all parents yen
For the carefree years
O, to be single again!

"You're lucky to have so many girls,"
I smiled, and I believed them.
But never is one of them around
When I desperately need them.

There are those rare occasions, though,
A mixed blessing from which I shrink,
When one of them does the laundry
And all the whites turn pink!

The Pep Club bid--the first date trauma
A boyfriend lost--to a SISTER drama.
The car totalled out; a "D" in health,
Insurance people accrue all our wealth.
With six teen drivers--a new one next year,
Bankruptcy is our main great fear.

It's four new dresses for the dance,
But then my greatest sorrow
Is to learn they all need them
By eight o'clock tomorrow!

The doorbell rings. There he stands
So handsome, bold and tall.
My, is this the romeo
To escort Susan to the ball?

About the time I've sized him up
As a great flamboyant spender,
He smiles, and cautiously asks:
"Which one's the baby tender?"

Their emotions are high gear,
Their memories poor--
Their getting up--low gear
And this is for sure--

Plan a weekend with your friends
And this I'll guarantee,
Here come the kids from college
With a roommate, two or three.

Here is where parenting
Takes on a serious role,
How to meet next quarter's needs
Without the public dole!

"Save the fuss and ride the bus"
Is a cliche of great renown.
But no bus has ever gone
To their destination in town!

It's "Take me here!"
"I'm late for work!"
"Mother, where's my keys?"
If we had a fleet of cars,

It might begin to please
Their important wants; their many needs
Despite the new gas hike--
I'd love to read the headlines:
"MOTHER DRIVERS STRIKE!"

An honorable proposal of marriage,
Tears fill our worried eyes.
I thought you both were waiting
For those missionary guys!

Now rearing boys is different,
It's not the same at all.
It's worrying about the zits he got
For the upcoming Preference Ball.

It's watching lanky arms and legs
Grow inches over night, and long
Before the new suit is cleaned
It presents an inglorious sight!

It's taxiing half the noisy crowd
To the furthest baseball game,
And screaming till your voice is gone
To bring Horman name to fame!

The telephone's another thing
It rings right off the wall.
There's never a five second lull
For mother's waiting call.

It's fixing that special meal
(This could incite a riot),
When two show up for dinner
And both are on a diet!

Or if I've prepared chili
Sufficient for our bunch,
I'm bound to hear them echo,
"That was today's school lunch."

Each morning of every day
We need to call inspection
Of clothes going out the door
Just for everyone's protection.

"Hey, that's my blouse!"
"You creep, those shoes are mine!"
"Why don't you ask permission
Before taking it off the line?"

The accusations thunder,
The chorus sounds alarm,
Teaching not to borrow clothes
Will put me in the funny farm!

And just about the time
We're praying for relief,
Three more announce in jubilation:
"I need braces on my teeth."

The diagnosis--simple,
The symptoms they are sure,
The cure is very complicated
But boldly I demure--

The talking till wee morning hours
The praying, crying too; the laughing
Entwine hearts with webs of love
Like nothing else can do.

Though fraught with fear and trepidation,
For me there is no other
Vocation I'd choose in all the world
Than the blessed one of "Mother."

APPENDIX G--RESUMES

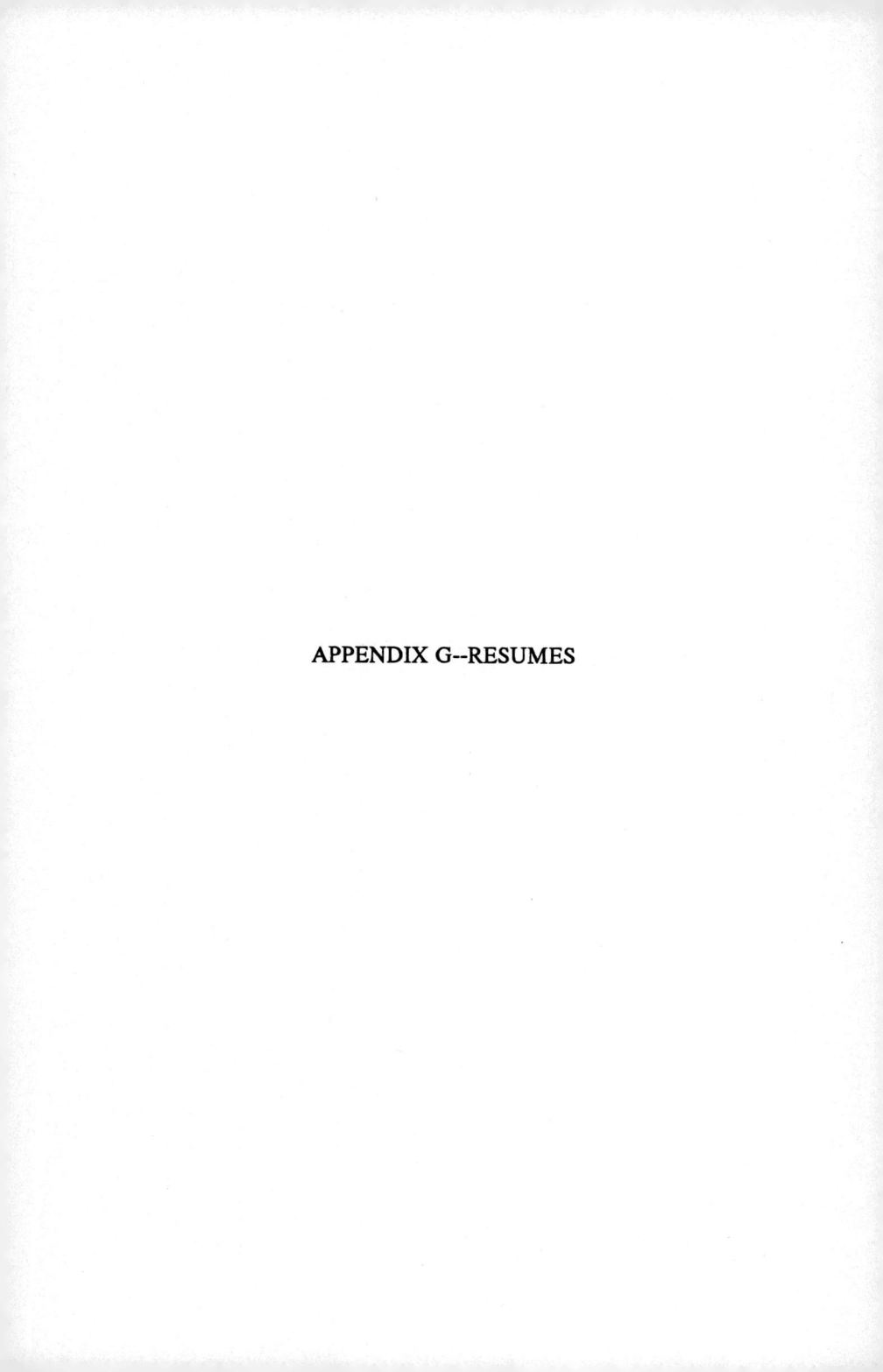

RESUMES

While serving in the Canada-Halifax Mission, my husband and I conducted a series of eleven Thursday night lectures open to the general public. When I was to be the featured speaker, I felt the need to sell myself over and above the obvious. When Phares read the following credentials, no one guessed who the speaker was to be!

While written "with-tongue-in-cheek," the events described in the resume are based in fact and provided spirited queries for introduction of my subject matter. It also resulted in some reflective thinking.

RESUME #1

Next week's speaker is a many-faceted individual. By way of introduction:

Has spent time in a state penitentiary
Has had an audience with the Pope in the Vatican City
Globe-trotter, international business tycoon and financier
A returned missionary
Expert on child development, marriage, family relations and spouse abuse
Editor and author of numerous Church books and publications
Survivor of three near-fatal accidents
Founder and director of private non-profit organization for unwed mothers, homeless and needy individuals
Private tutor of distinguished visitors from the Orient
International hostess to men of authority
Sponsor of five foreign missionaries
Personal secretary to at least two General Authorities
Survived combat duty as seminary teacher and teacher in public education
Has piloted boats and explored the Colorado and Green Rivers
Playwright and theatrical director who served on the Drama and Camp Committee of the General Board of the MIA
Blue Ribbon winner in Home Economics competition
Worked on the Alcan Highway
Will walk on water, if the water is hard enough!

YOU WOULDN'T DARE MISS THURSDAY NIGHT'S SPEAKER, WOULD YOU?

RESUME #2

60 year-old housewife, thirty-year Weight Watcher dropout
Redheaded Canadian
Educated in a one-room school
Visiting Teacher and PTA worker
Mother of seven children

* * * *

Does the first resume encourage you, at the very least, to know more of this fascinating individual? Would you make every effort to meet this person in a lecture setting? I suspect you would.

Judging the second resume at face value, likely the reader would just as soon stay home and watch the grass grow as walk across the street to hear her declarations. Right?

Why the different reaction to these two resumes? Surprisingly, they both describe the same person. Is it only a matter of semantics, of accentuating the positive? Is the difference more subtle? Perhaps it is one of perception, the words we use to describe ourselves. HOW DO WE PERCEIVE OURSELVES? Surely there is a marked difference in the two resumes when one makes a self-evaluation. Our perception spills over into our spoken and unspoken communications, whether through behavior or body language. We can either motivate and inspire, impede or confuse, thoughts which might have contributed to the "world's store of knowledge."

Are we just mothers or housewives? Or are we builders, architects of destiny? The job description may be the same. But the challenges loom in spite of the attendant glories when we are framers of destiny. We achieve these feats practically unconsciously; nonetheless, we deserve--yes, are responsible to acknowledge--our contribution as destiny shapers.

Were we each to prepare a positive resume of our achievements to date, we might be astounded at the truly unique and interesting persons we are. In so doing, we would catch the vision of our potential, realize how exceptional are our credentials, not only to others, but to ourselves and certainly to our Heavenly Father. Let us take time each day to find joy in the journey. Let's live it to the fullest. LOVE IT ALL THE WAY! Then our HEARTSTRINGS will create a symphonic, joyful sound!

CREDITS

Carol Clark Ottesen granted permission for inclusion of her poem, "Progress," from her book <u>Line Upon Line. . . .</u>

The following three articles are © by the Church of Jesus Christ of Latter-day Saints and are used by permission:

"Unto Every Man. . ." <u>The Improvement Era,</u> July 1958.

"Be Quiet and Pray," <u>The New Era,</u> October 1979.

"God, I Hate You," <u>The Liahona,</u> 1989, international publication of the Church of Jesus Christ of Latter-day Saints.

TOPICAL LISTINGS

TENDER VINES
What Made Our House
    a Home 3
Homesick 12
"One, Two, Buckle
    My Shoe!" 13
The Fence Sitter 17
An Early Lesson in Discipline 16
Apprentice Carpenter 21
Sunday School Sleigh Ride 22
The Windmill and
    My Mind . . . 24
From the Horse's Mouth 26
Right Between the Eyes 27
In Praise of Lehi School 29
Sex Education (?) At Lehi
    School! 35
Little Brown Jug 49
A Harey Story 50
If Wishes Were Horses, I'd Ride
    Again 52
Farming and "Liking" it 55
Daddy 58
The Great Horse Race 59
He Who Laughs Last . . . 60
"Hacking" It 61
Trouble! Trouble! Trouble!
    (Right Here in
    "The Garden City") 64

SAND IN MY SHOES MY SHOES
    Edmonton, Alberta 69
    Calgary, Alberta 76
A Letter to Santa Claus 77
The Snow Storm 78
    Whitehorse, Yukon
    Territory 82
My "Fight with Joe Louis" 82
A Bear-faced Story 83
To Those Who Enter 84

THE GREEN YEARS
    Southern States Mission
    (1946-1948) 99
    Waycross, Georgia 100
    Savannah, Georgia 100

THE GREEN YEARS con't
    Dothan, Alabama 101
    Mobile, Alabama 101
    Miami, Florida 104
    Ft. Lauderdale,
    Florida 105
    Winter Haven,
    Florida 106
My Testimony 108
The Night Prowler 109
BYU and Me 110
Dream Girl? 117
Utah General Depot,
    Ogden, Utah 122
BYU--Again 122
Dont's for Secretaries 124
Odd-Man-Out 125

IS MR. HORMAN MR RIGHT?
"When You Wish Upon a Star--
    Hope for a Blind
    Date" 133

A PEEK IN THE SHOE
On Seasons and
    Reasons. . . 178
A Serious Charge 198
Double Trouble 200
Of Scissors, Strollers
    and Sears. . . 201
Serendipity 203
Kidnapped? 205
. . . .And We Did It Again! 207
Lost: "Boomer" 208
It All Began When . . . 220
Things are Seldom as
    They Seem 222
A Bird in the Fireplace 223
Unique Company 224
How to Save Sanity Though
    Camping 225
"God, I Hate You!" 228

TOPICAL LISTINGS con't

A TIME OF HARVEST
Culture Shock 258
Bulawayo to Zimbabwe 260
Look Before You Leap 261
Personal Revelation 272
A Long, Long Night 273
The Magician Suffers Some
    Sleight-of-Hand 274
Let Not Your Yearning Exceed
    Your Earning 275
A Stolen Passport 276
Mission Farewell Talk 285
Reclaimed from the Sea 293
Ode to a Mosquito 315
Blessings of Filling
    a Mission 330
Self-fulfilling Prophecy 336
Surprise Entrepreneur 341

NOSTALGIA
Twentieth Century Pioneer 349
Can One Person Make a
    Difference? 351
Without Prejudice 354
    Black Man 354
    Japanese 354
    German and Italian 355
    Black Majority 357
    German 357
    Jewish: "Aunt
    Bertha" 357
    Japanese Students 358
    German Student
    Exchange 358
    Horman Hostel--League
    of Nations 359
Mother and the Hutterites 359
For Name's Sake 362
I Have a Story to "Tell" 364
The Stone was Rolled Away 366
A Holy War 367
A Reasonable, Patriotic
    American 369
"My Sheep Know
    My Voice". . 371

APPENDICIES
A--LEHI SCHOOL 373
    - 1933-36 378
    - 1936-37 380
    - 1937-38 381
    - 1938-40 382

B--THE HUTTERITES 387

C--PINPOINTS 391
    Destinations 393
    Ideals 394
    Let Peace Prevail 395
    "Leave Us Not to
    Sow Alone". . 396
    "Lives of
    Great Men". . 397
    In Search of Truth 398
    Vision is More
    than Sight 399
    "All Hoods Make Not
    Monks" 400
    A Teacher's Gift 401
    Look Up to
    the Light! 402
    The Price of Genius 403
    All the World's
    a Stage. . . 404
    Be Young this
    Spring 405
    Lest We Forget. . . 407

D--ONE TIME CELEBRITIES
    413

E--TRIBUTE TO MY
    CHILDREN AND MY
    BROTHERS AND
    SISTERS 421
    Memories of
    Grandma Briggs 423
    A Canadian Blizzard 424
    The May Storm
    of 1903 425
    Nostalgia 426
    My Celebration 428

HEART STRINGS 459

TOPICAL LISTINGS con't

F--FRIENDS FOREVER AND
    MY "POMES" 431
    Another Spring. . . 433
    Ode to Joan 434
    Tribute to
    June Meiners Horman 435
    John Heidenreich 436
    John the Beloved 437
    To All of You 438
    Love Letters 439
    My Prayer 440
    To Mother and
    Daddy 440
    Spring Song 441
    Far Away Places 441
    Life's
    Mountain Climb 442
    Fantasy 443
    On Being a Bird. . . 444
    Renaissance Woman 445
    Before Thou Thirst. . 446
    To April 446
    Mothers 447
    To All Mothers
    of Teens 447

G--RESUMES 453